Petite
PATISSERIE

First published in the United States of America in 2020 by
Rizzoli International Publications, Inc.
300 Park Avenue South
New York, NY 10010
www.rizzoliusa.com

Originally published in French in 2019 by Éditions de La Martinière
© 2019 Éditions de La Martinière, a brand of EDLM

Printed in Slovenia

2020 2021 2022 2023 / 10 9 8 7 6 5 4 3 2 1

ISBN: 978-0-8478-6915-2
Library of Congress Control Number: 2020935356

French to English Translation: Carmella Abramowitz Moreau
Copy Editing: Jane Sigal
Typesetting: Jordan Wannemacher
Proofreading: Kelli Rae Patton

Visit us online:
Facebook.com/RizzoliNewYork
Twitter: @Rizzoli_Books
Instagram.com/RizzoliBooks
Pinterest.com/RizzoliBooks
Youtube.com/user/RizzoliNY
Issuu.com/Rizzoli

CHRISTOPHE FELDER
CAMILLE LESECQ

Petite
PATISSERIE

180
EASY RECIPES FOR
ELEGANT FRENCH TREATS

Photography
Laurent Fau

Styling
Sarah Vasseghi

RIZZOLI
NEW YORK

New York · Paris · London · Milan

Simple Things are Always the Best

"When you make a cake at home, it's just like what you can get from the pastry shop, but better!" Now there's a compliment we dream of hearing.

It's true that baked goods made in your kitchen always have a special taste, one that's unique and irreplaceable.

The home baker must carefully select a recipe that everyone who'll be sharing will like.

When we bake at home, we need to take each one's likes into account: Louis is a chocolate lover, Lucie is a fan of raspberries, and Marie will want almonds. Romane is crazy for pistachios, and then Camille's favorite flavor is vanilla. Some go for soft, melting textures, while others prefer crisp and crunchy. But we'll make sure that everyone's kept happy.

Baking at home means you'll be producing a beautiful cake, a true labor of love.

It means following a recipe to the letter and then being able to say, "I made it myself!"

It means making a creation that's simple yet utterly delicious.

We're happy to throw open the doors to our little pastry shop to you and we hope that you enjoy every scrumptious mouthful.

Christophe Felder
Camille Lesecq

Table of Contents

Basic
Recipes
8

Monday
20

Tuesday
54

Wednesday
98

Thursday
138

Friday
182

Saturday
224

Sunday
274

Funday
324

Basic Recipes

The old adage about building on solid foundations is true in pastry making too.

With these luscious creamy fillings and pastry crusts—simple, sweet, or nut-based—you'll be a true pastry champion.

In this chapter, we let you in on all the secrets of our basic recipes.

And if you're already familiar with them, think of this section as a review of the building blocks of classic French pastry.

CRISP PLAIN PASTRY

Prep: 20 minutes   *Chill:* 2 hours

Makes about 1 lb. 5 oz. (600 g) pastry, enough for two 8- or 9-inch (20 or 22-cm) tart shells

1¼ teaspoons (6 g) fine salt

⅓ cup (2 oz. / 60 g) granulated sugar

2¾ cups (9 oz. / 250 g) cake flour

⅛ teaspoon vanilla bean powder

1½ sticks (6 oz. / 180 g) unsalted butter, diced, room temperature

¼ cup (60 ml) cold water

1 tablespoon plus 1 teaspoon (20 g) lightly beaten egg

1. Make sure you take the butter out of the refrigerator in time to let it soften well.

2. In a large bowl, whisk the salt with the sugar, flour, and vanilla. Rub in the butter until grainy. Add the water and egg and knead gently until just combined.

3. Shape the dough into a disk and cover with plastic wrap. Chill for at least 2 hours before using.

SWEET AND SALTY CARAMELIZED PEANUTS

Prep: 15 minutes   *Cook:* 10 minutes

Makes about 10 oz. (300 g) peanuts

⅓ cup (80 ml) water

½ cup (3½ oz. / 100 g) granulated sugar

1⅓ cups (7 oz. / 200 g) roasted salted peanuts

1. In a medium saucepan, bring the water to a boil with the sugar over high heat. Cook to 244°F (118°C).

2. Add the peanuts and stir until the sugar recrystallizes. Heat gently until the mixture caramelizes; the peanuts should not stick together. Carefully transfer to a baking sheet and let cool. Separate any clusters. Use for decoration or as a snack.

BRETON SHORT PASTRY

Prep: 10 minutes

Cook: 20 minutes

Chill: 20 minutes

Makes about 1 lb. 5 oz. (600 g) pastry, enough for two 9- or 10-inch (22- or 24-cm) cakes

3 egg yolks

⅔ cup (4½ oz. / 130 g) granulated sugar

1¼ sticks (5 oz. / 150 g) unsalted butter, diced, softened

1⅔ cups (7 oz. / 200 g) all-purpose flour, or

1 cup plus 2 tablespoons (5¼ oz. / 150 g) all-purpose flour plus generous ½ cup (1¾ oz. / 50 g) ground almonds or hazelnuts

Heaping ½ teaspoon (3 g) fine salt

1 scant tablespoon (11 g) baking powder

Equipment

Two 9- or 10-inch (22- or 24-cm) tart rings

1. In a medium bowl, whisk the egg yolks with the sugar until pale and thick. Using a wooden spoon, beat in the butter.

2. Sift the flour with the salt and baking powder into the yolk-butter mixture and fold in.

3. Shape the dough into a disk, cover with plastic wrap, and chill for about 20 minutes.

4. Preheat the oven to 340°F (170°C) convection.

5. On a lightly floured sheet of parchment paper, roll out the pastry about ¼ inch (4 to 5 mm) thick. Using the tart ring, press out a pastry disk and leave the disk in the ring. Remove the excess pastry and brush off the flour.

6. Carefully transfer with the paper to the baking sheet and bake for 15 to 20 minutes, until golden. Let cool in the ring.

7. Shape the remaining pastry into a disk, wrap well, and freeze to use later.

SWEET ALMOND PASTRY

Prep: 20 minutes   *Chill:* 2 hours

**Makes about 1 lb. (460 g) pastry, enough for
two 8- or 9-inch (20- or 22-cm) tart shells**

1 stick plus 1 teaspoon (4¼ oz. / 120 g) unsalted butter,
softened

Generous ½ cup (2¾ oz. / 75 g) confectioners' sugar

¼ cup (1 oz. / 25 g) ground natural almonds

1 pinch vanilla bean powder

1 pinch fleur de sel

2 tablespoons plus 2 teaspoons (1½ oz. / 40 g)
lightly beaten egg

2¼ cups (7 oz. / 200 g) cake flour

1. Place the butter in a large bowl and sift the confectioners' sugar over it. Add the ground almonds, vanilla bean powder, and fleur de sel.

2. Using a wooden spoon, beat until the texture is creamy. Stir in the beaten egg.

3. Sift the flour into the bowl and stir until just incorporated; do not overmix.

4. Shape the pastry into a disk, cover with plastic wrap, and chill for 2 hours, then use according to directions. If not using immediately, divide in half, wrap, and freeze.

ALMOND MERINGUE BASE

Prep: 15 minutes   *Cook:* 30 to 35 minutes

Makes a cake base for 8

1 scant cup (3 oz. / 90 g) almond flour

Scant ⅔ cup (3 oz. / 90 g) confectioners' sugar

1½ tablespoons (15 g) all-purpose flour

5 egg whites

Scant ¼ cup (1½ oz. / 45 g) granulated sugar

Equipment

A pastry bag fitted with a plain ¾-inch (18-mm) tip, optional

A 9- to 10-inch (22- to 24-cm) tart ring,
1¾ inches (4.5 cm) deep

1. Preheat the oven to 320°F (160°C) convection. Line a rimmed baking sheet with parchment paper, spread the almond flour on top, and lightly toast for about 10 minutes. Carefully remove the paper with the almond flour and let cool.

2. Increase the oven temperature to 340°F (170°C) convection. Do not brush the tart ring with butter; you want the meringue to stick to the sides and form a shell for filling.

3. Whisk the almond flour with the confectioners' sugar and all-purpose flour. In a large bowl, whisk the egg whites with the granulated sugar until they hold a soft peak. Fold in the dry ingredients.

4. Pipe or spread the batter in the tart ring, then pipe or spoon dollops of the batter around the rim. Bake for 30 to 35 minutes until a thin crust forms and the meringue base is springy to the touch.

5. Let cool in the ring. Carefully run a knife around the inside of the ring and remove it.

PISTACHIO MERINGUE BASE

Use ¾ cup (2½ oz. / 75 g) toasted almond flour and a scant ½ cup (1½ oz. / 40 g) raw ground pistachios, and sprinkle the unbaked meringue with chopped pistachios.

HAZELNUT MERINGUE BASE

Replace the almond flour with toasted finely ground hazelnuts.

ALMOND–HAZELNUT MERINGUE BASE

Use a scant ½ cup (1½ oz. / 45 g) each toasted ground hazelnuts and almond flour.

COCONUT MERINGUE BASE

Sprinkle the unbaked meringue with unsweetened shredded coconut.

Note: It's best to store coconut in the freezer.

CHOCOLATE LADYFINGER SPONGE CAKE

Prep: 10 minutes   *Cook:* 10 to 15 minutes

**Makes 2 disks plus a ladyfinger rim
for a charlotte for 12, or biscuits for 8**

1¾ cups (5½ oz. / 160 g) cake flour

3½ tablespoons (1 oz. / 25 g) unsweetened cocoa powder

6 eggs, separated

1 cup minus 2½ tablespoons (6 oz. / 170 g) granulated sugar

1 tablespoon pure vanilla extract

Confectioners' sugar for dusting

Equipment

A pastry bag fitted with a plain
½-inch (10-mm) tip, optional

1.   Preheat the oven to 440°F (210°C) convection.
Line a baking sheet with parchment paper. Draw two
9-inch (22-cm) circles on the paper and turn it over.
Sift the cake flour with the cocoa powder.

2.   In a large bowl, using an electric beater, whisk
the egg whites until frothy. Gradually whisk in the
granulated sugar, then the vanilla, until the mixture
holds a medium-firm peak. Gently stir in the egg
yolks, one by one. Fold in the dry ingredients.

3.   Using the circles as a guide, pipe or spread the
batter into 2 disks on the baking sheet. Pipe or spoon
the remaining batter into 3-inch (8-cm) long biscuits.

4.   Dust with confectioners' sugar and place in the
oven. Reduce the oven temperature to 350°F (180°C)
convection and bake for 10 to 15 minutes, until a thin
crust forms and the biscuits are springy to the touch.
Switch the oven off and transfer the biscuits to a
rack. Bake the disk for another 2 to 3 minutes, then
let cool. If not using them immediately, cover each
disk separately with plastic wrap, wrap the biscuits,
and store in the refrigerator or freezer.

Note: You can pipe out only biscuit shapes to serve
with coffee.

PINK LADYFINGER SPONGE CAKE
Biscuit à la Cuillère Rose

Prep: 10 minutes   *Cook:* 10 to 15 minutes

**Makes 2 disks plus a ladyfinger rim for
a charlotte for 12, or biscuits for 8**

6 eggs, separated

1 cup minus 2½ tablespoons (6 oz. / 170 g) granulated sugar

1 tablespoon vanilla extract

Red food coloring as needed

1¾ cups (5½ oz. / 160 g) cake flour

Confectioners' sugar for dusting

Equipment

A pastry bag fitted with a plain
½-inch (10-mm) tip, optional

1.   Follow the directions for Chocolate Ladyfinger
Sponge Cake (opposite), omitting the cocoa powder
and whisking in a few drops of red food coloring
after the vanilla in Step 2.

CHOUX PASTRY

Prep: 10 minutes   *Cook:* 25 to 30 minutes

Makes 50 choux puffs

½ cup minus 1 tablespoon (100 ml) water

½ cup minus 1 tablespoon (100 ml) whole milk

5 tablespoons plus 1 teaspoon (3 oz. / 80 g)
unsalted butter, diced

Scant ½ teaspoon (2 g) fine salt

1¼ teaspoons (5 g) granulated sugar

¼ teaspoon (2 g) trimoline or acacia honey

1⅓ cups (4¼ oz. / 120 g) cake flour

¾ to 1 scant cup lightly beaten egg, well chilled

Equipment
A pastry bag fitted with a plain tip (for Chouquettes)
or a finely fluted tip (for Eclairs)

CHOUX PASTRY

1. In a large saucepan, bring the water to a simmer
with the milk, butter, salt, sugar, and trimoline over
medium heat and cook until the butter melts.

2. Remove from the heat and, using a wooden
spoon, beat in the flour until smooth. Return the pan
to low heat and cook, stirring constantly, for about 5
minutes, to dry out the batter.

3. Transfer the batter to a large bowl and beat in the
eggs in 3 to 4 additions, until the mixture is shiny and
drops easily from the spoon.

4. Preheat the oven to 340°F (170C°) convection
for chouquettes and conventional for eclairs. Line 2
baking sheets with parchment paper.

CHOUQUETTES WITH PEARL SUGAR

1. Using the pastry bag fitted with the plain tip,
pipe 1½ inch (4-cm) choux puffs on the baking sheets,
spacing them well apart Sprinkle immediately with
the pearl sugar. Bake for 30 minutes, until well puffed
and golden. Transfer to a rack and let cool.

ECLAIRS

1. Using the fluted tip, pipe 5½ to 6-inch (14- to
15-cm) logs on the baking sheet. Bake for 25 to 30
minutes, until well puffed and golden. Transfer to a
rack and let cool.

QUICK PUFF PASTRY

Prep: 20 minutes   *Chill:* 30 minutes

Makes 1 lb. 5 oz. (600 g) puff pastry

1¾ sticks (7 oz. / 200 g) unsalted butter, well chilled

1 teaspoon (5 g) fine salt

½ cup (125 ml) cold water

2 cups (9 oz. / 250 g) cake flour

1. Cut the butter into ½-inch (1-cm) dice and chill.
In a small bowl, dissolve the salt in the water.

2. In a medium bowl, toss the butter with the flour.

3. Mound the mixture on a work surface and make
a well in the center. Pour the salt water into the well.

4. Gently knead until the ingredients come
together, but do not work the butter too much—some
should remain in dice.

5. On a lightly floured work surface, roll out the
dough into a rectangle about 16 by 12 inches (40 by
30 cm) long. Fold the top third down to the center,
then the bottom third up and over that. Roll out
again to 3 times the length. Repeat 4 times so that
you will have made 5 "turns."

6. Chill the pastry for 30 minutes. You can then use
it as you would any other puff pastry. Roll it out to
the desired thickness and size.

Notes: Use this recipe instead of making traditional
puff pastry. It's far simpler to prepare and is suitable
for many desserts. Good as it is, though, it won't rise
quite as much as traditional puff pastry when baked.

Well covered with plastic wrap, this pastry keeps
for several days in the refrigerator, and can also be
frozen.

BRETON HAZELNUT PASTRY

Prep: 15 minutes   *Cook:* 25 to 30 minutes

Makes 15 oz. (420 g) pastry

7 tablespoons (3½ oz. / 100 g) unsalted butter, softened
2½ teaspoons (15 g) egg yolk
½ cup (3½ oz. / 100 g) granulated sugar
Scant ½ teaspoon (2 g) fine salt
¾ cup (2¼ oz. / 65 g) ground hazelnuts
1 cup plus 1 tablespoon (4¾ oz. / 135 g) all-purpose flour
1 scant teaspoon (3.5 g) baking powder (see Note)

Equipment
Tart ring or pan according to your recipe

1.   In a medium bowl, whisk the butter with the egg yolk, sugar, and salt until smooth.

2.   Sift the ground hazelnuts with the flour and baking powder into the butter-egg yolk mixture and fold in. Cover with plastic wrap and chill for 30 minutes.

3.   Preheat the oven to 340°F (170°C) convection. If using a tart ring, line a baking sheet with parchment paper and place the ring in the center. On a lightly floured work surface, roll out the pastry ⅛- inch (3 mm) thick. Cut out a 9-inch (22-cm) disk and place in the tart ring. Bake for 25 to 30 minutes, until golden.

Note: Do try to weigh out the ingredients for the Breton hazelnut pastry, particularly the baking powder. Weight measures are more accurate than volume, so you'll get a better result.

RICH PASTRY CREAM

Prep: 30 minutes   *Cook:* 10 minutes

Makes about 2½ cups (800 g) pastry cream

2 cups (500 ml) whole milk
Scant ⅔ cup (4 oz. / 120 g) granulated sugar, divided
1 vanilla bean, split lengthwise and seeds scraped
6 egg yolks
⅓ cup (1¾ oz. / 50 g) cornstarch
3 tablespoons plus 1 teaspoon (1¾ oz. / 50 g) unsalted butter, diced

1.   In a medium saucepan, heat the milk with half of the sugar over medium-high heat, stirring, until bubbles appear around the edge and the sugar dissolves; remove from the heat. Add the vanilla bean and seeds, cover, and let infuse for 30 minutes. Remove the vanilla bean.

2.   In a medium bowl, whisk the egg yolks with the remaining sugar and the cornstarch until the sugar and cornstarch dissolve.

3.   Gently reheat the infused milk. Pour a little of the milk into the egg yolk mixture, whisking briskly. Return to the pan with the remaining milk.

4.   Cook over high heat, whisking constantly, until the mixture thickens. Remove from the heat and whisk in the butter.

5.   Line a baking sheet with plastic wrap, letting it hang generously over the two short sides. Spread the pastry cream on the baking sheet. Fold the plastic over the pastry cream to cover it completely.

6.   Place in the freezer for 10 minutes to cool rapidly, then transfer to the refrigerator.

Note: The quicker you cool the cream, the better it will keep.

PASTRY CREAM

Prep: 30 minutes   *Cook:* 10 minutes

Makes about 2½ cups (800 g) pastry cream

2 cups (500 ml) whole milk, divided
1 vanilla bean, split lengthwise and seeds scraped
2 teaspoons (5 g) powdered milk
Scant ½ cup (3 oz. / 80 g) granulated sugar
2 egg yolks
Generous ¼ cup (1½ oz. / 45 g) cornstarch

1. In a medium saucepan, heat 1⅓ cups (375 ml) of the whole milk over medium-high heat with the vanilla bean and seeds, powdered milk, and 3½ tablespoons (1½ oz. / 40 g) of the sugar, stirring, until bubbles appear around the edge and the sugar dissolves; remove from the heat. Remove the vanilla bean.

2. In a medium bowl, whisk the egg yolks with the remaining 3½ tablespoons (1½ oz. / 40 g) sugar, the cornstarch, and remaining ⅔ cup (125 ml) of the whole milk.

3. Pour a little of the hot milk into the egg yolk mixture, whisking briskly. Return to the pan with the remaining milk. Cook over high heat, whisking constantly, until the mixture thickens. Remove from the heat.

4. Line a baking sheet with plastic wrap, letting it hang generously over the two short sides. Spread the pastry cream on the baking sheet. Fold the plastic over the pastry cream to cover it completely. Chill until cooled.

CHANTILLY PASTRY CREAM

5. Whip ½ cup minus 1 tablespoon (100 ml) of heavy cream until it holds a medium-firm peak. Fold into the chilled Pastry Cream (above) in Step 4. Chill for at least 1 hour.

RASPBERRY MOUSSELINE CREAM

Prep: 15 minutes
Cook: 5 minutes

3 egg yolks
2 tablespoons (20 g) cornstarch
1 tablespoon plus 2 teaspoons (20 g) granulated sugar
9 oz. (250 g) raspberry purée, divided (strained and unsweetened, or low-sugar)
4 tablespoons plus 1 teaspoon (2½ oz. / 65 g) unsalted butter, diced
½ cup (130 ml) heavy cream

1. Place a medium bowl, preferably metal, in the freezer. You'll need it to whip the cream. In a separate bowl, whisk the egg yolks with the cornstarch, sugar, and 2 oz. (50 g) of the raspberry purée.

2. In a large saucepan, warm the remaining 7 oz. (200 g) raspberry purée over low heat. Pour a little into the egg yolk mixture and whisk briskly to combine.

3. Return the egg yolk-raspberry mixture to the pan with the remaining milk. Cook over high heat, whisking constantly, until the mixture thickens.

4. Remove from the heat and whisk in the butter.

5. Line a baking sheet with plastic wrap, letting it hang generously over the two short sides. Spread the pastry cream on the baking sheet. Fold the plastic over the pastry cream to cover it completely. Chill until cooled.

6. In the chilled mixing bowl, whip the cream until it holds a medium-firm peak.

7. Using an electric beater, briskly whisk the raspberry pastry cream until it's as soft as mayonnaise. Using a silicone spatula, immediately fold the whipped cream into the raspberry pastry cream. Refrigerate for 1 hour, until lightly set.

LIGHT PASTRY CREAM (DIPLOMAT CREAM)

Prep: 20 minutes
Cook: 10 minutes
Chill: 50 minutes + 1 hour

Makes 1½ to 2 cups (500 g) light pastry cream

1 vanilla bean
1 cup (250 ml) whole milk
3 egg yolks
⅓ cup (2 oz. / 60 g) granulated sugar
2½ tablespoons (1 oz. / 25 g) cornstarch
1 tablespoon plus 2 teaspoons (1 oz. / 25 g) unsalted butter
½ sheet (1 g) 200 bloom gelatin
Scant ⅓ cup (75 ml) heavy cream

1. Split the vanilla bean lengthwise and scrape out the seeds. In a medium saucepan, heat the milk over medium-high heat with the vanilla bean and seeds until bubbles appear around the edge; remove from the heat. Remove the vanilla bean.

2. In a medium bowl, whisk the egg yolks with the sugar and cornstarch. Pour a little of the hot milk into the egg yolk mixture, whisking briskly. Return to the pan with the remaining milk. Cook over high heat, whisking constantly, until the mixture thickens. Remove from the heat and whisk in the butter.

3. Line a baking sheet with plastic wrap, letting it hang generously over the two short sides. Spread the pastry cream on the baking sheet. Fold the plastic over the pastry cream to cover it completely. Chill until cooled.

4. In a medium bowl of very cold water, soften the gelatin. In a chilled bowl, using an electric beater, whip the cream until it holds a firm peak.

5. In a medium bowl, using the electric beater, whip the chilled pastry cream until it's as soft as mayonnaise. Squeeze the gelatin dry and melt in a large bowl set over a saucepan of simmering water or in the microwave; it should barely heat. Remove the bowl from the heat. Briskly whisk in the pastry cream in 3 additions.

6. Using a silicone spatula, fold in the whipped cream. Refrigerate until lightly set.

Note: Light Pastry Cream is best prepared a day ahead.

LIGHT LIME PASTRY CREAM

Add the finely grated zest of ¼ lime.

LIGHT COCONUT PASTRY CREAM

Stir in a dash of Malibu® or other coconut liqueur.

LIGHT CITRUS PASTRY CREAM

Stir in the finely grated zest of ¼ orange and ¼ lime.

LIGHT PISTACHIO PASTRY CREAM

Stir in 1¾ oz. (50 g) Pistachio Paste (p. 19), well softened.

ALMOND CREAM

Prep: 20 minutes

Makes about 8 oz. (230 g) almond cream

4 tablespoons (2 oz. / 60 g) unsalted butter, softened
⅓ cup (2 oz. / 60 g) granulated sugar
¾ cup (2 oz. / 60 g) almond flour
1 egg, lightly beaten
1 teaspoon dark rum

1. In a medium bowl, whisk the butter with the sugar and almond flour until light and fluffy.

2. Whisk in the egg, beating briskly, then the rum.

3. Transfer to an airtight container and store in the refrigerator. Bring to room temperature before using.

SET VANILLA CREAM

Prep: 10 minutes   *Chill:* 12 hours

Makes about 2½ servings (700 g)

3½ sheets (7 g) 200 bloom gelatin
4 vanilla beans
8 oz. (225 g) white chocolate, chopped
¾ cup plus 1 tablespoon (190 ml) whole milk
1⅔ cups (385 ml) heavy cream

1. In a medium bowl of very cold water, soften the gelatin. Split the vanilla beans lengthwise and scrape out the seeds. Place the white chocolate in a bowl.

2. In a medium saucepan, heat the milk over medium-high heat with the vanilla beans and seeds until bubbles appear around the edge; remove from the heat. Remove the vanilla beans. Squeeze the gelatin dry and stir into the hot milk until completely dissolved. Pour the hot liquid over the white chocolate and stir until smooth. Let cool to about 85°F (30°C), then stir in the cream.

3. Transfer to a bowl and press plastic wrap directly on the surface. Chill for 12 hours. Whisk before using.

VANILLA PASTE

Prep: 15 minutes

Use according to directions, or to add a strong vanilla taste to your baking.

5 fresh vanilla beans
5 used vanilla beans (seeds scraped, washed, and dried)
2 teaspoons (10 ml) vanilla extract
(or acacia honey, or glucose)
1 tablespoon (20 g) honey

1. Place the fresh vanilla beans in a warm place to dry out for a few days.

2. Cut all the vanilla beans into small pieces. In a small food processor, blend them with the vanilla extract and honey until a paste forms with a few small chunks. Transfer to a small jar, seal, and store in the refrigerator.

PURE HAZELNUT PRALINE PASTE

Prep: 20 minutes
Cook: about 30 minutes

Makes about 1 lb. (450 g) paste

1½ cups (9½ oz. / 270 g) whole hazelnuts
1 cup (7 oz. / 200 g) sugar, divided

1. Preheat the oven to 340°F (170°C) convection. Line a rimmed baking sheet with a silicone mat or parchment paper. Spread the hazelnuts on the baking sheet and toast for at least 20 minutes. Let cool.

2. Wrap the hazelnuts in a kitchen towel and rub the nuts together to remove the skins.

3. In a medium saucepan (preferably copper), melt half of the sugar over medium heat, stirring with a wooden spoon or spatula, until the sugar melts and begins to color.

4. Add the remaining sugar and cook, stirring, until a deep caramel color. Remove from the heat.

5. Add the peeled hazelnuts and stir to coat with the caramel. Spread on the lined baking sheet and let cool.

6. Break the caramelized hazelnuts into chunks. In a food processor, finely grind them until a smooth paste forms. Transfer to an airtight container and store in a dark place

Note: For the best possible taste, choose the finest hazelnuts. If possible, make the caramel-hazelnut mixture 2 days before grinding so the sugar can fully absorb the taste of the nuts. But for everyday use, simply process as soon as the coated caramelized hazelnuts have cooled.

FONDANT ICING

Prep: 10 minutes

Makes about 1 lb. 2 oz. (500 g) icing

1 lb. 2 oz. (500 g) white fondant
A little water (see Note)
Liquid food coloring or flavoring of your choice

1. In a medium heatproof bowl (nonmetallic if using the microwave), stir the white fondant with a little water. Heat gently, using short bursts in the microwave or over a saucepan of simmering water, stirring occasionally to warm evenly. The mixture should be thick yet pourable. Keep heating until the fondant reaches 95°F (35°C), has a flowing texture, and is still shiny. If overheated, it loses its sheen.

2. If the fondant looks like it's too thick to pour, stir in a little more water.

3. Pour at 95°F (35°C); reheat or keep warm if necessary.

Note: Some brands of white fondant are pre-softened and may need very little water. If you add too much, simply stir in more white fondant to get the right texture.

CHOCOLATE FONDANT ICING

Prep: 15 minutes

Makes about 1 lb. 10 oz. (750 g) icing

2 tablespoons plus 2 teaspoons (40 ml) water
¼ cup (2 oz. / 60 g) granulated sugar
9 oz. (250 g) white fondant
3½ oz. (100 g) 80% chocolate, preferably Valrhona® Coeur de Guanaja, melted
1¾ oz. (50 g) neutral glaze or strained apricot jelly
1 oz. (30 g) 100% dark chocolate or same weight unsweetened cocoa powder

1. In a small saucepan, bring the water to a boil with the sugar, stirring until the sugar dissolves, creating a syrup.

2. In a medium bowl, stir the fondant with the syrup and melted chocolate. Stir in the neutral glaze and dark chocolate. Heat gently, using short bursts in the microwave or over a saucepan of simmering water, stirring occasionally to warm evenly. The mixture should be thick yet pourable. Keep heating until the fondant reaches 95°F (35°C), has a flowing texture, and is still shiny. If overheated, it loses its sheen.

3. Pour at 95°F (35°C); reheat or keep warm if necessary.

BARELY SWEET RASPBERRY JAM

Prep: 15 minutes   *Cook:* 10 minutes

Makes one 8-ounce (250-g) jar

9 oz. (250 g) fresh or frozen raspberries
¾ cup (5¼ oz. / 150 g) granulated sugar, divided
¾ teaspoon (3 g) pectin NH
2 teaspoons (10 ml) lemon juice

1. Place a small plate in the freezer.

2. In a food processor, purée the raspberries with half of the sugar for 2 to 3 minutes, until smooth. Pour into a saucepan and bring to a boil.

3. In a small bowl, thoroughly combine the remaining sugar with the pectin. Stir into the boiling raspberry mixture. Add the lemon juice and boil for 2 minutes.

4. Check the consistency: drop a little jam onto the chilled plate; it should hold its shape. If it doesn't, cook a little longer. Pour into jar, cover, and let cool. Chill until using.

Note: If you don't have pectin NH, either replace all the sugar with special jam sugar (also known as gelling sugar), or simply use ordinary sugar and continue cooking until the consistency is right.

RHUBARB COMPOTE

Prep: 15 minutes   *Cook:* 30 to 40 minutes

Serves 6

2 lb. 3 oz. (1 kg) rhubarb
Scant ⅔ cup (4 oz. / 120 g) granulated sugar
2 tablespoons plus 1 teaspoon (1¾ oz. / 50 g) pine honey
(or other flavorful honey)
1 vanilla bean, split lengthwise and seeds scraped
1 sheet (2 g) gelatin, optional

1.   Preheat the oven to 350°F (180°C) convection.

2.   Peel the rhubarb and slice it ¾ inch (2 cm) thick.
In a shallow baking dish, toss the rhubarb with the
sugar. Stir in the honey and add the vanilla bean and
seeds. Bake for 30 to 40 minutes, until the rhubarb
is soft and compotelike. Let cool, remove the vanilla
bean, and chill.

3.   For a firmer texture, soften the gelatin in a bowl
of cold water, then squeeze it dry and add to the
compote as soon as it comes out of the oven, stirring
until completely dissolved. But if the rhubarb has
been correctly cooked, it should hold on its own.

FRUITY GLAZE

Prep: 10 minutes

Makes about 1 cup (250 ml) glaze

5 sheets (10 g) 200 bloom gelatin
¼ vanilla bean
⅔ cup (150 ml) mineral water
1 cup (7 oz. / 200 g) granulated sugar
Finely grated zest of ¼ orange
Finely grated zest of ½ lemon

1.   In a medium bowl of very cold water, soften the
gelatin. Split the vanilla bean lengthwise and scrape
out the seeds.

2.   In a medium saucepan, bring the water to a boil
with the vanilla bean and seeds, sugar, and citrus
zest, stirring until the sugar dissolves; remove from
the heat. Remove the vanilla bean.

3.   Squeeze the gelatin dry and gently whisk into the
hot liquid until completely dissolved. Strain through
a fine sieve. Let cool and chill until needed.

4.   To use the glaze, heat gently in a bowl set over a
saucepan of simmering water until pourable.

Note: The glaze keeps for 2 or 3 weeks in the freezer
or a few days in the refrigerator.

PISTACHIO CREAM

Prep: 10 minutes   *Cook:* 5 minutes
Chill: 4 hours minimum, preferably 12 hours

Makes about 1 lb. 6 oz. (630 g) pistachio cream

1¼ teaspoons (4 g) gelatin powder
5¼ oz. (150 g) white chocolate, preferably Valrhona® Ivoire
⅓ oz. (10 g) cocoa butter
1¾ oz. (50 g) pistachio paste, preferably Fabbri®
½ cup plus 1 tablespoon (140 ml) whole milk
1 cup plus 2 tablespoons (280 ml) heavy cream

1.   Dissolve the gelatin powder in a little very cold water.

2.   Place the white chocolate, cocoa butter, and pistachio
paste in a medium bowl.

3.   In a small saucepan, heat the milk over medium-high
heat until bubbles appear around the edge. Remove from
the heat and stir in the gelatin until completely dissolved.
Pour the hot liquid into the white chocolate mixture. Using
an immersion blender, process until smooth. Let cool.

4.   Pour in the cream and process again. Chill for at least
4 hours, but preferably 12. Whisk well before using.

Note: If you don't have cocoa butter, add an extra ½ oz.
(15 g) white chocolate to the recipe.

PISTACHIO–ALMOND PASTE

Prep: 10 minutes

Makes about 7 oz. (200 g) paste

¾ cup (7 oz. / 200 g) whole, peeled,
unsalted pistachios
2 to 3 tablespoons orgeat syrup

1. In a food processor, finely chop the pistachios,
then drizzle in the orgeat syrup.

2. Process for 4 to 5 minutes, until a paste forms.

COFFEE PASTE

Prep: 15 minutes   *Cook:* 10 minutes

Makes 10½ oz. (300 g) paste

3½ oz. (100 g) coffee beans
½ cup (3½ oz. / 100 g) granulated sugar, divided
½ cup minus 1 tablespoon (100 ml) neutral oil

1. Preheat the oven to 320°F (160°C) convection.

2. Line a rimmed baking sheet with a silicone mat
or parchment paper. Spread the coffee beans on the
baking sheet and roast for about 10 minutes, then
let cool.

3. In a small saucepan, melt half of the sugar over
medium heat, stirring with a silicone spatula or
wooden spoon, until the sugar melts and begins
to color.

4. Add the remaining sugar and cook, stirring,
until a deep caramel color. Remove from the heat.

5. Add the roasted coffee beans and stir to coat.
Spread on the lined baking sheet and let cool.

6. Break the caramelized coffee beans into chunks.
In a food processor, finely grind them, gradually
drizzling in the oil, until a smooth paste forms.

7. Transfer the paste to an airtight container and
store in the refrigerator.

Note: This recipe was created by Augustin Steiner,
head pastry chef at the Mutzig pastry shop.

PURE PISTACHIO PASTE

Prep: 10 minutes   *Cook:* 10 minutes

Makes about 10½ oz. (300 g) paste

1¼ cups (5¼ oz. / 150 g) whole, peeled, unsalted pistachios
⅔ cup (4½ oz. / 130 g) granulated sugar
Scant ⅓ cup (70 ml) water

1. Preheat the oven to 320°F (160°C) convection.
Line a baking sheet with parchment paper and spread
the pistachios on it. Toast for 10 minutes and let cool.

2. In a small saucepan, heat the sugar and water,
stirring, until the sugar dissolves and the temperature
registers 285°F (140°C). Add the pistachios and stir to
coat. Let cool on the baking sheet.

3. In a small food processor, finely grind the
pistachios.

Monday

Start the week off with something
easy, yet elegant - pink biscuits
(p. 23) perhaps? All the cookies here
keep well ... if you don't finish
them immediately!

Prep:
30 minutes

Rest:
30 minutes

Cook:
10 to 12 minutes

PINK BISCUITS
Biscuits Roses

···

Makes 20 biscuits

Unsalted butter for brushing
All-purpose flour for dusting and the biscuits
3 extra-large eggs
Granulated sugar
½ vanilla bean
A few drops pink or red food coloring
Confectioners' sugar for dusting

Equipment
A kitchen scale
A pastry bag fitted with a plain ¼- to ⅓-inch (7- to 8-mm) tip, optional
Twenty 2 by 1¼-inch (5 by 3-cm) molds

1. Brush the pans with butter and dust with flour. Set on a baking sheet.

2. Weigh the eggs in their shells. Weigh out exactly the same weight of granulated sugar and of flour. Sift the flour. Split the vanilla bean lengthwise and scrape out the seeds.

3. In a medium bowl, combine the eggs with the granulated sugar and food coloring. Using an electric beater, mix at high speed for 15 minutes, then at medium speed for 5 minutes.

4. Using a silicone spatula, carefully fold the flour and vanilla seeds into the egg mixture.

5. Pipe or spoon the batter into the financier pans, filling three-quarters full. Dust generously with the confectioners' sugar. Let the batter stand at room temperature for 30 minutes to dry. Preheat the oven to 350°F (180°C) convection.

6. Bake the biscuits for 10 to 12 minutes. They should remain pink but be lightly golden on the bottom.

7. Let the biscuits cool in the pans before removing carefully.

Note: These biscuits can be stored in an airtight container.

BUCKWHEAT FINANCIER CAKE

Serves 8

1¼ sticks (5¼ oz. / 150 g) unsalted butter, plus more for brushing

¼ cup plus 2 teaspoons (1¾ oz. / 50 g) buckwheat flour, plus more for dusting

1 cup (3½ oz. / 100 g) almond flour

1⅓ cups (6 oz. / 170 g) confectioners' sugar

5 egg whites

1 tablespoon (20 g) apricot or quince purée

Apricot jam, warmed for brushing

⅓ cup (1¾ oz. / 50 g) whole toasted almonds

Equipment

An 8-inch (20-cm) round metal cake pan, nonstick if you prefer (see Note)

A pastry bag fitted with a plain ⅓-inch (8-mm) tip, optional

1. Preheat the oven to 340°F (170°C) convection. Brush the cake pan with butter and dust with buckwheat flour. In a small saucepan, melt the butter over medium heat, then cook until it begins to brown and smells a little like hazelnuts. Strain the brown butter through a fine sieve. You'll need to use the brown butter while still warm.

2. Sift the almond flour with the confectioners' sugar and buckwheat flour into a medium bowl. Stir in the egg whites. Whisk in the brown butter and apricot purée.

3. Pipe or spoon the batter into the cake pan, filling three-quarters full. (The cake must be at least ¾- inch / 2- cm thick.) Bake for 35 to 40 minutes, until golden on top and springy.

4. Immediately turn out the cake onto a rack and brush the top with the apricot jam. Finely grate the whole almonds around the edge. Serve warm.

Note: For a nice, crisp crust, use a metal pan. You get a better result with metal than silicone, which is why most professional pastry chefs use metal pans to make this type of cake.

Prep:
30 minutes

Chill and rest:
2 hours + 24 hours

Cook:
15 to 20 minutes

MINI RUM BABAS

Makes 15 babas

Baba dough	Baba syrup	Equipment
1⅔ cups (7 oz. / 200 g) all-purpose flour	¾ cup (200 ml) water	Fifteen 2-inch (5-cm) baba molds or muffin cups
2½ teaspoons (½ oz. / 15 g) dry yeast	1½ cups (10½ oz. / 300 g) granulated sugar	
¾ teaspoon (4 g) fine salt	Zest of ¼ orange peeled, in long strips	
1 tablespoon plus 2 teaspoons (20 g) granulated sugar	1 pinch vanilla bean powder	
1 teaspoon pure vanilla extract	Scant ½ cup (100 ml) dark rum	
2 eggs		
3 tablespoons plus 1 teaspoon (1¾ oz. / 50 g) unsalted butter, room temperature, cubed, plus more for brushing		

BABA DOUGH

1. In the bowl of a stand mixer fitted with the dough hook, combine the flour with the yeast, sugar, salt, and vanilla. Working at medium speed, add the eggs one by one, then knead for 2 minutes. Add the butter and knead at medium speed for 7 minutes, until the dough pulls away from the sides of the bowl. Cover the bowl with a kitchen towel and let rise for 1 hour, until doubled in volume.

2. Brush the baba molds with butter. Transfer the dough to a work surface and knead until smooth and elastic. Shape into a log and cut into 15 equal pieces.

3. Place 1 piece of dough in each mold. Set on a baking sheet.

4. Let the dough rise for 1 hour. Preheat the oven to 350°F (180°C) convection. Bake the babas for 15 to 20 minutes, until golden and well risen. Turn the babas out onto a rack and let dry at room temperature, preferably for a whole day, so they can better absorb the syrup later.

BABA SYRUP

5. In a medium saucepan, bring the water to a boil with the sugar, orange zest, and vanilla. Remove from the heat and add the rum. Place the babas in a 2-cup (16-fl.-oz. / 500-ml) jar, pour in the syrup, and close.

Note: These babas can be stored in the syrup for up to 4 weeks.

PETITS FOURS
WITH ALMOND PASTE AND SOUR CHERRIES

Makes about 40 petits fours

1¾ oz. (50 g) canned sour cherries

1 lb. 2 oz. (500 g) 50% almond paste, well softened

½ egg white

2½ tablespoons (1¾ oz. / 50 g) glucose

3 tablespoons (1¾ oz. / 50 g) apricot purée

3½ oz. (100 g) slivered almonds

Confectioners' sugar for dusting

Equipment

A pastry bag fitted with a fluted ⅜-inch (1-cm) tip

1. Drain the cherries and dry them on paper towels. Cut them into small dice. In a medium bowl, using an electric beater, mix the almond paste with the egg white.

2. In a small saucepan, heat the glucose with the apricot purée to 113°F (45°C), then carefully stir into the almond paste mixture. Stir in the sour cherries.

3. Line a baking sheet with parchment paper. Pipe long strips of dough on the baking sheet. Press in the almonds and dust with the confectioners' sugar. Let dry at room temperature for about 12 hours; if the outside of the dough dries somewhat after only a few hours—simply touch them to check—they are ready to bake.

4. Preheat the oven to 480°F (250°C) convection. If you like, cut the dough strips into 1¾-inch (4-cm) pieces. Bake for 2 to 3 minutes, keeping an eye on them so they don't burn. Let the petits fours cool slightly on the baking sheet, then transfer to racks and let cool completely.

Note: These petits fours can be stored in an airtight container.

MOOIST CHESTNUT CAKE

Serves 10 to 12

1 stick (4¼ oz. / 120 g) unsalted butter, melted and cooled, plus more for brushing

3 tablespoons (1 oz. / 30 g) all-purpose flour, plus more for dusting

4 eggs, separated

1 lb. 2 oz. (500 g) chestnut spread (*crème de marrons*)

1 teaspoon Vanilla Paste (p. 16)

A few candied chestnuts, broken into pieces

Equipment

A 10-inch (24-cm) round cake pan or 10 by 5-inch (24 by 13-cm) loaf pan

Kitchen torch (optional)

1. Preheat the oven to 350°F (180°C) convection. Brush the cake pan with butter and dust with flour. Chill until needed.

2. In a small saucepan, melt the butter over medium heat. In the bowl of a stand mixer fitted with the whisk, whip the egg whites until they hold a soft peak. In a large bowl, beat the chestnut spread with the melted butter. Beat in the egg yolks, flour, and vanilla. Carefully fold in the egg whites.

3. Spread the batter in the cake pan and bake for 40 minutes. Let the cake cool slightly in the pan, then turn out onto a rack and let cool completely. Decorate with the candied chestnuts.

4. You can add texture to this soft, moist cake by topping it with threads of Italian meringue piped from a very fine tip or a Mont Blanc (multi-opening) tip. If you like, brown the meringue using a kitchen torch or under the broiler.

ITALIAN MERINGUE

5. In a small saucepan, cook 3 tablespoons plus 1 teaspoon (50 ml) water with ½ cup (3½ oz. / 100 g) sugar over medium heat, stirring with a silicone spatula. You will be cooking this syrup to 244°F (118°C)—use an instant-read thermometer to check. Meanwhile, place the egg white of an extra-large egg in the bowl of a stand mixer. When the temperature of the syrup reaches 237°F (114°C), begin whisking the egg white at high speed.

6. As soon as the temperature of the syrup reaches 244°F (118°C), reduce the speed of the whisk and drizzle in the syrup, taking care to pour it down the side of the bowl so it doesn't splatter. Increase the speed to high and whisk until the Italian meringue reaches room temperature.

Notes: Chestnut spread (*crème de marrons*) comprises chestnuts, sugar, crushed candied chestnuts, glucose syrup, a little water, and vanilla extract.

Chestnut paste (*pâte de marrons*) comprises chestnuts, sugar, glucose, and vanilla extract.

Recipe by Françoise Vauzeilles.

Prep:
30 minutes

Rest:
12 hours or overnight
for the caramel

Cook:
10 minutes

PRALINE–PEANUT COOKIES

Makes 20 cookies

Salted butter caramel

3 tablespoons plus 1 teaspoon
(50 ml) heavy cream

¼ vanilla bean

Scant ⅔ cup (4¼ oz. / 120 g)
granulated sugar

½ teaspoon (2 g) fleur de sel

5 tablespoons (3 oz. / 80 g)
unsalted butter, well chilled
and diced

Cookie dough

1⅔ cups (7 oz. / 200 g)
all-purpose flour

1 teaspoon baking soda

4 tablespoons plus 2 teaspoons
(2½ oz. / 70 g) unsalted butter,
room temperature

1¾ oz. (50 g) hazelnut paste,
well softened

⅓ cup (2½ oz. / 75 g)
granulated sugar

½ cup (3½ oz. / 100 g) light
brown sugar

2 pinches fine salt

1 teaspoon pure vanilla extract

1 pinch vanilla bean powder

1 egg

1¾ oz. (50 g) gianduja chocolate

1¾ oz. (50 g) 50%
dark chocolate

½ cup (3 oz. / 80 g)
salted peanuts

5¼ oz. (150 g) Sweet and Salty
Caramelized Peanuts (p. 9)

SALTED BUTTER CARAMEL

1. Make the caramel a day ahead: In a small saucepan, heat the cream over medium-high heat until bubbles appear around the edge; remove from the heat. Split the vanilla bean lengthwise and scrape out the seeds. In a small saucepan, cook the sugar over low heat, stirring occasionally, until it's a lovely caramel color. Increase the heat to medium. Carefully pour in the cream and add the vanilla seeds. Using a wooden spoon or silicone spatula, stir until smooth and cook until the temperature reaches 223°F (106°C).

2. Remove the pan from the heat and stir in the fleur de sel and butter.

3. Transfer the caramel to a jar, close, and let set at room temperature, preferably for 12 hours or overnight.

COOKIE DOUGH

4. Preheat the oven to 400°F (200°C) convection. Line 2 baking sheets with parchment paper. Sift the flour with the baking soda. In a large bowl, beat the butter with the hazelnut paste, granulated sugar, brown sugar, salt, vanilla extract, and vanilla bean powder. Beat in the egg. Stir in the dry ingredients.

5. Using a knife, roughly chop the two chocolates. Stir into the cookie dough with the salted peanuts.

6. Using a tablespoon or, even better, a small ice cream scoop, place balls of dough on the baking sheets. Bake for about 10 minutes, rotating the pans halfway through; the center should remain soft. Let the cookies cool on the baking sheets.

7. Drizzle spirals of caramel over the tops and decorate with the caramelized peanuts.

Note: This caramel can be stored at room temperature in an airtight container.

COFFEE FINANCIER LOAF

Serves 8

1 stick plus 2 tablespoons (5¼ oz. / 150 g) unsalted butter, plus more for brushing

½ cup (2 oz. / 55 g) all-purpose flour, plus more for dusting

⅓ cup (1¾ oz. / 50 g) raisins

A little dark rum for soaking

¾ cup (2½ oz. / 70 g) almond flour

Generous ⅓ cup (1 oz. / 30 g) ground hazelnuts

1⅓ cups (6 oz. / 170 g) confectioners' sugar

1 pinch vanilla bean powder

5 egg whites

½ oz. (15 g) Coffee Paste (p. 19)

1 tablespoon (15 g) apricot purée

Equipment

An 8 by 4-inch (20 by 10-cm) loaf pan

A pastry bag, optional

1. Preheat the oven to 340°F (170°C) convection. Brush the loaf pan with butter and dust with flour. Rinse the raisins under hot water. In a small bowl, soak the raisins in the rum. Drain before using.

2. In a small saucepan, melt the butter over medium heat, then cook until the brown butter begins to brown and smells a little like hazelnuts. Strain the brown butter through a fine sieve. You'll need to use it while it's still warm.

3. Sift the almond flour with the ground hazelnuts, confectioners' sugar, vanilla, and flour into a medium bowl. Stir in the egg whites. Whisk in the brown butter, Coffee Paste, and apricot purée.

4. Pipe or spoon the batter into the loaf pan, filling three-quarters full. Sprinkle the raisins along the length. Bake for about 30 minutes, until golden on top and springy. Immediately turn out the loaf onto a rack and let cool completely.

GIANT MUESLI COOKIES

CRUSTY ALMOND TART

Makes 2 to 3 giant cookies

1⅔ cups (7 oz. / 200 g) all-purpose flour
Heaping ½ teaspoon (2.5 g) baking powder
2 teaspoons (5 g) unsweetened cocoa powder
1 scant cup (3½ oz. / 100 g) muesli with red berries
1 stick plus 1 tablespoon (4½ oz. / 130 g) unsalted butter,
room temperature
½ cup (3½ oz. / 100 g) granulated sugar
⅓ cup (2½ oz. / 70 g) brown sugar
½ teaspoon (2 g) fine salt
1 teaspoon pure vanilla extract
1 egg
3½ oz. (100 g) 60 to 70% dark chocolate
2 oz. (60 g) 40% milk chocolate

Serves 8 to 10

9 oz. (250 g) Sweet Almond Pastry (p. 10),
room temperature
About 3 egg whites (you may need a little extra)
1½ cups (10½ oz. / 300 g) granulated sugar
A few drops green food coloring
2⅔ cups (8 oz. / 225 g) ground almonds

Equipment
A 5½ by 7½-inch (14 by 19-cm) tart pan
or 6-inch (16-cm) square cake pan

1. Preheat the oven to 350°F (180°C)
convection. On a lightly floured work surface,
roll out the pastry about ⅛ inch (3 to 4 mm)
thick. Line the tart pan with the pastry. Bake the
tart shell for about 15 minutes. Transfer the pan
to a rack and let cool.

2. In a medium bowl, using a wooden spoon,
combine the egg whites with the sugar. Stir in
the food coloring, then the ground almonds. If
the mixture is very firm, add a little more egg
white to soften it slightly.

3. Spread the ground almond mixture in the
tart shell and bake for 45 to 50 minutes, until the
top is lightly browned. Transfer the tart to a rack
and let cool. Cut into small rectangles.

Notes: This recipe, from Lamballe baker and
pastry chef Philippe Lemercier, can be frozen
raw and baked the day you serve it. It keeps very
well and is perfect for picnics or alongside a
warming cup of tea in winter.

1. Preheat the oven to 400°F (200°C) convection.
Line a baking sheet with parchment paper. Sift the
flour with the baking powder and cocoa powder.
Spread the muesli on a large plate.

2. In a medium bowl, beat the butter with the
granulated sugar, brown sugar, salt, and vanilla.
Beat in the egg. Stir in the dry ingredients.

3. Roughly chop the two chocolates. Stir them into
the dough. Shape into large balls and flatten them
partially with the palm of your hand. Press them
into the muesli and place on the baking sheet.

4. Bake for about 15 minutes; the center should
remain soft. Let the cookies cool slightly on the
baking sheet.

Recipe by Philippe Lemercier, baker and pastry
chef in Lamballe, France.

GIANT MUESLI COOKIES

GIANT CHOCOLATE–CITRUS COOKIES

GIANT CHOCOLATE–CITRUS COOKIES

————————————

Makes six 8-inch (20-cm) cookies

4¼ cups (1 lb. 1½ oz. / 530 g) all-purpose flour

½ teaspoon baking powder

10½ oz. (300 g) dark chocolate of your choice

2 sticks plus 1½ tablespoons (9 oz. / 250 g) unsalted
butter, room temperature

Scant ½ cup (3 oz. / 90 g) granulated sugar

1¼ cups (9 oz. / 250 g) light brown sugar

2 eggs

1 teaspoon fine salt

2 teaspoons pure vanilla extract

Candied orange or lemon peel, chopped

1. Preheat the oven to 350°F (180°C) convection.
Line 2 baking sheets with parchment paper. Sift
the flour with the baking powder. Using a large
knife, roughly chop the chocolate.

2. In a food processor, combine the butter with
the two sugars. Add the eggs, salt, and vanilla and
process for a few seconds.

3. Incorporate the dry ingredients, taking care
not to overmix, then pulse in the chocolate. Using
your hands, shape the dough into large balls,
place them on the baking sheets, and flatten
them partially with the palm of your hand.

4. Press the candied citrus peel into the top just
deep enough to stick. Bake for 10 to 15 minutes,
rotating the pans halfway. Let the cookies cool
slightly on the baking sheet. These are delicious
when served warm.

SPICED BAKED APPLES

————————————

Serves 7

7 Golden Delicious apples

Juice of 1 lemon

Julienned zest and juice of 2 oranges

2 teaspoons vanilla sugar (see Note)

2 pinches freshly grated nutmeg

2 pinches freshly ground pepper

2 pinches cinnamon

2 teaspoons unsalted butter

2 tablespoons honey

Cinnamon sticks for decorating, optional

1. Preheat the oven to 300°F (150°C) convection.
Peel the apples and core them. Brush with lemon
juice to discourage browning.

2. In a small saucepan, warm the orange juice
with the zest, vanilla sugar, spices, butter, and
honey, swirling the pan, until melted.

3. Fit the apples snugly into an ovenproof dish.
Drizzle with the spiced orange juice and cover
with foil. Reduce the oven temperature to 250°F
(120°C) and bake for 2 hours, turning the apples
occasionally. If you like, decorate them with
cinnamon sticks just before serving.

Note: If you don't have ready-made vanilla
sugar, prepare your own by storing used, dried
vanilla beans in a closed jar of sugar for at least 1
week. Simply replace any sugar you use to have a
permanent supply on hand.

SPICED BAKED APPLES

PISTACHIO CUSTARD TART

———————————————

Serves 8

10½ oz. (300 g) Crisp Short Pastry (p. 9), room temperature,
or Quick Puff Pastry (p. 12), chilled

8 egg yolks

½ cup plus 1 tablespoon (4 oz. / 110 g) granulated sugar, divided

Generous ⅓ cup (2 oz. / 60 g) cornstarch

7 oz. (200 g) Pistachio Paste (p. 19), or store-bought, well softened

2 vanilla beans, split lengthwise and seeds scraped

¾ cup (200 ml) heavy cream

3 cups (700 ml) milk

½ teaspoon (2 g) fleur de sel

7 tablespoons (3½ oz. / 100 g) unsalted butter, diced, room temperature

Equipment

An 8-inch (20-cm) tart ring or pan with removable bottom, 1¾ inches (4 cm) deep

1. If using a tart ring, line a baking sheet with parchment paper and place the ring in the center. On a lightly floured work surface, roll out the pastry ⅛ inch (3 mm) thick. Line the ring with the pastry. Chill for at least 10 minutes. Preheat the oven to 340°F (170°C) convection. Cover the pastry with parchment paper and fill with baking beans. Bake for 30 minutes, then carefully remove the paper with the beans and let cool.

2. In a medium bowl, whisk the egg yolks with half of the sugar, the cornstarch, pistachio paste, and vanilla seeds but don't let the mixture lighten in color. Stir in the cream.

3. In a medium saucepan, heat the milk with the fleur de sel and remaining sugar over medium-high heat, whisking until bubbles appear around the edge and the sugar dissolves. Remove from the heat. Gradually whisk into the egg yolk mixture. Return to the pan and cook over medium heat, whisking continuously, until the custard thickens. Remove from the heat and stir in the butter. Spread the custard in the tart shell. Let cool completely.

4. Preheat the oven to 425°F (220°C) convection. Bake the tart for 20 minutes, then increase the oven temperature to 465°F (240°C) convection and bake for 10 minutes. If the top is still pale and you prefer it lightly browned, slide the tart under the broiler for a few minutes. Let cool completely.

CRISP VANILLA SWIRLS

Prep:
20 minutes

Cook:
20 minutes

Chill:
40 + 30 minutes

CRISP VANILLA SWIRLS

Makes about 20 swirls

½ cup minus 1 tablespoon (2¾ oz. / 80 g) vanilla sugar
10½ oz. (300 g) Quick Puff Pastry (p. 12), chilled
Confectioners' sugar for dusting

1. Sprinkle a work surface with about one-third of the vanilla sugar. Working on the sugar, roll out the pastry to an 8 by 16-inch (20 by 40-cm) rectangle ⅛-inch (4 mm) thick.

2. Sprinkle the pastry with another third of the vanilla sugar and press it in lightly with your palms. Fold the pastry in three to make an envelope and roll out again to the same dimensions. Sprinkle with the remaining vanilla sugar and lightly press it in with the rolling pin.

3. Roll up the pastry along the longer side into a log. Cover with plastic wrap and chill for 40 minutes.

4. Line 2 baking sheets with parchment paper. Cut the log into slices just under ½ inch (1 cm) thick and place on the baking sheets, spacing well apart. Chill for 30 minutes.

5. Preheat the oven to 400°F (200°C) convection. Bake the swirls for 30 minutes, until nicely golden. Dust with confectioners' sugar and return to the oven for a few minutes to caramelize, watching carefully so the swirls don't burn. You can also caramelize them under the broiler, but they'll absorb moisture more quickly after baking.

6. Let the swirls cool slightly on the baking sheets, then transfer to racks and let cool completely.

Prep:
20 minutes

Cook:
20 minutes

Rest:
1 hour

CRISP ALMOND COOKIES
Croquants de Cordes-sur-Ciel

Makes 20 cookies

1¼ cups (9 oz. / 250 g) granulated sugar
½ cup (3½ oz. / 100 g) natural almonds
3 to 4 tablespoons (30 to 40 g) all-purpose flour
About 2 egg whites
A few drops pure vanilla extract, optional

1. In a medium bowl, stir the sugar with the almonds and flour. Gradually stir in the egg whites, just enough for the dough to be fairly thick. Stir in the vanilla, if desired

2. Shape the dough into 1¼ by 8-inch (4 by 20-cm) strips. On a well-floured work surface, cut them into slices just under ½ inch (1 cm) thick.

3. Place the slices on a nonstick baking sheet or a baking sheet lined with a silicone mat or parchment paper, spacing well apart; you may have to work in batches. Let stand at room temperature for at least 1 hour, until a crust forms on the outside.

4. Preheat the oven to 350°F (180°C) convection. Bake for 20 minutes, until puffed and browned. Let cool slightly on the baking sheet, then transfer to racks and let cool completely.

Note: These cookies can be stored in an airtight container.

CRISP ALMOND COOKIES

MOLTEN CHOCOLATE MUG CAKE

Prep:
15 minutes

Chill:
1 hour + 1 hour

Cook:
7 to 8 minutes

MOLTEN CHOCOLATE MUG CAKES

Serves 2 to 3 hungry chocolate lovers

6 tablespoons (3 oz. / 90 g) unsalted butter,
plus more for brushing

¼ cup (1¼ oz. / 35 g) all-purpose flour,
plus more for dusting

3½ oz. (100 g) 70% dark chocolate

3 eggs

½ cup plus 1 tablespoon (4 oz. / 110 g) granulated sugar

1 teaspoon unsweetened cocoa powder, sifted

1 tablespoon milk

Equipment

3 heatproof mugs or cups

1. Brush the mugs with butter and dust with flour. Chill for at least 1 hour before starting the recipe.

2. Using a knife, chop the chocolate. In a medium bowl set over a saucepan of simmering water, melt the chocolate with the butter, stirring occasionally, until smooth and lukewarm.

3. In a medium bowl, using an electric beater, whisk the eggs with the sugar but don't let the mixture lighten in color. Whisk in the melted chocolate and butter. Whisk in the flour, cocoa powder, and milk.

4. Divide the batter among the mugs and chill for at least 1 hour. The cold batter will cook less in the center, creating a molten texture.

5. Preheat the oven to 400°F (200°C) convection. Bake for 7 to 8 minutes, until the surface starts to crack but the batter remains wobbly below.

EDMÉE'S ANISEED LOAF

Serves 8

Unsalted butter for brushing

5 ⅓ cups (1 lb. 1 oz. / 480 g) cake flour,
plus more for dusting

2 teaspoons baking soda

2 teaspoons ground aniseed,
plus whole aniseed for sprinkling

1 cup (250 ml) water

2 eggs, separated

1¼ cups (9 oz. / 250 g) granulated sugar

¾ cup (9 oz. / 250 g) pine honey or other flavorful honey

1 drop kirsch

Equipment

An 8½ by 4½-inch (22 by 11-cm) loaf pan

1. Preheat the oven to 400°F (200°C) convection. Brush the loaf pan with butter and dust with flour.

2. Sift the flour with the baking soda.

3. In a small saucepan, bring the ground aniseed and water to a boil and cook for 2 minutes. Remove the pan from the heat and let cool to lukewarm.

4. In a medium bowl, whisk the egg whites until they hold a firm peak. In a large bowl, combine the sugar with the honey, kirsch, and aniseed infusion. Beat in the egg yolks and the dry ingredients, but do not overmix. Carefully fold in the beaten egg whites.

5. Spread the batter in the loaf pan, filling three-quarters full. Sprinkle the top with whole aniseed and bake for about 1 hour, until well risen and a tester inserted into the center comes out clean. Let the loaf cool slightly in the pan, then turn out onto a rack and let cool completely.

EDMÉE'S ANISEED LOAF

SEMOLINA PUDDING CAKES

Serves 6

4 cups (1 liter) whole milk
¾ cup minus 2½ teaspoons (4 oz. / 140 g) granulated sugar
1 tablespoon vanilla sugar
1 teaspoon (5 g) cinnamon
3 tablespoons plus 1 teaspoons (1 ¾ oz. / 50 g) unsalted butter
1 cup (5½ oz. / 150 g) wheat semolina (farina)
2 egg yolks
2 tablespoons plus 2 teaspoon (1½ oz. / 40 g) melted butter
¼ cup (1¾ oz. / 40 g) light brown sugar

1. In a large saucepan, heat the milk with the granulated sugar, vanilla sugar, cinnamon, and butter over medium-high heat, whisking, until bubbles appear around the edge and the sugar dissolves.

2. Gradually pour in the semolina, whisking continuously, and cook until the mixture looks like thin porridge. Remove from the heat.

3. Stir in the egg yolks.

NOW, DECIDE ON THE SHAPE AND SIZE OF YOUR CAKES:

- Spread in ramekins and let cool slightly before serving.
- Spread in a shallow dish ¾ inch (1.5 cm) thick, let cool, and chill until set. Cut into rectangles or other shapes and place on a baking sheet. Brush with melted butter and sprinkle with light brown sugar. Slide under the broiler for a few minutes, until lightly browned.

4. Serve warm accompanied by any of the following: applesauce, fresh fruit, grated almonds, or fruit coulis.

Prep:
4 hours

Freeze:
1 hour

Cook:
12 minutes

DOUBLE CHOCOLATE ROULADE

Serves 10

Extra-dark chocolate sponge cake

2½ egg yolks

1½ whole eggs, lightly beaten

⅓ cup (2½ oz. / 75 g) granulated sugar, divided

3 egg whites

2½ tablespoons (25 g) all-purpose flour

3½ tablespoons (1 oz. / 25 g) unsweetened cocoa powder

Milk chocolate mousse

8 oz. (230 g) 40% milk chocolate, preferably Valrhona® Jivara, chopped

3 tablespoons plus 1 teaspoon (45 ml) whole milk

1 scant cup (235 ml) heavy cream, divided

1 egg yolk

1¼ teaspoons (5 g) granulated sugar

Cocoa syrup

3 tablespoons plus 1 teaspoon (50 ml) water

2 tablespoons (15 g) unsweetened cocoa powder

1 tablespoon plus 2 teaspoons (20 g) granulated sugar

Assembly

2 to 3 tablespoons (¾ oz. / 20 g) cocoa nibs or chopped hazelnuts

Unsweetened cocoa powder for dusting

Equipment

A kitchen scale

A rimmed 12 by 16-inch (30 by 40-cm) baking sheet

EXTRA-DARK CHOCOLATE SPONGE CAKE

1. Preheat the oven to 350°F (180°C) convection. Line the baking sheet with parchment paper. In a medium bowl, whisk the egg yolks with the whole eggs and ¼ cup (1¾ oz. / 50 g) of the sugar until pale and thick.

2. In a separate bowl, whisk the egg whites with the remaining 1 tablespoon plus 2 teaspoons (20 g) sugar until they hold a firm glossy peak. Sift the flour with the cocoa powder. Carefully fold half of the meringue into the egg mixture.

3. Fold in the remaining meringue, then the dry ingredients. Weigh out 11¾ oz. (335 g) of the batter and spread on the baking sheet, leaving a ½-inch (1-cm) border. Bake for 12 minutes, just until springy.

MILK CHOCOLATE MOUSSE

4. In a bowl set over a pan of simmering water, melt the chocolate, stirring until smooth.

5. In a small saucepan, heat the milk with 3 tablespoons (45 ml) of the cream over medium-high heat until bubbles appear around the edge; remove from the heat. In a small bowl, whisk the egg yolk with the sugar until pale and thick. Whisk into the milk mixture. Cook over low heat, whisking constantly, to 176°F (80°C); do not let boil. Remove from the heat.

6. Stir the custard into the melted chocolate. Let cool to 86°F (30°). In a separate bowl, whip the remaining ¾ cup minus 2 teaspoons (190 ml) cream until it holds a soft peak. Fold into the chocolate custard.

COCOA SYRUP

7. In a small saucepan, bring the water to a boil with the cocoa powder and sugar, stirring. Invert the sponge on a clean sheet of parchment; peel off the top parchment. Brush with the syrup.

ASSEMBLY

8. Spread the mousse on the sponge and sprinkle with the cocoa nibs. Roll up the cake and freeze for 1 hour. Dust with cocoa powder.

Tuesday

Go nuts! Almonds are an essential in any French pastry maker's pantry. For an exceptional almond experience, try pain de Gênes (p 79), a rich sponge cake that includes almond paste and often a dash of liqueur!

Prep:
1 hour

Chill::
about 1 hour

Cook:
about 45 minutes

LAYERED RHUBARB–ALMOND TART

Serves 8

Almond cream

4 tablespoons (2 oz. / 60 g)
unsalted butter, room
temperature

⅓ cup (2 oz. / 60 g)
granulated sugar

¾ cup (2 oz. / 60 g)
almond flour

1½ teaspoons (5 g) cornstarch

1 egg, lightly beaten

½ teaspoon (2 ml) dark rum

Almond meringue

1 cup (3½ oz. / 100 g)
almond flour

1 tablespoon plus 1 teaspoon
(10 g) all-purpose flour

Scant 1 cup (6 oz. / 180 g)
granulated sugar, divided

7 egg whites

Chopped almonds
for sprinkling

Confectioners' sugar
for dusting

Rum glaze

2 tablespoons plus 1 teaspoon
(35 ml) water

2 tablespoons (30 ml)
dark rum

1¼ cups (6 oz. / 160 g)
confectioners' sugar

Assembly

7 oz. (200 g) Sweet Almond
Pastry (p. 10), room
temperature

10 to 14 oz. (300 to 400 g)
Rhubarb Compote (p. 18)

Equipment

A pastry bag fitted with a plain
½-inch (1.2-cm) tip

A pastry bag fitted with
a fine tip

ALMOND CREAM

1. In the bowl of a stand mixer fitted with the whisk, whip the butter with the sugar, almond flour, and cornstarch until smooth. Gradually whisk in the egg and rum. Cover and chill for 1 hour.

ALMOND MERINGUE

2. Preheat the oven to 350°F (180°C) convection. Line a baking sheet with parchment paper. Draw an 8½-inch (22-cm) circle on the paper and turn it over. In a medium bowl, whisk the almond flour with the all-purpose flour and ½ cup (3½ oz. / 100 g) of the granulated sugar. In a large bowl, whisk the egg whites, gradually adding the remaining ½ cup minus 1 tablespoon (2¾ oz. / 80 g) granulated sugar, until they hold a soft peak. Carefully fold the dry ingredients into the meringue.

3. Using the ½-inch (1.2-cm) tip, pipe an 8½-inch (22-cm) open spiral on the baking sheet, leaving space between the swirls to pipe the almond cream. Using the fine tip, pipe the almond cream in a spiral, filling the gaps.

4. Sprinkle with the chopped almonds and dust with confectioners' sugar. Bake for 15 to 20 minutes and let the spiral cool on the baking sheet.

RUM GLAZE

5. Reduce the oven temperature to 320°F (160°C) convection. In a small bowl, mix the water with the rum and confectioner's sugar. Pour evenly over the spiral. Place in the oven for 2 to 3 minutes, just until the glaze forms a crust.

ASSEMBLY

6. Increase the oven temperature to 340°F (170°C) convection. On a lightly floured work surface, roll out the pastry and cut out a disk the same diameter as the baked spiral. Chill for at least 10 minutes. Bake for 20 minutes and let cool.

7. Spread the rhubarb compote evenly over the pastry disk, then carefully top with the almond meringue spiral. Dust with confectioners' sugar.

CHURROS

Makes about 20 churros

Chocolate sauce
3½ oz. (100 g) 60 to 70% dark chocolate, chopped
½ cup (125 ml) heavy cream

Churros
1½ cups plus 2 tablespoons (380 ml) water
½ teaspoon fine salt
2¾ cups (9 oz. / 250 g) cake flour
1 pinch baking soda, optional
Finely grated zest of ½ lemon
⅓ cup (75 ml) olive oil
Neutral oil for frying
Granulated sugar for dredging

Equipment
A pastry bag fitted with a fluted ⅓-inch (8-mm) tip

CHOCOLATE SAUCE

1. In a medium bowl set over a saucepan of simmering water, melt the chocolate, stirring occasionally, until smooth.

2. In a small saucepan, heat the cream over medium-high heat until bubbles appear around the edge, then gradually stir into the chocolate. Keep warm.

CHURROS

3. In a small saucepan, bring the water and salt to a boil. Meanwhile, in a medium heatproof bowl, combine the flour with the baking soda and lemon zest. Pour in the boiling water and mix well.

4. Gradually beat in the olive oil to make a soft batter that's firm enough to pipe.

5. In a large pot, heat the neutral oil to 350°F (180°C). Pipe the batter in 6-inch (15-cm) lengths into the oil, cutting the batter off at the tip. You may need to work in batches.

6. Fry the churros, turning them occasionally, for about 5 minutes, until golden. Using a slotted spoon, transfer to paper towels to drain. Place the sugar in a large bowl. Dredge the churros in the sugar.

7. Serve the churros as soon as possible with the chocolate sauce in a bowl for dipping.

Prep:
1 hour 30 minutes

Chill:
12 hours

Cook:
30 minutes

VIENNESE APPLE STRUDEL

Serves 10

Strudel pastry

2¾ cups (12½ oz. / 350 g)
all-purpose flour, plus more
for dusting

1 egg

⅔ cup (150 ml) cold water

1 pinch fine salt

1⅔ cups plus 1 tablespoon
(415 ml) neutral oil

Filling and assembly

10 Golden Delicious or other
baking apples

1 tablespoon plus 1 teaspoon
(20 ml) dark rum

Scant ⅔ cup (4 oz. / 120 g)
granulated sugar, divided

1 teaspoon (5 g) cinnamon

½ cup (3 oz. / 80 g) raisins

Generous ½ cup (1¾ oz. / 50 g)
ground almonds

1 stick plus 2 teaspoons
(4½ oz. / 125 g) unsalted butter

Confectioners' sugar for
dusting

Equipment

A large white bed sheet

STRUDEL PASTRY

1. A day ahead, make the strudel dough: Sift the flour into the bowl of a stand mixer fitted with the dough hook. Add the egg, water, salt, and 1 tablespoon (15 ml) of the oil and knead at medium speed for 2 minutes. Shape into a ball and transfer to another bowl.

2. Pour the remaining oil over the dough and let stand for about 10 minutes. This prevents the dough from drying out as it rests and makes it easier to work with later. Discard the oil and cover the dough with plastic wrap. Chill for 12 hours. Thirty minutes before you begin working with it, bring the dough to room temperature.

FILLING AND ASSEMBLY

3. Peel, core, and halve the apples. Slice ⅛ inch (3 mm) thick. Place in a bowl, drizzle with the rum, and add ½ cup minus 1 tablespoon (2¾ oz. / 80 g) of the granulated sugar, the cinnamon, raisins, and ground almonds. Toss well to combine.

4. The rolled dough measures about 23 by 30 inches (70 by 80 cm), so make sure your work surface is large enough. Spread out the sheet on the work surface and dust with flour. On the sheet, roll out the dough a little with a rolling pin. Working from the center, begin pulling and stretching the dough; it should be as thin and smooth as possible. If it tears, don't worry; it won't be visible after baking.

5. Preheat the oven to 375°F (190°C) convection. Line a baking sheet with parchment paper. Melt the butter. Brush it evenly over the dough and sprinkle with the remaining 3½ tablespoons (1½ oz. / 40 g) granulated sugar.

6. Spoon the apple filling along the shorter side of the dough rectangle. Roll up the strudel tightly, tucking in the ends. Cut it in half crosswise and transfer to the baking sheet, seam side down. Bake for about 30 minutes, until crisp and lightly browned. Let the strudel cool on the baking sheet then dust with the confectioners' sugar.

Prep:
10 minutes

Chill:
2 to 12 hours

Cook:
25 to 35 minutes

PINK FONDANT BUTTER COOKIES

Makes 12 cookies

Cookie dough
2 cups (9 oz. / 250 g) all-purpose flour
½ teaspoon baking powder
⅔ cup (4½ oz. / 125 g) granulated sugar
1 stick plus 2 teaspoons (4½ oz. / 125 g) unsalted butter, diced
1 extra-large egg
Finely grated zest of ¼ lemon

Pink fondant icing
9 oz. (250 g) Fondant Icing (p. 17), warmed to 95°F (35°C)
A little kirsch for flavoring (see Note)
A drop red food coloring

Equipment
A 5-inch (12-cm) cookie cutter

COOKIE DOUGH

1. In a large bowl, whisk the flour with the baking powder and sugar. Rub in the butter until crumbly.

2. Knead in the egg and lemon zest. Transfer the dough to a lightly floured work surface and, using the heel of your hand, scrape the dough away from you until smooth.

3. Shape the dough into a disk, cover with plastic wrap, and chill for at least 2 hours. If you're not in a hurry, chill for 12 hours, which is even better.

4. Bring the dough to room temperature. Preheat the oven to 340°F (170°C) convection. Line a baking sheet with parchment paper. On a lightly floured work surface, roll out the dough about ¼ inch (4 to 5 mm) thick.

5. Using the cookie cutter, press out rounds and place on the baking sheet. Bake for about 20 minutes, until golden. Let the cookies cool slightly on the baking sheet, then transfer to racks and let cool completely.

PINK FONDANT ICING

6. In a medium bowl, add a little water to thin the fondant and a little kirsch for flavoring. The fondant must be thicker for these cookies than for covering a cake. Beat in the food coloring. Using a spatula or flat knife, spread it over the cookies. Let dry at room temperature.

Note: My parents had a bakery when I was growing up in Schirmeck, and I used to eat loads of these cookies. In Alsace, children are introduced to kirsch's subtle taste early. In this kid-friendly recipe, the alcohol evaporates by the time the cookies are ready to eat.

Pistachio Panna Cotta + Basil-Almond Panna Cotta

Prep:
20 minutes

Cook:
5 minutes

Chill:
3 hours

BASIL–ALMOND PANNA COTTA

•••••••••••••••••••••••••••••

Serves 3

1½ sheets (3 g) 200 bloom gelatin

1 cup (250 ml) heavy cream

3 tablespoons plus 2 teaspoons (1½ oz. / 45 g)
granulated sugar, divided

¾ oz. (20 g) basil leaves, finely chopped, plus more
leaves for garnishing

3 tablespoons plus 1 teaspoon (50 ml) orgeat syrup

1 lime

14 oz. (400 g) peaches or nectarines

1. In a medium bowl of very cold water, soften
the gelatin. In a medium saucepan, heat the
cream over medium-high heat until bubbles
appear around the edge, then whisk in
2 tablespoons (1 oz. / 25 g) of the sugar and
the chopped basil. Remove from the heat.

2. Squeeze the gelatin dry and whisk into the
hot cream, followed by the orgeat syrup. Divide
the panna cotta among glasses. Chill for at least
3 hours.

3. Working over a small bowl to catch the juices
and using a small, sharp knife, peel the lime.
Cut in between the membranes to release
the segments.

4. Peel the peaches. Using a melon baller, scoop
out the flesh. Cut off the flesh around the pits
and process it with the remaining 1 tablespoon
plus 2 teaspoons (20 g) sugar and the lime juice
until puréed. Pour a little of this coulis in each
glass and decorate with the peach balls, lime
segments, and basil leaves.

PISTACHIO PANNA COTTA

•••••••••••••••••••••••••••••••••

Serves 6

2½ sheets (5 g) 200 bloom gelatin

2 cups (500 ml) heavy cream

5 tablespoons plus 1 teaspoon (2 oz. / 60 g)
granulated sugar, divided

1½ to 1¾ oz. (40 to 50 g) pistachio paste,
to taste, well softened

14 oz. (400 g) strawberries, halved, divided

3½ oz. (100 g) raspberries

1¾ oz. (50 g) red currants

A few pistachios

1. In a medium bowl of very cold water, soften the
gelatin. In a medium saucepan, heat the cream over
medium-high heat until bubbles appear around the
edge, then whisk in 3½ tablespoons (1½ oz. / 40 g) of
the sugar. Remove from the heat.

2. Squeeze the gelatin dry and whisk into the hot
cream, then the pistachio paste. Divide the panna
cotta among glasses. Chill for at least 3 hours.

3. Process or blend half of the strawberries with
the remaining 1 tablespoon plus 2 teaspoons (20 g)
sugar, then strain. Pour a little of this coulis in each
glass and add the remaining fruit and pistachios.

WALNUT–ALMOND CAKE

Serves 10

10½ oz. (300 g) Sweet Almond Pastry (p. 10), room temperature
2⅔ sticks (10½ oz. / 300 g) unsalted butter
1½ cups (6 oz. / 150 g) shelled walnuts, divided
2½ cups (9 oz. / 250 g) almond flour
1¼ cups (9 oz. / 250 g) granulated sugar, preferably coarse
8 egg whites
½ cup (2½ oz. / 75 g) potato starch
3½ tablespoons (2½ oz. / 75 g) honey, plus more for drizzling

Equipment
An 8-inch (20-cm) cake ring,
2½ inches (6 cm) deep, or springform pan

1. If using a cake ring, line a baking sheet with parchment paper and place the ring in the center. On a lightly floured work surface, roll out the pastry ⅛ inch (3 mm) thick. Line the ring with the pastry. Chill for at least 10 minutes. Preheat the oven to 340°F (170°C) convection.

2. In a small saucepan, melt the butter over medium heat, then cook until it begins to brown and smells a little like hazelnuts. Strain the brown butter through a fine sieve. You'll need to use it while it's still warm.

3. In a food processor, finely chop 1 scant cup (3½ oz. / 100 g) of the walnuts, making sure they don't become oily. You can also chop them using a large knife.

4. Combine the walnuts with the almond flour and sugar, then stir in the egg whites. Whisk in the potato starch and brown butter to combine, but do not overmix.

5. Whisk in the honey. (If your honey has crystallized, warm it slightly in the microwave.)

6. Spread the batter in the cake ring and decorate with the remaining scant ½ cup (1¾ oz. / 50 g) walnuts. Bake for 30 to 40 minutes, until a tester inserted into the center comes out clean. Let the cake cool slightly in the ring, then remove the ring and drizzle with honey.

Note: This cake can be stored in an airtight container for 2 to 3 days.

Prep:
20 minutes

Chill:
30 minutes

Cook:
40 to 45 minutes

RASPBERRY–ALMOND CUSTARD TART
Mirliton aux Framboises

Serves 8

10½ oz. (300 g) Sweet Almond Pastry (p. 10), room temperature

3 tablespoons plus 1 teaspoon (1¾ oz. / 50 g) unsalted butter

6 eggs

Generous ½ cup (1¾ oz. / 50 g) almond flour

1 tablespoon all-purpose flour

1 cup (7 oz. / 200 g) granulated sugar

1 cup (250 ml) heavy cream

½ cup minus 1 tablespoon (100 ml) orgeat syrup

1 tablespoon kirsch or amaretto

13 oz. (375 g) raspberries

Confectioners' sugar for dusting

Equipment

A 9-inch (24-cm) cake ring or pan, 1½ inches (3 to 4 cm) deep

1. If using a cake ring, line a baking sheet with parchment paper and place the ring in the center. On a lightly floured work surface, roll out the pastry ⅛ inch (3 mm) thick. Line the ring with the pastry. Chill for 30 minutes. If you like, prebake the tart shell. If not, make sure the baking sheet is perforated or very thin aluminum, so the pastry bakes all the way through.

2. Preheat the oven to 350°F (180°C) convection. Melt the butter in the microwave or in a small saucepan and let cool. In a medium bowl, whisk the eggs with the almond flour, all-purpose flour, melted butter, granulated sugar, cream, orgeat syrup, and kirsch.

3. Arrange the raspberries in the tart shell. Pour in the custard, filling to the rim. Dust with confectioners' sugar and bake for 40 to 45 minutes, until set and golden. Let the tart cool completely. Dust with confectioners' sugar.

Note: If you prebaked the pastry and see there are small holes, fill them in with a little custard (⅛ inch / 2 to 3 mm deep) and bake for a few minutes, until set. Then proceed as above.

CAMILLE'S PINEAPPLE UPSIDE-DOWN CAKE

Serves 6 to 8

Salted butter caramel	Pineapple cake	Equipment
4 tablespoons plus 1 teaspoon (2¼ oz. / 65 g) unsalted butter, diced, room temperature, plus more for brushing	1 ripe pineapple	An 8-inch (20-cm) cake pan
All-purpose flour for dusting	3 eggs	
¼ vanilla bean	½ cup (3½ oz. / 100 g) granulated sugar	
2 tablespoons plus 2 teaspoons (40 ml) heavy cream	¾ cup plus 2 tablespoons (3½ oz. / 100 g) all-purpose flour	
½ cup (3½ oz. / 100 g) granulated sugar	1 scant tablespoon (11 g) baking powder	
1 pinch fleur de sel	3 tablespoons plus 1 teaspoon (1¾ oz. / 50 g) unsalted butter, melted	

SALTED BUTTER CARAMEL

1. Brush the cake pan with butter and dust with flour. Split the vanilla bean lengthwise and scrape out the seeds. In a small saucepan, heat the cream with the vanilla bean and seeds over medium-high heat until bubbles appear around the edge. Remove from the heat, cover, and let infuse.

2. In a heavy saucepan, cook half of the sugar over medium heat, stirring with a wooden spoon, until melted. Add the remaining sugar and cook until it's a lovely caramel color. Remove the vanilla bean from the cream and carefully drizzle into the caramel, whisking, until smooth. This is a delicate operation, because the difference in temperatures makes the contents of the pan bubble up violently. If your pan isn't deep enough, you may get burned.

3. Remove from the heat. Whisk in the butter and fleur de sel. Pour the caramel into the cake pan in a thin layer.

PINEAPPLE CAKE

4. Peel and core the pineapple, then cut into slices just under ½ inch (about 1 cm) thick. Cut each slice in half.

5. Preheat the oven to 350°F (180°C) convection. In the bowl of a stand mixer fitted with a whisk, whip the eggs and sugar at medium-high speed for about 15 minutes, until pale and thick.

6. Sift the flour with the baking powder. Using a silicone spatula, stir the melted butter into the egg-sugar mixture, then fold in the dry ingredients.

7. Arrange the pineapple slices in concentric circles in the pan, starting from the center. Spread the batter on top.

8. Bake for 25 to 30 minutes, until well risen and a tester inserted into the center (without touching the pineapple) comes out clean. Let the cake cool in the pan to room temperature, then invert onto a serving platter. Dust confectioners' sugar on the sides of the cake.

Prep:
30 minutes

Cook:
about 20 minutes

LUCIEN PELTIER'S ORANGE TART

Prep:
15 minutes

Cook:
3 to 5 minutes per batch

CARNIVAL FRITTERS

Serves 8

10½ oz. (300 g) Sweet Almond Pastry (p. 10),
room temperature

3 whole eggs

3 egg yolks

1½ cups (10½ oz. / 300 g) granulated sugar

1½ tablespoons cornstarch or custard powder

Scant ⅓ cup (70 ml) orange juice

Finely grated zest of 1 orange, or blanched zest of
1 orange, finely chopped

1 stick (4 oz. / 120 g) unsalted butter, melted and cooled

Equipment

A 9-inch (22-cm) tart pan, 1¾ inches (2 cm) deep
Kitchen torch (optional)

Serves 8

2 cups (9 oz. / 250 g) all-purpose flour

1½ eggs, lightly beaten

1 small pinch fine salt

4 tablespoons (2 oz. / 60 g) unsalted butter,
melted and cooled

Ice water as needed

½ cup (3½ oz. / 100 g) granulated sugar

½ tablespoon vanilla bean powder or cinnamon

Neutral oil for frying

1. On a lightly floured work surface, roll out the pastry ⅛ inch (3 mm) thick. Line the tart pan with the pastry. Chill for 30 minutes. Preheat the oven to 350°F (180°C) convection. Bake for 20 to 25 minutes.

2. In a medium bowl, using an electric beater, whisk the whole eggs, egg yolks, and sugar for 5 minutes, until pale and thick. Beat in the cornstarch. Whisk in the orange juice, zest, and melted butter. Transfer to a medium saucepan and cook for 2 minutes; let cool.

3. Spread the cream in the tart shell. Using a kitchen torch, lightly brown the top.

1. Mound the flour on a work surface and make a well in the center. Add the eggs and salt to the well. Working with one hand, combine the ingredients, gradually drawing the flour into the well while adding the melted butter. Work the dough gently, adding just enough water to make a fairly firm dough. Chill for a few minutes.

2. In a large bowl, whisk the sugar with the vanilla.

3. On a lightly floured work surface, roll out the dough as thinly as possible. Cut into 1¼ by 4-inch (3 by 10-cm) strips.

4. In a large pot, heat the oil to 340°F (170°C). Working in batches, fry the fritters, turning them occasionally, for about 4 minutes, until golden.

5. Using a slotted spoon, transfer the fritters to paper towels to drain. Dredge in the vanilla sugar. Serve as soon as possible.

CARNIVAL FRITTERS

SBRISOLONA

Prep:
15 minutes

Cook:
40 minutes

CRUMBLY ITALIAN ALMOND TORTE
Sbrisolona

Prep:
10 minutes

Cook:
10 minutes

Chill:
12 hours

Serves 8 to 10

2 sticks minus 1 teaspoon (7¾ oz. / 220 g) unsalted
butter, diced, room temperature,
plus more for brushing

2¼ cups (7 oz. / 200 g) cake flour,
plus more for dusting

1¼ cups (7 oz. / 200 g) corn flour

¾ cup (5¼ oz. / 150 g) granulated sugar

2⅓ cups (7 oz. / 200 g) ground almonds

2 egg yolks

Finely grated zest of 1 lemon

Confectioners' sugar for dusting

Equipment

A 10-inch (24-cm) cake pan

PRUNES IN RED WINE

Serves 6

2 cups (500 ml) full-bodied red wine

1½ cups (350 ml) water

⅔ cup (4½ oz. / 130 g) granulated sugar

½ orange, unpeeled, cut in chunks

½ lemon, unpeeled, cut in chunks

2 bay leaves

2 sticks cinnamon

1 lb. (500 g) unpitted prunes

Vanilla ice cream for serving, optional

1. Preheat the oven to 350°F (180°C) convection.
Brush the cake pan with butter and dust with
flour. On a work surface, mix the cake and corn
flours and make a well in the center. Add the
granulated sugar, ground almonds, egg yolks,
and lemon zest to the well. Using your hands, mix
all the ingredients and again make a well in the
center. Add the butter to the well and rub into the
almond mixture until crumbly.

2. Transfer the dough to the pan and crumble
it to distribute evenly. Rap the pan on the work
surface a few times to eliminate any gaps. Bake for
about 40 minutes, until golden. Let the cake cool
slightly in the pan, then turn out onto a rack and
let cool completely. Dust with confectioners' sugar.

Note: The chef of the Hotel Cipriani in Venice
shared this easy, excellent recipe.

1. In a large saucepan, combine the wine and
water with the sugar. Bring to a boil and let cook
for only a few seconds.

2. Add the orange and lemon chunks, bay
leaves, and cinnamon sticks and bring to a boil.
Remove from the heat and add the prunes. Let
cool, cover, and chill for at least 12 hours.

3. Serve plain or with ice cream.

Note: This dish tastes far better if the prunes
have their pits, especially after they've been
marinating a few days.

PRUNES IN RED WINE

ALMOND PASTE CAKE

Prep:
25 minutes

Cook:
30 minutes

ALMOND PASTE CAKE
Pain de Gênes

Serves 6 to 8

6 tablespoons (3 oz. / 90 g) unsalted butter, melted and cooled, plus more for brushing

2½ tablespoons (1 oz. / 25 g) all-purpose flour, plus more for dusting

10½ oz. (300 g) 50% almond paste, well softened

4 eggs

2½ tablespoons (1 oz. / 25 g) potato starch

1 teaspoon (5 ml) dark rum

1 teaspoon (5 ml) Grand Marnier or other orange liqueur

1 drop bitter almond extract

Candied orange and lemon peel strips and natural almonds for decorating

Confectioners' sugar for dusting

Equipment

An 8- to 9-inch (20- to 22-cm) cake pan

1. Preheat the oven to 350°F (180°C) convection. Brush the cake pan with butter and dust with flour. In the bowl of a stand mixer fitted with the paddle, beat the almond paste with 1 egg until smooth and soft. Using the whisk, whip in the remaining 3 eggs, one by one, at high speed for 10 minutes, until pale and very creamy. In a medium bowl, combine the butter with the flour, potato starch, rum, liqueur, and almond extract. Fold into the egg mixture.

2. Bake for 30 minutes, until a tester inserted into the center comes out clean. Let cool slightly in the pan, then turn out onto a rack and let cool completely. Decorate with the candied citrus peel and almonds and dust with confectioners' sugar.

Note: The percentage of almonds in the almond paste is important so you get the right texture and balance of almond flavor and sweetness.

Prep:
20 minutes

Cook:
40 minutes

SIMPLE CHOCOLATE CAKE

Serves 8

3 tablespoons plus 1 teaspoon (1¾ oz. / 50 g) unsalted butter, plus more for brushing

2 tablespoons (20 g) all-purpose flour, plus more for dusting

5 eggs, separated

¾ cup (5¼ oz. / 150 g) granulated sugar, divided

3½ oz. (100 g) 70% dark chocolate

1 pinch fine salt

2 tablespoons (20 g) cornstarch

Unsweetened cocoa powder for dusting, optional

Equipment

A 9-inch (22-cm) cake pan

1. Preheat the oven to 400°F (200°C) convection. Butter the cake pan and dust with flour. In a large bowl, using an electric beater, whisk the egg yolks with ½ cup (3½ oz. / 100 g) of the sugar until pale and creamy.

2. In a large bowl set over a pan of simmering water, melt the chocolate with the butter, stirring occasionally, until smooth. Meanwhile, in a separate bowl, whisk the egg whites with the salt and remaining ¼ cup (2 oz. / 50 g) sugar until they hold a soft peak. Stir the egg yolk mixture into the melted chocolate and butter.

3. Sift the flour with the cornstarch and fold into the chocolate mixture. Carefully fold in the beaten egg whites. Spread the batter in the cake pan.

4. Bake for 10 minutes, then reduce the oven temperature to 300°F (150°C) and bake for 30 minutes. If you like, dust the cake with cocoa powder.

SIMPLE CHOCOLATE CAKE

QUINCE–PEAR UPSIDE-DOWN TART

Prep:
35 minutes

Cook:
1 hour + 1 hour
10 minutes

QUINCE–PEAR
UPSIDE–DOWN TART

Serves 8 to 10

9 oz. (250 g) Quick Puff Pastry (p. 12), chilled,
or Crisp Short Pastry (p. 9), room temperature
2 lb. 3 oz. (1 kg) firm ripe pears
1 lb. 2 oz. (500 g) quince
1 cup plus 2 tablespoons
(7¾ oz. / 220 g) granulated sugar

Equipment
A 10-inch (24-cm) cake pan

1. Line a baking sheet with parchment paper or
a silicone mat. On a lightly floured work surface,
roll out the pastry to make a 10-inch (24-cm)
round ⅛ inch (3 mm) thick. Transfer to the
baking sheet and chill.

2. Peel, core, and halve the pears. Peel, core,
and cut the quince into 1¼-inch (3-cm) slices. In
a large saucepan of boiling water, cook the quince
slices for about 1 hour, until tender.

3. Lightly oil a baking sheet. Have ready a large
bowl of cold water. In a medium heavy saucepan,
cook half of the sugar over medium heat, stirring
with a wooden spoon, until melted. Add the
remaining sugar and cook until it's a lovely
caramel color. Remove from the heat and let
darken to a deep caramel. Immediately dip the
the pan in the cold water for 2 seconds to stop the
cooking. Carefully pour half of the caramel into
the cake pan in a thin layer. Drizzle the remaining
caramel on the oiled baking sheet to make drops.
Let cool, then carefully peel them off. Reserve the
caramel drops on the same sheet.

4. Preheat the oven to 400°F (200°C) convection.
Arrange the pear halves, cut sides down, and
quince slices in the cake pan, packing them as
tightly as possible. Place in the lower third of the
oven and bake for 40 minutes. Remove the pan
from the oven and carefully place the pastry on
the fruit. Reduce the oven temperature to 350°F
(180°C) and bake for 30 minutes.

5. Let the tart cool in the pan. Invert onto a
serving platter. Decorate with the caramel drops.

Prep:
25 minutes

Cook:
30 to 40 minutes

GOLD BAR ALMOND CAKES

Makes 3 large cakes

1¾ sticks (7 oz. / 200 g) unsalted butter,
plus more for brushing
1 cup (7 oz. / 200 g) granulated sugar
1¼ cups (5¼ oz. / 150 g) almond flour
⅔ cup (2½ oz. / 75 g) all-purpose flour
5 egg whites
A few drops yellow food coloring
Finely grated zest and juice of 1 lemon
1 lb. 2 oz. (500 g) Fondant Icing (p. 17),
warmed to 95°F (35°C)

Equipment
Three 3 by 9-inch (8 by 22-cm) oval pans

1. Preheat the oven to 350°F (180°C) convection.
Brush the pans with butter and chill until firm;
repeat. In a small saucepan, melt the butter over
medium heat, then cook until it begins to brown and
smells a little like hazelnuts. Strain the brown butter
through a fine sieve. You'll need to use it while it's
still warm.

2. In a medium bowl, whisk the sugar with the
almond flour and all-purpose flour. Whisk in the egg
whites, then the brown butter.

3. Divide the batter among the pans. Bake the large
cakes for 30 to 40 minutes, until a tester inserted
into the center comes out clean. Let cool slightly
in the pans, then turn out onto racks and let cool
completely.

4. In a medium bowl, beat the food coloring and
lemon zest and juice into the fondant. Using a spatula
or flat knife, spread it over the cakes. Let dry at
room temperature.

Note: These cakes are a variation of the Coffee
Financier Loaf (p. 34).

GOLD BAR ALMOND CAKES

Prep:
20 minutes

Cook:
1 hour

CRÈME CARAMEL

Serves 6

1½ cups (10½ oz. / 300 g) granulated sugar, divided
3 extra-large eggs or 4 medium eggs
2 cups (500 ml) whole milk

Equipment
A 7-inch (18-cm) heatproof dish or round pan

1. Have ready a large bowl of cold water. In a small heavy saucepan, cook ¼ cup plus 2 tablespoons (2½ oz. / 75 g) of the sugar over medium heat, stirring with a wooden spoon, until melted.

2. Add ¼ cup plus 2 tablespoons (2½ oz. / 75 g) of the sugar and cook until it's a lovely caramel color. Remove from the heat and let darken to a deep caramel.

3. Immediately dip the pan in the cold water for 2 seconds to stop the cooking. Pour the caramel into the heatproof dish in a thin layer. Let cool completely.

4. Preheat the oven to 350°F (180°C) convection. In a medium bowl, whisk the eggs with the remaining ¾ cup (5¼ oz. / 150 g) sugar. Whisk in the milk. Strain through a fine sieve into a glass measuring cup.

5. Pour the custard into the dish. Place in a larger heatproof dish and pour water around the smaller dish, filling the larger dish halfway. Bake for at least 1 hour, until the custard no longer jiggles and a tester inserted into the center comes out clean. Let cool completely in the dish.

6. Run a small knife around the inside of the dish and carefully invert the custard onto a serving dish, so the melted caramel doesn't splash.

Note: This crème caramel comes from Margaux at the excellent Anatable restaurant in Dinsheim. It's her grandmother's recipe.

VANILLA VISITING LOAF

Serves 8

6 tablespoons (3 oz. / 90 g) unsalted butter, softened,
plus more for brushing

1 cup plus 1 tablespoon (5 oz. / 140 g) all-purpose flour,
plus more for dusting

1 cup minus 2½ teaspoons (6¾ oz. / 190 g) granulated sugar

1 extra-large egg

1 tablespoon pure vanilla extract

1 vanilla bean, split lengthwise and seeds scraped

1 pinch fine salt

½ cup (120 ml) heavy cream

1 teaspoon baking powder

5¼ oz. (150 g) white chocolate

Confectioners' sugar for dusting

Equipment
An 8 by 3-inch (19 by 7-cm) loaf pan

1. It's important for all the ingredients in this recipe—yes, even the cream—to be at room temperature, so take them out of the refrigerator the evening before (or 12 hours ahead).

2. Preheat the oven to 320°F (160°C) convection. Brush the loaf pan with butter and dust with flour. In a food processor, blend the butter with the flour, granulated sugar, egg, vanilla extract, vanilla seeds, salt, cream, and baking powder.

3. Spread the batter in the loaf pan and bake for 40 minutes, until well risen and a tester inserted into the center comes out clean. Let the loaf cool slightly in the pan, then turn out on a rack and let cool completely.

4. Using a large knife, chop 2½ oz. (70 g) of the chocolate. In a medium bowl set over a saucepan of simmering water, melt the remaining 2¾ oz. (80 g) chocolate, stirring occasionally, until smooth. Brush the melted chocolate over the top of the loaf. Sprinkle with the chopped chocolate and dust with confectioners' sugar.

Note: A visiting, or travel, cake is a sturdy, homemade food gift that you might take to new parents or to friends hosting you at their weekend house.

Prep:
30 minutes

Cook:
25 to 30 minutes

ALMOND BISCOTTI

Makes about 40 cookies

Unsalted butter for brushing

¾ cup plus 1 tablespoon (9 oz. / 255 g) cake flour,
plus more for dusting

3 medium eggs

1¼ cups (9 oz. / 250 g) granulated sugar

Finely grated zest of 1 orange

3 to 4 cardamom seeds, crushed

½ teaspoon vanilla bean powder

1 cup (7 oz. / 200 g) natural almonds

¾ cup plus 2 tablespoons (1¾ oz. / 50 g) chopped walnuts

1 cup (3½ oz. / 100 g) sliced almonds

Equipment
A pastry bag, optional

1. Preheat the oven to 350°F (180°C) convection. Brush 2 baking sheets with butter and dust with flour. In a medium bowl, using an electric beater, whisk the eggs with the sugar for 20 minutes. Whisk in the orange zest, cardamom, and vanilla.

2. Using a large knife, roughly chop the natural almonds. Stir the chopped almonds and walnuts into the egg-sugar mixture, then fold in the flour. The batter should be fairly thick.

3. Pipe or spoon the batter into 1¼-inch (3-cm) wide strips on the baking sheets, spacing well apart.

4. Sprinkle the strips with the sliced almonds and remove any excess. Bake for 25 to 30 minutes, until golden. Immediately cut the strips into ½-inch (1-cm) slices on the diagonal and let cool.

5. Note: In this faux-but-simple biscotti recipe, the cookies are baked only once.

RASPBERRY CUSTARD TART

Serves 10

10½ oz. (300 g) Crisp Short Pastry (p. 9), room temperature,
or Quick Puff Pastry (p. 12), chilled

8 egg yolks

¾ cup (5¼ oz. / 150 g) granulated sugar, divided

Generous ⅓ cup (2 oz. / 60 g) cornstarch

½ teaspoon (2 g) fleur de sel

1 teaspoon pure vanilla extract

1 cup (250 ml) heavy cream

1 lb. 10 oz. (750 g) raspberry purée

7 tablespoons (3½ oz. / 100 g) unsalted butter, diced, room temperature

Equipment

A 9-inch (22-cm) tart ring or pan, 1¾ inches (4 cm) deep

1. If using a tart ring, line a baking sheet with parchment paper and place the ring in the center. On a lightly floured work surface, roll out the pastry ⅛ inch (3 mm) thick. Line the ring with the pastry. Chill for at least 10 minutes. Preheat the oven to 340°F (170°C) convection. Cover the pastry with parchment paper and fill with baking beans. Bake for 30 minutes, then carefully remove the paper with the beans and let cool.

2. In a medium bowl, whisk the egg yolks with ⅓ cup (2½ oz. / 75 g) of the sugar, the cornstarch, fleur de sel, and vanilla but don't let the mixture lighten in color. Stir in the cream.

3. In a medium saucepan, bring the raspberry purée and remaining ⅓ cup (2½ oz. / 75 g) sugar to a boil over medium-high heat. Immediately remove from the heat. Gradually whisk into the egg yolk mixture. Return to the pan and cook over medium heat, whisking continuously, until the custard thickens. Remove from the heat and stir in the butter. Spread the custard in the tart shell. Let cool completely.

4. Preheat the oven to 425°F (220°C) convection. Bake the tart for 20 minutes, then increase the oven temperature to 465°F (240°C) convection and bake for 10 minutes. Let the tart cool completely.

BLACK CURRANT CUSTARD TART

Serves 10

10½ oz. (300 g) Crisp Short Pastry (p. 9), room temperature,
or Quick Puff Pastry (p. 12), chilled

8 egg yolks

¾ cup (5¼ oz. / 150 g) granulated sugar, divided

Generous ⅓ cup (2 oz. / 60 g) cornstarch

½ teaspoon (2 g) fleur de sel

1 teaspoon pure vanilla extract

1¼ cups (300 ml) heavy cream

1 lb. 10 oz. (750 g) black currant purée

7 tablespoons (3½ oz. / 100 g) unsalted butter, diced, room temperature

Equipment
A 9-inch (22-cm) tart ring or pan, 1¾ inches (4 cm) deep

1. If using a tart ring, line a baking sheet with parchment paper and place the ring in the center. On a lightly floured work surface, roll out the pastry ⅛ inch (3 mm) thick. Line the ring with the pastry. Chill for at least 10 minutes. Preheat the oven to 340°F (170°C) convection. Cover the pastry with parchment paper and fill with baking beans. Bake for 30 minutes, then carefully remove the paper with the beans and let cool.

2. In a medium bowl, whisk the egg yolks with ⅓ cup (2½ oz. / 75 g) of the sugar, the cornstarch, fleur de sel, and vanilla but don't let the mixture lighten in color. Stir in the cream.

3. In a medium saucepan, bring the black currant purée and remaining ⅓ cup (2½ oz. / 75 g) sugar to a boil over medium-high heat. Remove from the heat. Gradually whisk into the egg yolk mixture. Return to the pan and cook over medium heat, whisking continuously, until the custard thickens. Remove from the heat and stir in the butter. Spread the custard in the tart shell. Let cool completely.

4. Preheat the oven to 425°F (220°C) convection. Bake the tart for 20 minutes, then increase the oven temperature to 465°F (240°C) convection and bake for 10 minutes. Let the tart cool completely.

Prep:
15 minutes

Cook:
35 to 40 minutes

YOGURT CAKE WITH STRAWBERRIES AND RASPBERRIES

Serves 8 to 10

1 stick plus 2 teaspoons (4½ oz. / 125 g) unsalted butter,
room temperature, plus more for brushing

2½ cups (10½ oz. / 300 g) all-purpose flour, plus more for dusting

½ cup (125 g) plain yogurt

3 eggs

1¼ cups (9 oz. / 250 g) granulated sugar

2¾ teaspoons (10 g) baking powder

1 tablespoon (15 ml) dark rum

3½ oz. (100 g) strawberries

3½ oz. (100 g) raspberries

Barely Sweet Raspberry Jam with Seeds (p. 17),
or 8 oz. (250 g) homemade or store-bought jam for brushing

Equipment
A 10-inch (24-cm) loaf pan

1. Preheat the oven to 410°F (210°C) convection. Brush the loaf pan with butter and dust with flour.

2. Soften the butter by beating it or heating it using brief pulses in the microwave. Do not let it melt. In a food processor, blend the butter with the yogurt, eggs, and sugar.

3. Sift the flour with the baking powder and add to the yogurt mixture. Pour in the rum and process until creamy.

4. Spread the batter in the loaf pan, filling halfway. Distribute the strawberries and raspberries over the batter and spread the remaining batter in the pan.

Bake for 35 to 40 minutes, until a tester inserted into the center comes out clean.

5. Immediately turn the cake out of the pan onto a rack.

6. In a small saucepan, heat the jam, then brush it over the cake. Let the jam set, then brush the cake with a second coating of jam.

Notes: You can play around with this recipe by changing the fruit: try apricots with apricot jam, or blueberries with blueberry jam. Or change the shape: Bake the batter in a muffin pan, filling the cups three-quarters full.

CHOCOLATE MOUSSE WITH
LANGUES DE CHAT COOKIES

Serves 12

Chocolate mousse	Cookies	Equipment
½ cup minus 1 tablespoon (100 ml) heavy cream	4 tablespoons (2 oz. / 60 g) unsalted butter, softened	An 8-inch (20-cm) serving bowl, at least 2½ inches (6 cm) deep
9 oz. (250 g) 60 to 70% dark chocolate	⅔ cup (3 oz. / 80 g) confectioners' sugar	A pastry bag fitted with a plain ¼-inch (5-mm) tip
6 egg whites	2 extra-large egg whites	A nonstick baking sheet
1 pinch fine salt	½ cup (2 oz. / 60 g) all-purpose flour	
3½ tablespoons (1½ oz. / 40 g) granulated sugar	1 teaspoon pure vanilla extract	
2 egg yolks		

CHOCOLATE MOUSSE

1. In a small saucepan, heat the cream over medium-high heat until bubbles appear around the edge; remove from the heat. Chop the chocolate and transfer to a medium bowl. Pour in the hot cream and let stand for 1 minute, then whisk until smooth to make a shiny ganache. Let cool to lukewarm.

2. In a large bowl, whisk the egg whites with the salt until frothy. Gradually whisk in the sugar, whisking until the egg whites hold a soft peak.

3. In a small bowl, lightly beat the egg yolks. Stir them into the ganache. Carefully fold the ganache-yolk mixture into the beaten egg whites. Spread in the large serving bowl. Chill for at least 2 hours.

COOKIES

4. Preheat the oven to 350°F (180°C) convection. Place the butter in a medium bowl. Working in two or three additions, beat in the confectioners' sugar, alternating with the egg whites. Sift in the flour and fold in the vanilla until just blended.

5. Pipe 2½-inch (6-cm) lengths of batter onto the baking sheet. Bake for 10 minutes, until golden. The cookies should be crisp, so make sure they're well baked. Let the cookies cool slightly on the baking sheet, then transfer to racks and let cool completely.

6. Just before serving, stand the cookies in the chocolate mousse.

Notes: To make chocolate langues de chat (cat's tongues) cookies, sift 1½ tablespoons (10 g) unsweetened cocoa powder with the flour.

For chocoholics, top the mousse with more ganache, prepared by stirring ½ cup minus 1 tablespoon (100 ml) hot heavy cream into 3½ oz. (100 g) chopped 60% dark chocolate. Please note that the chocolate mousse contains raw eggs.

Wednesday

A day for mixing things
up! Go exotic with a
passion fruit custard tart
(p 129) — a refreshing twist
on a traditional dessert.

JUST–SWEET–ENOUGH ALSATIAN CHEESECAKE

Serves 8 to 10

Unsalted butter for brushing

10½ oz. (300 g) Crisp Short Pastry (p. 9), room temperature

1 lb. 2 oz. (500 g) fromage blanc, quark, or ricotta, preferably whole milk

1 cup (7 oz. / 200 g) granulated sugar

¾ cup plus 2 tablespoons (3½ oz. / 100 g) all-purpose flour

1 tablespoon pure vanilla extract

2 eggs

1 cup (250 ml) whole milk

1 cup (250 ml) crème fraîche

⅓ cup (1¾ oz. / 50 g) golden or dark raisins, optional

Confectioners' sugar for dusting

Equipment

A 10-inch (24-cm) tart ring or pan, or pie dish,
1½ inches (3 to 4 cm) deep

1. Preheat the oven to 400°F (200°C) convection. If using a tart ring, line a baking sheet with parchment paper and place the ring in the center. Brush the tart ring with butter. On a lightly floured work surface, roll out the pastry ⅛ inch (3 mm) thick. Line the ring with the pastry. Prick the dough evenly with a fork. Chill for at least 10 minutes.

2. Prebake the tart shell for 30 minutes or simply skip this step.

3. Increase the oven temperature to 410°F (210°C) convection. In a large bowl, whisk the fromage blanc with the granulated sugar, flour, vanilla, and eggs. Whisk in the milk and crème fraîche.

4. Spread the filling in the tart shell and sprinkle with the raisins. Bake for 20 minutes. Let cool for 10 minutes, then return to the oven for 15 to 20 minutes. Let the cheesecake cool in the ring. Dust with confectioners' sugar.

Notes: My parents used to make this old family recipe in their bakery in Schirmeck, Alsace.

If you like, sprinkle the raisins on the tart after baking, then dust with confectioners' sugar.

Prep:
1 hour 30 minutes

*Refrigerate
and freeze*
2 hours

Cook:
20 + 25 minutes

COFFEE MICE

Makes 10 mice

Coffee cream

¾ cup (200 ml) whole milk

4 egg yolks

⅓ cup (2½ oz. / 75 g)
granulated sugar

2½ tablespoons (1 oz. / 25 g)
cornstarch or potato starch

1 stick plus 2 tablespoons
(5 oz. / 140 g) unsalted
butter, softened

1¾ oz. (50 g) Coffee Paste (p. 19)

Coffee mice

9 oz. (250 g) Sweet Almond
Pastry (p. 10), room
temperature

7 oz. (200 g) Almond Cream
(p. 15)

1 lb. 2 oz. (500 g) Fondant Icing,
colored brown or flavored
with coffee extract

Toasted sliced almonds

About 35% almond paste,
well kneaded

Unsweetened cocoa powder

Equipment

Ten 2½-inch (6-cm)
barquette molds

Pastry bag, optional

COFFEE CREAM

1. In a medium saucepan, heat the milk over medium-high heat until bubbles appear around the edge; remove from the heat. In a medium bowl, whisk the egg yolks with the sugar and cornstarch. Gradually whisk in the hot milk.

2. Return the yolk-milk mixture to the pan and cook over medium heat, whisking continuously, until thickened. Let simmer very briefly, still whisking, then remove from the heat. Transfer to a bowl, press plastic wrap directly on the surface, and refrigerate for 1 hour, until cold.

3. Let the pastry cream warm up very slightly. In a large bowl, whisk the butter with the Coffee Paste. Whisk the pastry cream into the butter-coffee mixture in 2 or 3 additions. If the coffee cream seems too soft, chill for a few minutes. Using an electric beater, whisk until light and airy.

COFFEE MICE

4. On a lightly floured work surface, roll out the pastry ⅛ inch (3 mm) thick. Line the molds with the pastry. Transfer to a baking sheet and chill for at least 10 minutes. Preheat the oven to 350°C (180°C) convection. Bake the tartlet shells for 10 to 15 minutes, until golden. Spread the almond cream in the tartlet shells and bake for 10 minutes, then let cool.

5. Pipe or spoon the coffee cream over the almond cream to form mice. Freeze for 1 hour, until set, so the mice are easier to glaze.

6. In a medium bowl, beat the fondant with the coffee. Spread it over the coffee cream and let set. Decorate with the sliced almonds and almond paste. To make the eyes, mix a little almond paste with cocoa powder to darken it.

Prep:
40 minutes

Chill:
2 to 12 hours

Cook:
20 to 25 minutes

JAM-FILLED SANDWICH COOKIES

Makes about 10 cookies

Cookies	Red currant and raspberry jam	Equipment
2 cups (9 oz. / 250 g) all-purpose flour	1½ cups (10½ oz. / 300 g) granulated sugar, divided	A 4-inch (10-cm) cookie cutter, a 1¼-inch (3-cm) cookie cutter, and a ¾-inch (2-cm) cookie cutter
½ teaspoon baking powder	2 teaspoons (8 g) pectin NH	
⅔ cup (4½ oz. / 125 g) granulated sugar	10½ oz. (300 g) raspberries	
1 stick plus 2 teaspoons (4½ oz. / 125 g) unsalted butter, diced	7 oz. (200 g) redcurrants	
1 extra-large egg	2 teaspoons (10 ml) lemon juice	
Finely grated zest of ¼ lemon		
Confectioners' sugar for dusting		

COOKIES

1. In a medium bowl, whisk the flour with the baking powder and granulated sugar. Rub in the butter until crumbly.

2. Knead in the egg and lemon zest. Transfer the dough to a lightly floured work surface and, using the heel of your hand, scrape the dough away from you until smooth.

3. Shape the dough into a disk, cover with plastic wrap, and chill for at least 2 hours. If you're not in a hurry, chill for 12 hours, which is even better.

RED CURRANT AND RASPBERRY JAM

4. Place a plate in the freezer to test the jam for doneness. In a small bowl, combine half of the sugar with the pectin NH. In a food processor, blend the raspberries and red currants with the remaining sugar for 1 minute. In a medium saucepan, bring the fruit purée to a boil over medium heat. Stir in the sugar-pectin mixture and cook for 5 minutes.

5. Stir in the lemon juice and cook for about 1 minute. To test for doneness, drop a little jam on the chilled plate. It should hold its shape without spreading.

6. Bring the dough to room temperature. Preheat the oven to 340°F (170°C) convection. Line a baking sheet with parchment paper. On a lightly floured work surface, roll out the dough just under ¼ inch (4 to 5 mm) thick.

7. Using the 4-inch (10-cm) cookie cutter, press out rounds in the dough. Using the two smaller cookie cutters, cut decorative holes in half of the rounds. Place them on the baking sheet. Bake for about 20 minutes, until golden. Let the cookies cool slightly on the baking sheet, then transfer to racks and let cool completely.

8. If the jam has set, heat it slightly, whisking well. Spread on the whole cookies.

9. Generously dust the cookies with the decorative holes with the confectioners' sugar and place them on the jam layer. Press lightly so the cookies hold together and the jam fills the holes.

Notes: These are childhood memory joggers for me. I would eat two of them a day!

If you can't locate red currants, substitute the same amount of strawberries or more raspberries.

If you can't locate pectin NH, substitute a favorite berry jam.

ORANGE ROULADE

Serves 10 to 12

Moist sponge cake

6 whole eggs

4 egg yolks

⅔ cup (4½ oz. / 125 g)
granulated sugar

1 cup (4½ oz. / 125 g)
all-purpose flour, sifted

Orange cream

⅓ cup (2½ oz. / 75 g)
granulated sugar

3 whole eggs

2 egg yolks

2½ tablespoons (1 oz. / 25 g)
cornstarch

1 cup (240 ml) orange juice

Finely grated zest of 2 oranges

1⅔ sticks (6¾ oz. / 190 g)
unsalted butter, well chilled
and diced

Assembly

Granulated sugar for
sprinkling

Finely grated orange zest for
sprinkling

Equipment

Two rimmed 12 by 16-inch
(30 by 40-cm) baking sheets

MOIST SPONGE CAKE

1. Preheat the oven to 410°F (210°C) convection. Line the baking sheets with parchment paper. In a large bowl, combine 1 whole egg with the 4 egg yolks. Using an electric beater, whisk in the sugar. Whisk in the remaining 5 whole eggs, one by one, for 5 to 8 minutes, until the mixture is light and creamy.

2. Using a silicone spatula, carefully fold in the flour.

3. Using an offset spatula, spread the batter evenly over the 2 baking sheets, leaving a ½ inch (1 cm) border.

4. Bake for 7 to 8 minutes, until very lightly browned. Leave the sponges on the parchment paper, slip each one onto a rack, and let cool.

ORANGE CREAM

5. In a medium bowl, whisk the sugar with the whole eggs, egg yolks, and cornstarch.

6. In a medium saucepan, bring the orange juice and zest to a boil over medium heat. Remove from the heat.

7. Whisk the egg-sugar mixture into the orange juice. Return to medium heat and cook, stirring continuously, until the cream thickens and comes to a simmer. Let simmer for 20 seconds, then remove from the heat.

8. Whisk in the butter until the cream is smooth and shiny. Let cool completely.

ASSEMBLY

9. Invert each sponge cake on a clean sheet of parchment paper and carefully peel off the top parchment. Spread the orange cream evenly over each one. Using the parchment paper as a guide, roll up the cake tightly along the shorter side. Sprinkle with the sugar and orange zest.

Prep:
50 minutes

Chill:
1 hour

Cook:
15 to 20 minutes

STACKED ALSATIAN COOKIE CAKE
Mandelbari

Serves 8

Cookie dough

1 teaspoon (4 g) baking powder

4 cups (13¼ oz. / 375 g) cake flour

⅔ cup (4½ oz. / 125 g) granulated sugar

2 sticks plus 1½ tablespoons (9 oz. / 250 g) unsalted butter,
room temperature

2 egg yolks

1 teaspoon pure vanilla extract

1½ vanilla beans, split lengthwise and seeds scraped

Meringue

2 egg whites

⅔ cup (4½ oz. / 125 g) granulated sugar

2 cups (7 oz. / 200 g) sliced almonds

1½ vanilla beans, split lengthwise and seeds scraped

Assembly

Red currant jelly

Confectioners' sugar for dusting

Red currants or raspberries

Equipment

A set of graduated plain round cookie cutters

STACKED ALSATIAN COOKIE CAKE
Mandelbari

COOKIE DOUGH

1. In a large bowl, whisk the baking powder with the flour and sugar. Rub in the butter until crumbly. Knead in the egg yolks, vanilla extract, and vanilla seeds. Transfer the dough to a lightly floured work surface and, using the heel of your hand, scrape the dough away from you until smooth. Alternatively, use a stand mixer fitted with the dough hook to knead until smooth. Shape the dough into a disk, cover with plastic wrap, and chill for at least 1 hour.

2. Bring the dough to room temperature. Line at least 2 baking sheets with parchment paper. On a lightly floured work surface, roll out the dough ⅛ inch (4 mm) thick. Beginning with the largest cookie cutter plus a size that enables you to cut out a disk to form a ring, cut out two cookie rings.

3. Using the next size down, cut out two cookie rings. Continue to cut out increasingly smaller pairs of rings. In each case, you need two same-size rings to form the meringue cookies with red currant jelly. Arranging the cookies by size, place on the baking sheets. Chill until needed.

MERINGUE

4. Preheat the oven to 320°F (160°C) convection. In the bowl of a stand mixer fitted with the whisk, whip the egg whites until frothy, then add a little of the sugar. Whip until they hold a soft peak. Gradually add the remaining sugar, then whisk for 5 minutes, until the egg whites hold a firm peak.

5. Using a silicone spatula, carefully fold in the sliced almonds and vanilla seeds.

6. Spoon the meringue on most of the rings; the plain ones will be used to make jam sandwich cookies after they're baked.

7. Bake for 15 to 20 minutes, rotating the pans halfway through, until nicely golden. Let cool on the baking sheet.

ASSEMBLY

8. Prepare a few meringue cookies with jam: spread the plain cookies with a little red currant jelly. Sandwich with a same-size meringue cookie.

9. Dust all the meringue cookies with confectioners' sugar and stack them, starting from the largest to the smallest. Decorate with a few red currants.

Note: This recipe, created by Christelle Aron, is a variation of traditional *mandelbari*. Some of the cookies are sandwiched with red currant jelly and then stacked to create the traditional *mandelbari* tower. This is a particularly delicious, fruity version and is dedicated to all fans of jam sandwich cookies.

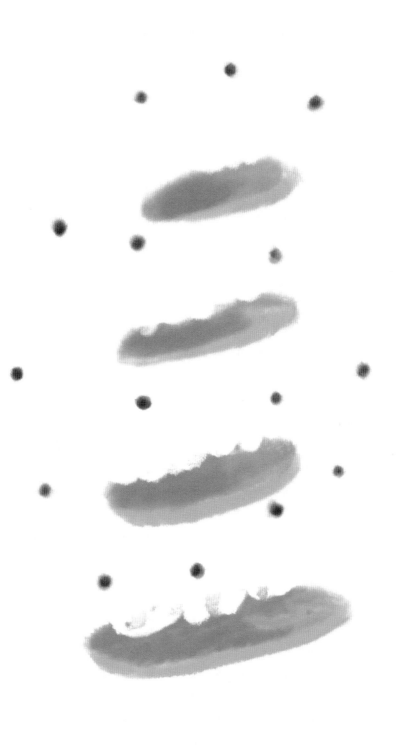

Prep:
40 minutes

Cook:
10 to 15 minutes

ALMOND BRIOCHE SLICES
Bostock aux Amandes

Serves 6

Scant ½ cup (100 ml) water

¾ cup minus 1 teaspoon (5 oz. / 140 g) granulated sugar

2 tablespoons plus 2 teaspoons (15 g) ground almonds

A drop bitter almond extract

1 tablespoon plus 1 scant tablespoon (15 g) confectioners' sugar,
plus more for dusting

2 teaspoons (10 ml) orange flower water

Generous 1 cup (3½ oz. / 100 g) sliced almonds

A 1-lb. (500-g) round brioche

Almond Cream (p. 15)

Equipment

A small, plain tip

1. In a small saucepan, bring the water to a boil with the sugar, stirring until the sugar dissolves. Remove from the heat and stir in the ground almonds, bitter almond extract, and confectioners' sugar. Return to the heat and bring to a boil, skimming. Remove from the heat and add the orange flower water. Pour into a medium bowl and let cool to lukewarm.

2. Preheat the oven to 400°F (200°C) convection. Using the pastry tip, cut out disks in the sliced almonds.

3. Cut slices of brioche 1½ inches (3 to 4 cm) thick. Dip them in the syrup. Spread the almond cream on one side of each slice and dot with the almonds. Dust with confectioners' sugar.

4. Transfer to baking sheets. Bake for 10 to 15 minutes, until lightly browned, and serve warm.

Note: To vary the decoration, use a mix of sliced almonds disks and whole sliced almonds.

PISTACHIO BLONDIES

ⁿⁿⁿⁿⁿⁿⁿⁿⁿⁿⁿⁿⁿⁿⁿⁿⁿⁿⁿⁿⁿⁿⁿⁿⁿⁿⁿⁿⁿⁿⁿⁿⁿⁿⁿⁿ

Serves 10

1 stick plus 3 tablespoons (5¾ oz. / 165 g) unsalted butter,
softened, plus more for brushing

¾ cup plus 2 tablespoons (3½ oz. / 100 g) all-purpose flour,
plus more for dusting

1¼ cups (5¾ oz. / 165 g) confectioners' sugar

1¼ cups (4¼ oz. / 120 g) almond flour

2¾ oz. (75 g) Pure Pistachio Paste (p. 19), well softened

2 tablespoons (30 ml) neutral oil

4 egg yolks

1 whole egg, lightly beaten

⅓ cup (1¾ oz. / 50 g) peeled pistachios,
plus chopped pistachios for sprinkling, optional

2 tablespoons (30 ml) milk

3 egg whites

Scant ¼ cup (1½ oz. / 45 g) granulated sugar

Equipment
An 8-inch (20-cm) square brownie pan

1. Preheat the oven to 350°F (180°C) convection. Brush the brownie pan with butter and dust with flour. In a medium bowl, whisk the butter until light and airy. Whisk in the confectioners' sugar, almond flour, and pistachio paste. Whisk in the oil, egg yolks, and whole egg.

2. Beat until foamy. Chop the pistachios and incorporate with the milk.

3. In a medium bowl, whisk the egg whites with the granulated sugar until they hold a soft peak. Using a silicone spatula, carefully fold into the batter, then fold in the all-purpose flour.

4. Spread in the brownie pan and bake for 20 to 25 minutes, until lightly browned. Transfer the pan to a rack and let the brownies cool completely. Sprinkle with chopped pistachios, if desired, and cut into squares.

Prep:
20 minutes

Chill:
30 minutes

Cook:
40 to 45 minutes

APRICOT–ALMOND CUSTARD TART
Mirliton aux Abricots

Serves 8

10½ oz. (300 g) Sweet Almond Pastry (p. 10),
room temperature

8 large ripe apricots

6 eggs

Generous ½ cup (1¾ oz. / 50 g) almond flour

1 tablespoon all-purpose flour

3 tablespoons plus 1 teaspoon (1¾ oz. / 50 g) unsalted butter,
melted and cooled

1 cup plus 2½ tablespoons (8 oz. / 230 g) granulated sugar

1¼ cups (300 ml) heavy cream

1 tablespoon dark rum

Confectioners' sugar for dusting

Equipment
A 9-inch (24-cm) cake ring or pan, 1½ inches (3 to 4 cm) deep

1. If using a cake ring, line a baking sheet with parchment paper and place the ring in the center. On a lightly floured work surface, roll out the pastry ⅛ inch (3 mm) thick. Line the ring with the pastry. Chill for 30 minutes. If you like, prebake the tart shell; if not, make sure the baking sheet is perforated or very thin aluminum so the pastry bakes all the way through.

2. Preheat the oven to 350°F (180°C) convection. Cut the apricots in half and pit them.

3. In a medium bowl, whisk the eggs with the almond flour, all-purpose flour, melted butter, granulated sugar, cream, and rum.

4. Arrange the apricot halves, round side up, in the tart shell. Pour in the custard, filling to the rim. Dust with confectioners' sugar and bake for 40 to 45 minutes, until set and golden. Let the tart cool completely. Dust with confectioners' sugar.

Note: If you prebaked the base and see there are small holes, fill them in with a little custard (⅛ inch / 2 to 3 mm deep) and bake for a few minutes, until set. Then proceed as above.

GIANDUJA–HAZELNUT LOAF

Serves 8

1 stick plus 2 tablespoons (5¼ oz. / 150 g) unsalted butter,
softened, plus more for brushing

¾ cup plus 2 tablespoons (3½ oz. / 100 g) all-purpose flour,
plus more for dusting

1 cup (4½ oz. / 125 g) confectioners' sugar

2 tablespoons (30 ml) neutral oil

1½ cups minus 1 tablespoon (2¾ oz. / 80 g) light brown sugar, divided

1¼ cups (4¼ oz. / 120 g) ground hazelnuts, toasted

6½ oz. (180 g) hazelnut paste or praline paste, well softened, divided

4 egg yolks

2 tablespoons (30 ml) heavy cream

3½ egg whites

4½ oz. (125 g) hazelnuts, toasted and chopped

14 oz. (400 g) gianduja spread, well softened

Caramelized almonds and hazelnuts
(see Sweet and Salty Caramelized Peanuts, p. 9) or Marcona almonds

Equipment
A 3 by 9-inch (7 by 22-cm) loaf pan
A pastry bag fitted with a Saint-Honoré tip or other tip, optional

1. Preheat the oven to 320°F (160°C) convection. Brush the loaf pan with butter and dust with flour. In a medium bowl, beat the butter with the confectioners' sugar, oil, 3 tablespoons (1¼ oz. / 35 g) of the light brown sugar, the ground hazelnuts, 3½ oz. (100 g) of the hazelnut paste, the egg yolks, and cream.

2. In a medium bowl, whisk the egg whites with a scant ¼ cup (1½ oz. / 45 g) of the light brown sugar until they hold a soft peak. Carefully fold into the hazelnut mixture, then fold in the flour. Stir in the chopped hazelnuts.

3. Spread the batter in the pan and bake for 40 minutes, until a cake tester inserted into the center comes out clean.

4. In a medium bowl, whisk the gianduja with the remaining 3 oz. (80 g) hazelnut paste until smooth and let stand until the mixture thickens. Whisk again and pipe it in waves or, using a spatula, spread over the top of the loaf. Decorate with caramelized almonds and hazelnuts.

ORANGE FLOWER FRITTERS

Prep:
10 minutes

Cook:
5 minutes per batch

Chill:
1 hour

ORANGE FLOWER FRITTERS
Croustillons

Makes 20 fritters

2¾ cups (9 oz. / 250 g) cake flour

4 tablespoons (2 oz. / 60 g) unsalted butter,
diced, room temperature

1 egg

3½ tablespoons (1½ oz. / 40 g) granulated sugar

1 tablespoon dark rum

A pinch fine salt

1½ teaspoons (6 g) baking powder

1 tablespoon orange flower water

1 tablespoon cold water

Neutral oil for frying

Confectioners' sugar for dredging

1. Place the flour in the bowl of a stand mixer fitted with the paddle. Gradually beat in the butter, egg, granulated sugar, rum, salt, and baking powder at medium-low speed. Add the orange flower water and cold water and beat until the dough is quite firm. Shape into a disk, cover with plastic wrap, and chill for 1 hour.

2. Bring the dough to room temperature. On a lightly floured work surface, roll out the dough about ¼ inch (6 mm) thick. Cut into 2-inch (5-cm) squares. In a large pot, heat the oil to 320°F (160°C). Working in batches, fry the fritters, turning them occasionally, for about 5 minutes, until golden. Using a slotted spoon, transfer to paper towels to drain. Place the confectioners' sugar in a large bowl. Dredge the fritters in the confectioners' sugar and serve as soon as possible.

STRAWBERRY–BASIL
MUFFINS

Makes 15 muffins

1¼ sticks (5¼ oz. / 150 g) unsalted butter,
room temperature, plus more for brushing

3½ cups (11¼ oz. / 320 g) cake flour, plus more for dusting

1 cup minus 2½ tablespoons (6 oz. / 170 g)
granulated sugar

1½ tablespoons (17 g) baking powder

2 eggs

¾ cup plus 1 tablespoon (190 ml) whole milk

3 egg whites, lightly beaten

7 oz. (200 g) strawberries, sliced

1 sprig basil, leaves chopped

Confectioners' sugar for dusting

Equipment

A 15-cup muffin pan

1. Preheat the oven to 350°F (180°C) convection. Brush the muffin cups with butter and dust with flour. In a medium bowl, beat the butter with the granulated sugar, then place the bowl over a saucepan of simmering water until the mixture is soft but not melted.

2. Sift the flour with the baking powder. Beat the whole eggs into the butter-sugar mixture, then beat in the milk. Carefully fold in the dry ingredients.

3. Carefully fold in the egg whites.

4. Divide the batter among the muffin cups. Arrange the strawberries and basil on top.

5. Bake for 25 to 30 minutes, until a cake tester inserted into the center of a muffin comes out with a few moist crumbs attached. Let the muffins cool slightly in the pan, then turn out onto a rack and let cool completely. Dust with confectioners' sugar.

STRAWBERRY–BASIL MUFFINS

TRIPLE-CHOCOLATE MUFFINS

Prep:
15 minutes

Cook:
20 to 25 minutes

TRIPLE-CHOCOLATE MUFFINS

Makes 15 muffins

5 tablespoons plus 2 teaspoons (3 oz. / 85 g) unsalted butter, melted and cooled, plus more for brushing

2 cups (9 oz. / 250 g) all-purpose flour, plus more for dusting

3½ tablespoons (25 g) unsweetened cocoa powder

1 scant tablespoon (11 g) baking powder

½ teaspoon (2.5 g) baking soda

3 oz. (90 g) dark chocolate

3 oz. (90 g) milk chocolate

3 oz. (90 g) white chocolate

2 eggs

1¼ cups (300 ml) heavy cream

Scant ½ cup (3 oz. / 85 g) light brown sugar

Equipment

A 15-cup muffin pan

1. Preheat the oven to 375°F (190°C) convection. Brush the muffin cups with butter and dust with flour. Sift the flour with the cocoa powder, baking powder, and baking soda. Roughly chop the dark, milk, and white chocolates.

2. In a medium bowl, beat the eggs with the cream, brown sugar, and melted butter. Fold in the dry ingredients; do not overmix. Fold in the chopped chocolate.

3. Divide the batter among the muffin cups and bake for 20 to 25 minutes, until a cake tester inserted into a center comes out clean. Let the muffins cool in the pan for 10 minutes. Carefully turn them out onto a rack—they're fragile—and let cool completely.

Prep:
20 minutes

Cook:
12 to 15 minutes

JACKY'S COCONUT MACAROONS

Makes 15 macaroons

1⅓ cups (3½ oz. / 100 g) unsweetened shredded coconut

2 cups (14 oz. / 400 g) granulated sugar

7 egg whites, lightly beaten

½ cup (2 oz. / 60 g) all-purpose flour

Equipment

A pastry bag, optional

1. Preheat the oven to 400°F (200°C) convection. Line a baking sheet with parchment paper. In a medium bowl, using a wooden spoon, stir the shredded coconut with the sugar, then beat in the egg whites.

2. Place the bowl over a saucepan of simmering water and heat to 140°F (60°C), stirring constantly, until the ingredients form a batter. Remove from the heat and stir in the flour. Pipe or spoon large balls onto the baking sheet.

3. Bake for 12 to 15 minutes, until golden, rotating the pan halfway through, so the macaroons color evenly. Transfer carefully to a rack to cool.

JACKY'S COCONUT MACAROONS

Prep:
20 minutes

Chill:
1 hour

Cook:
55 minutes

PECAN–MAPLE TART

Serves 6 to 8

3 tablespoons plus 1 teaspoon (1¾ oz. / 50 g) unsalted butter,
melted and cooled, plus more for brushing

All-purpose flour for dusting

10½ oz. (300 g) Sweet Almond Pastry (see p. 10), room temperature

3 eggs

1 pinch fine salt

1 cup minus 2½ tablespoons (6 oz. / 170 g) granulated sugar

1 cup (250 ml) pure maple syrup

2½ cups (10½ oz. / 300 g) pecan halves

Equipment
A nonstick 9- to 10-inch (22- to 24-cm) tart pan
with a removable bottom

1. Preheat the oven to 350°F (180°C) convection. Brush the tart pan with butter and dust with flour. On a lightly floured work surface, roll out the pastry ⅛ inch (3 mm) thick. Line the tart pan with the pastry. Bake for 15 minutes. Let cool until needed.

2. Reduce the oven temperature to 340°F (170°C) convection. In a medium bowl, whisk the eggs with the salt. Whisk in the sugar, melted butter, maple syrup, and pecans.

3. Spread the filling in the tart shell, arranging the pecans evenly, and bake for 40 minutes. Let the tart cool slightly in the pan, then remove the rim and transfer the tart to a rack and let cool completely.

PASSION FRUIT CUSTARD TART

Serves 10

10½ oz. (300 g) Crisp
Short Pastry (p. 9),
room temperature, or Quick
Puff Pastry (p. 12), chilled

9 egg yolks

¾ cup (5¼ oz. / 150g)
granulated sugar, divided

Generous ⅓ cup (2 oz. / 60 g)
cornstarch or custard powder

½ teaspoon (2 g) fleur de sel

1 teaspoon pure vanilla extract,
if custard powder is not used

¾ cup (200 ml) heavy cream

1 lb. 10 oz. (750 g) passion
fruit purée

7 tablespoons (3½ oz. / 100 g)
unsalted butter, diced, room
temperature

Equipment

A 9-inch (22-cm) tart ring or
pan, 1¾ inches (4 cm) deep

1. If using a tart ring, line a baking sheet with parchment paper and place the ring in the center. On a lightly floured work surface, roll out the pastry ⅛ inch (3 mm) thick. Line the ring with the pastry. Chill for at least 10 minutes. Preheat the oven to 340°F (170°C) convection. Cover the pastry with parchment paper and fill with baking beans. Bake for 30 minutes, then carefully remove the paper with the beans and let cool.

2. In a medium bowl, beat the egg yolks with ⅓ cup (2½ oz. / 75 g) of the sugar, the cornstarch, fleur de sel, and vanilla but don't let the mixture lighten in color. Stir in the cream.

3. In a medium saucepan, bring the passion fruit purée and remaining ⅓ cup (2½ oz. / 75 g) sugar to a boil over medium-high heat. Immediately remove from the heat. Gradually whisk into the egg yolk mixture. Return to the pan and cook over medium heat, whisking continuously, until the custard thickens. Remove from the heat and stir in the butter. Spread the custard in the cooled tart shell. Let cool completely.

4. Preheat the oven to 425°F (220°C) convection. Bake the tart for 20 minutes, then increase the oven temperature to 465°F (240°C) convection and bake for 10 minutes. If the top is still pale, slide the tart under the broiler for a few minutes. Let cool completely.

Prep:	Chill:	Cook:
30 minutes	40 minutes	20 minutes

DUTCH BUTTER COOKIES

Makes 20 cookies

1 stick plus 1½ tablespoons (4¾ oz. / 135 g)
unsalted butter, softened

½ cup (3½ oz. / 100 g) granulated sugar

1 egg yolk

A pinch baking soda

½ teaspoon (2 g) pure vanilla extract

Finely grated zest and juice of ¼ lemon

1 tablespoon whole milk

2¾ cups (9 oz. / 250 g) cake flour

1 egg, lightly beaten

Equipment
A 4-inch (10-cm) fluted round cookie cutter

1. In a medium bowl, cream the butter with the sugar. In a small bowl, combine the egg yolk with the baking soda. Stir into the butter-sugar mixture.

2. Beat in the vanilla, lemon zest and juice, and milk. Fold in the flour; do not overmix or the dough will be tough.

3. Shape into a disk, cover with plastic wrap, and chill for at least 40 minutes, until firm.

4. Preheat the oven to 340°F (170°C) convection. Line two baking sheets with parchment paper. On a lightly floured work surface, roll out the dough ⅛ inch (4 to 5 mm) thick and cut out the cookies.

5. Brush the tops with the beaten egg and, using the tines of a fork, make crisscross marks on each one.

6. Bake for about 20 minutes, until golden. Let the cookies cool slightly on the baking sheets, then transfer to a rack and let cool completely.

Note: These cookies are a classic at our pastry store in Mutzig.

Prep:
35 minutes

Rise and chill:
3 hours 30 minutes
+ 2 hours

Cook:
15 minutes

CINNAMON BRIOCHE LOAF

Serves 10

2 cups (9 oz. / 250 g) all-purpose flour

2½ tablespoons (1 oz. / 30 g) granulated sugar

1 teaspoon (5 g) fine salt

½ oz. (15 g) fresh yeast

3 whole eggs

1¾ sticks (7 oz. / 200 g) unsalted butter, diced and softened,
plus more for brushing

½ teaspoon cinnamon, plus more for dusting

1 egg yolk, lightly beaten

1. Pour the flour into the bowl of a stand mixer fitted with the dough hook. On one side, place the sugar and salt, and, on the other, the yeast—the yeast should not touch the salt or sugar.

2. Add the eggs. Knead at low speed for 2 to 3 minutes to make a very dense dough. Add the butter and cinnamon and knead until smooth.

3. Increase the speed to medium and knead for 5 to 10 minutes, until the dough is elastic and pulls away from the sides of the bowl.

4. Cover the bowl with a kitchen towel and let dough rise at room temperature for 1 hour, until doubled in volume.

5. Chill the dough for 3 hours, until firm.

6. Brush a baking sheet very lightly with butter. On a lightly floured work surface, roll the dough into a fat log. Transfer to the baking sheet and let rise. Brush with the beaten egg and, using a pair of scissors, make angled cuts along the top.

7. Bake for 15 minutes, until golden on the bottom and sides. Dust with cinnamon. Let cool slightly on the baking sheet, then transfer the loaf to a rack and let cool completely.

HAZELNUT–CHOCOLATE CHIP CAKE

Serves 6

1 stick plus 5 tablespoons (6½ oz. / 185 g) unsalted butter,
melted and cooled, plus more for brushing

⅔ cup plus 1 tablespoon (3 oz. / 90 g) all-purpose flour, plus more for dusting

6 eggs, separated

1 cup minus 1 tablespoon (6½ oz. / 185 g) granulated sugar

1 tablespoon vanilla sugar

1 scant tablespoon (11 g) baking powder

1 cup (3 oz. / 90 g) ground hazelnuts

5¼ oz. (150 g) dark chocolate chips or chopped dark chocolate

3½ oz. (100 g) praline paste, well softened

⅓ cup (1¾ oz. / 50 g) toasted hazelnuts, cut in half

Confectioners' sugar for dusting

Equipment

A 7- to 8-inch (18- to 20-cm) cake pan

1. Preheat the oven to 350°F (180°C). Brush the cake pan with butter and dust with flour. In a medium bowl, whisk the egg yolks with the granulated and vanilla sugars until pale and thick. Using a silicone spatula, stir in the melted butter.

2. In a medium bowl, whisk the egg whites until they hold a soft peak. Using a silicone spatula, carefully fold them into the egg yolk mixture. Fold in the flour, baking powder, ground hazelnuts, and chocolate. Do not overmix.

3. Spread the batter in the cake pan and bake for 45 minutes, until nicely browned and a cake tester inserted into the center comes out clean.

4. Immediately turn out the cake onto a rack and let cool. Spread the top with the praline paste, dot with the hazelnut halves, and dust with confectioners' sugar.

Note: This homey yet sophisticated recipe was created by Virginie Masse.

BANANA–CHOCOLATE SANDWICH COOKIES

Makes two 8-inch (20-cm) cookies

Cookies	Banana ganache	Equipment
1⅔ cups (7 oz. / 200 g) all-purpose flour	7¼ oz. (210 g) white chocolate, chopped	An 8-inch (20-cm) pastry ring or cutter
3½ tablespoons (1 oz. / 25 g) unsweetened cocoa powder, plus more for dusting	1¼ oz. (35 g) cocoa butter, chopped	A 4-inch (10-cm) pastry ring or cutter
1¼ sticks (5¼ oz. / 150 g) unsalted butter, softened	½ cup (3½ oz. / 100 g) granulated sugar	
½ cup plus 1 tablespoon (4 oz. / 110 g) granulated sugar	1½ bananas, peeled and puréed	
¾ cup plus 1½ teaspoons (2¾ oz. / 75 g) almond flour	2 tablespoons plus 2 teaspoons (40 ml) heavy cream	
2 tablespoons (1 oz. / 30 g) lightly beaten egg	2 tablespoons plus 1 teaspoon (1¼ oz. / 35 g) unsalted butter, diced, room temperature	
	1 teaspoon (5 ml) dark rum	

COOKIES

1. Preheat the oven to 320°F (160°C) convection. Line a baking sheet with parchment paper. Sift the all-purpose flour with the cocoa powder. In a medium bowl, cream the butter with the sugar, almond flour, and egg. Rub in the flour mixture.

2. On a lightly floured work surface, roll out the dough ⅛ inch (4 mm) thick. Press out four 8-inch (20 cm) rounds. Using the 4-inch (10-cm) cutter, cut out a disk from the center of two of the rounds to form rings. Transfer to the baking sheet and bake for 20 minutes. Let cool slightly on the baking sheet, then transfer to a rack and let cool completely.

BANANA GANACHE

3. In a medium heatproof bowl, combine the white chocolate with the cocoa butter. In a medium heavy saucepan, cook half of the sugar over medium heat, stirring with a wooden spoon, until melted. Add the remaining sugar and cook until it's a lovely caramel color. Remove from the heat and carefully stir in the puréed banana, cream, and butter.

4. Pour the hot caramel mixture over the white chocolate and cocoa butter and stir until smooth. Let cool, then stir in the rum.

5. Dust the rings with cocoa powder. Spread the banana ganache evenly over each entire cookie. Carefully place the cookie rings on the ganache.

Thursday

Madeleines (p. 178) are a must. Traditionally baked in a scalloped mold, they emerge from the oven bearing a little bump on the top, a sign that the recipe has done its magic.

CHERRY–RASPBERRY CHEESECAKE

Serves 8 to 10

Unsalted butter for brushing

10½ oz. (300 g) Crisp Short Pastry (p. 9), room temperature

1 lb. 5 oz. (600 g) fromage blanc, quark, or ricotta, preferably whole milk

1 cup (7 oz. / 200 g) granulated sugar

½ teaspoon pure vanilla extract

2 tablespoons (20 g) cornstarch

4 eggs

¾ cup (200 ml) heavy cream

7 oz. (200 g) sweet cherries, pitted

3½ oz. (100 g) raspberries

Apricot jelly, warmed, for brushing

Equipment

A 10-inch (24-cm) tart dish

1. Preheat the oven to 350°F (180°C) convection. Brush the tart dish with butter. On a lightly floured work surface, roll out the pastry ⅛ inch (4 mm) thick. Line the dish with the pastry. Prick the pastry evenly with a fork. Chill for at least 10 minutes.

2. Cover the pastry with parchment paper and fill with baking beans. Bake for 30 minutes. Let cool, then carefully remove the paper with the beans. Leave the oven on.

3. In a large bowl, whisk the fromage blanc with the sugar, vanilla, and cornstarch, then whisk in the eggs and cream.

4. Spread the filling in the tart shell. Arrange the cherries and raspberries evenly on top. The filling should be at least 1¼ inches (3 cm) deep.

5. Bake for 30 to 40 minutes and let cool to room temperature.

6. Brush the cake very lightly with the apricot jelly.

Prep: 25 minutes

Cook: 40 minutes

APPLE CAKE WITH ROSEMARY

Serves 8

Apples

1 lb. 2 oz. (500 g) peeled and cored Golden Delicious apples

1 tablespoon (15 g) unsalted butter

2½ tablespoons (1 oz. / 30 g) light brown sugar

Cake batter

1¾ sticks (7 oz. / 200 g) unsalted butter, softened, plus more for brushing

2¾ cups (9 oz. / 250 g) cake flour, plus more for dusting

1 teaspoon baking powder

1 generous cup (5¼ oz. / 150 g) confectioners' sugar, plus more for dusting

2½ egg yolks

1 teaspoon pure vanilla extract

2 tablespoons (1½ oz. / 40 g) honey

5 egg whites

¼ cup (1¾ oz. / 50 g) granulated sugar

¼ cup (1¾ oz. / 50 g) light brown sugar

2 teaspoons (1.5 g) chopped rosemary, plus rosemary sprigs for decorating

Equipment

A 9-inch (22-cm) cake pan

APPLES

1. Cut some of the apples into cubes and the others into wedges. Make sure you have at least 14 oz. (400 g) of cubes. In a large skillet, melt the butter with the light brown sugar over high heat. Add all the apple pieces and cook, stirring often, for 15 minutes, then remove from the heat.

CAKE BATTER

2. Preheat the oven to 350°F (180°C) convection. Brush the cake pan with butter and dust with flour. Sift the cake flour with the baking powder. In a large bowl, whisk the butter with the confectioners' sugar, egg yolks, vanilla, and honey.

3. In a separate bowl, whisk the egg whites with the granulated and light brown sugars until they hold a soft peak. Fold into the batter.

4. Fold in the dry ingredients. Weigh out 12 oz. (350 g) of the cubed apples and fold them carefully into the cake batter with the chopped rosemary.

5. Spread the batter in the cake pan and bake for 40 minutes, watching the cake carefully.

6. Let the cake cool slightly in the pan, then turn out onto a rack and let cool completely. Dust with the confectioners' sugar. Decorate with the apple wedges, remaining 1¾ oz. (50 g) apple cubes, and rosemary sprigs.

Prep:
20 minutes

Cook:
5 minutes

Chill:
3 hours

PANNA COTTA
WITH FRESH FRUIT

Serves 10

3½ sheets (7 g) 200 bloom
gelatin

1 vanilla bean

2 cups (500 ml) heavy cream

½ cup (125 g) fromage blanc
or Greek yogurt

⅔ cup (4½ oz. / 125 g)
granulated sugar

**Pink grapefruit and
coconut topping**

1 tablespoon plus 2 teaspoons
(20 g) granulated sugar

1 teaspoon Malibu® or other
coconut liqueur

7 oz. (200 g) pink grapefruit
segments

Coconut shavings

**Orange, passion fruit,
mango, and lime topping**

5 oz. (150 g) orange segments

Pulp of 2 passion fruits

3½ oz. (100 g) diced mango

1 tablespoon plus 2 teaspoons
(20 g) granulated sugar

A little orange juice

Finely grated lime zest

**Cherry and green
almond topping**

7 oz. (200 g) sweet cherries,
halved and pitted

1 tablespoon plus 2 teaspoons
(20 g) granulated sugar

A few green almonds, peeled,
or natural almonds

Equipment

10 glasses or ramekins

Egg trays

PANNA COTTA

1. In a medium bowl of very cold water, soften the gelatin.

2. Split the vanilla bean lengthwise and scrape out the seeds. In a medium saucepan, heat the cream with the vanilla bean and seeds over medium-high heat until bubbles appear around the edge. Remove from the heat. Remove the vanilla bean. Squeeze the gelatin dry and whisk into the hot cream until dissolved.

3. In a large bowl, whisk the fromage blanc with the sugar. Whisk in the hot cream.

4. Tilting the glasses, divide the panna cotta among them. Carefully place in egg trays and chill so the cream sets at an angle. Decorate with the fruit topping of your choice.

PINK GRAPEFRUIT AND COCONUT TOPPING

Stir the sugar and Malibu into the grapefruit, then add the coconut.

ORANGE, PASSION FRUIT, MANGO, AND LIME TOPPING

Combine the orange segments with the passion fruit and mango and stir in the sugar. Add the orange juice and lime zest.

CHERRY AND GREEN ALMOND TOPPING

Combine the cherries with the sugar and add the almonds.

JAPANESE-STYLE MILK ROULADE WITH WHIPPED CREAM

Serves 8

5 egg yolks

Scant ½ cup (3 oz. / 90 g) granulated sugar, divided

4 egg whites

½ cup minus 1 tablespoon (2 oz. / 55 g) all-purpose flour

2 tablespoons plus 1 teaspoon (35 ml) whole milk

1¼ cups (300 ml) heavy cream

1 tablespoon plus 2 teaspoons (20 g) sugar

Confectioners' sugar for dusting

Unsweetened cocoa powder for sifting

Equipment

A small piece of light cardboard or paper with holes cut out

1. Preheat the oven to 375°F (190°C) convection. Line a 12 by 16-inch (30 by 40-cm) rimmed baking sheet with parchment paper. In the bowl of a stand mixer fitted with the whisk, whip the egg yolks with 3 tablespoons (1¼ oz. / 35 g) of the granulated sugar at high speed for 15 minutes.

2. In a separate bowl, whisk the egg whites, gradually adding the remaining ¼ cup (1¾ oz. / 50 g) sugar, until they hold a soft peak.

3. Carefully fold the whipped egg whites into the egg yolk-sugar mixture, then fold in the flour and milk. Spread evenly over the baking sheet.

4. Bake for 10 to 12 minutes, then reduce the oven temperature to 280°F (140°C) convection and bake for 2 minutes. Let cool completely.

5. Meanwhile, place the bowl of a stand mixer, a whisk, and the cream in the freezer. Or set the bowl in a larger bowl half-filled with ice water.

6. Whisk the cream at high speed for 3 to 4 minutes, gradually adding the sugar. The cream is ready when it forms a little peak that droops ever so slightly when you lift the whisk.

7. Invert the cake onto a clean sheet of parchment paper and carefully peel off the top parchment. Spread the whipped cream evenly over the cake. Using the parchment paper as a guide, roll up the cake tightly along the shorter side.

8. Dust the cake with confectioners' sugar, then sift the cocoa powder through the holes in the cardboard on top.

Notes: This recipe comes from Takahiro Komai, pastry chef with Henri Charpentier in Japan. During strawberry season, you can dot the cream with a few strawberries before rolling up the cake.

Prep:
1 hour

Chill:
1 hour

Cook:
20 to 25 minutes

CAMILLE'S CHESTNUT BOATS

Makes 10 individual cakes

7 tablespoons (3½ oz. / 100 g) unsalted butter,
room temperature

9 oz. (250 g) chestnut spread (*crème de marrons*)

9 oz. (250 g) Sweet Almond Pastry (p. 10),
room temperature

7 oz. (200 g) Almond Cream (p. 15)

Chocolate Fondant Icing (p. 17),
warmed to 95°F (35°C)

Equipment

Ten 3-inch (7 to 8-cm) barquette molds

1. In a medium bowl, whip the butter. Gradually add the chestnut spread and whip until very creamy.

2. Preheat the oven to 350°F (180°C) convection. On a lightly floured work surface, roll out the pastry ⅛ inch (4 mm) thick. Line the barquette molds with the pastry. Transfer to a baking sheet and chill for at least 10 minutes. Bake for 5 minutes. Remove from the oven and leave the oven on.

3. Spread the Almond Cream about ¼ inch (5 mm) thick in the banquette molds. Return to the oven for 15 to 20 minutes. Let cool slightly in the molds, then turn out carefully onto a rack and let cool completely.

4. Spread the chestnut filling over the Almond Cream. Chill for 1 hour, until set.

5. Glaze the cakes with the fondant and chill until set. Bring to room temperature before serving.

Prep:
45 minutes

Chill:
1 hour

Cook:
25 to 30 minutes

HONEYED PEAR TART

Serves 8

10½ oz. (300 g) Sweet Almond Pastry (p. 10),
room temperature

1 recipe Almond Cream (p. 15)

2 lb. 2 oz. (1 kg) Bartlett pears (see Note)

Lemon juice for drizzling

¼ cup (3 oz. / 80 g) pine honey or other flavorful honey

1 vanilla bean

2 tablespoons (1 oz. / 30 g) unsalted butter

Pear jelly or apricot jelly, warmed, for brushing

Confectioners' sugar for dusting

Equipment

A 10-inch (24-cm) tart ring or pan

1. Preheat the oven to 350°F (180°C) convection. If using a tart ring, line a baking sheet with parchment paper and place the ring in the center. On a lightly floured work surface, roll out the pastry about ⅛ inch (3 to 4 mm) thick. Line the ring with the pastry. Chill for at least 10 minutes. Bake the tart for about 15 minutes. Spread the Almond Cream fairly thickly in the tart shell.

2. Peel and halve the pears, then scoop out the cores but keep the stems. Drizzle with the lemon juice.

3. In a large skillet, sauté the pears in the honey until they are caramelized. Split the vanilla bean lengthwise and scrape out the seeds; reserve the bean. Add the seeds and butter to the skillet and

cook over low heat for about 10 minutes. Remove from the heat and let cool slightly; the pears should be barely warm for the next step.

4. Arrange the pears, slightly overlapping them in the tart shell and letting the stems peek out. Bake for 25 to 30 minutes.

5. Let the tart cool and brush the pears with the jelly. Cut the reserved vanilla bean into thin strips and use to decorate the tart. Dust the rim with confectioners' sugar.

Note: This tart can only be truly delicious if you have sweet, ripe pears that are still a little firm.

APPLE–STRAWBERRY CRUMBLE

Serves 8

Fruit

7 baking apples

Juice of 1 lemon

1 tablespoon vanilla sugar

½ teaspoon cinnamon

7 oz. (200 g) strawberries

Crumble topping

1⅓ cups (5½ oz. / 165 g) all-purpose flour

Scant ⅔ cup (4 oz. / 120 g) light brown sugar

3½ tablespoons (1½ oz. / 40 g) granulated sugar

1 stick plus 2 tablespoons (5 oz. / 140 g)
unsalted butter, diced

Equipment

9-inch (22-cm) shallow baking dish

FRUIT

1. Peel, core, and halve the apples. Cut the apples into large cubes.

2. In a large bowl, toss the apple cubes with the lemon juice, coating them well, then stir in the vanilla sugar and cinnamon.

3. Cut the strawberries in half and stir gently into the apples. Spread the fruit in the baking dish.

CRUMBLE TOPPING

4. Preheat the oven to 350°F (180°C) convection. In a medium bowl, whisk the flour with the two sugars. Squeeze in the butter until the dough forms large crumbs.

5. Sprinkle the crumble evenly over the fruit. Bake for at least 30 minutes, until the fruit is bubbling and the topping is golden.

CLAFOUTIS

Serves 8 to 10

8 eggs

2 pinches fine salt

1 tablespoon plus 2 teaspoons (20 g) vanilla sugar,
plus more for sprinkling

1¾ cups plus 1½ tablespoons (8 oz. / 230 g) all-purpose flour

2 tablespoons dark rum, divided

3¼ cups (775 ml) whole milk

2 cups (500 ml) heavy cream

1 lb. (450 g) cherries (see Notes)

1 cup minus 1½ tablespoons (6¼ oz. / 180 g) granulated sugar

Equipment
A 10-inch (24 cm) pie dish

1. Preheat the oven to 425°F (220°C) convection. In a large bowl, using an electric beater, whisk the eggs with the salt, vanilla sugar, and flour for 5 minutes, until smooth.

2. Stir in 1 tablespoon of the rum with the milk and cream. Blend the batter for a few minutes, until smooth. If you have time, chill the batter thoroughly so the flour thoroughly absorbs the milk.

3. If using pitted cherries, pour the batter into the dish and arrange the cherries evenly on top. Bake for 30 to 35 minutes.

4. If using unpitted cherries, pour some of the batter into the dish, ½ to ¾ inch (1 to 2 cm) deep, and bake for 15 minutes. Let cool for 5 minutes, then pour in the remaining batter. Arrange the cherries evenly on top and bake for 15 to 20 minutes.

5. Immediately sprinkle with vanilla sugar and drizzle with the remaining rum.

Notes: To pit or not to pit the cherries? Many think the taste is superior if the pits are left in; others prefer to remove them and avoid the risk of breaking a tooth. Leaving in the pits does seem to have more pros than cons. The pit is thought to preserve the full flavor of the cherries, and whole cherries don't leak their juice into the batter. Of course, it's your call. We also like to leave on the stems.

Next choice: serve hot, warm, or cold? This simple dessert is easy to prepare at the last minute and serve warm. Again, you can experiment to decide what you prefer. To give this everyday dessert a hint of decadence, dip the cherries into jam and dot over the baked clafoutis.

MY FATHER'S LOAF CAKE
WITH A LITTLE CANDIED FRUIT

Serves 8

1 stick plus 1 tablespoon (4½ oz. / 130 g) unsalted butter,
melted and cooled to about 115°F (45°C), plus more for brushing

3 eggs

1 cup minus 1 tablespoon (6½ oz. / 185 g)
granulated sugar

2 tablespoons plus 2 teaspoons (40 ml)
whole milk, room temperature

3 cups plus 1½ tablespoons (9¾ oz. / 280 g) cake flour

1 tablespoon (12 g) baking powder

Assorted candied fruit (but just a little)

5 oz. (150 g) Fondant Icing (p. 17), warmed to 95°F (35°C)
and flavored with a drop of kirsch

Equipment

A 3 by 9-inch (8 by 22-cm) loaf pan

A paper decorating cone

1. Preheat the oven to 425°F (220°C) convection.
Brush the loaf pan with butter and line with
parchment paper. In a stand mixer fitted with the
whisk, whip the eggs with the sugar for 20 minutes.

2. Whisk in the milk, cake flour, baking powder,
and candied fruit, one by one, in order, finishing
with the melted butter. Spread the batter in the pan.

3. Place the cake in the oven and reduce the oven
temperature to 400°F (200°C) convection. Bake for
40 to 50 minutes, until a tester inserted into the
center comes out clean. Let cool completely.

4. Using the paper decorating cone, draw fine lines
with the fondant over the cake.

Notes: My father began making this cake in the 1970s
at his bakery in Schirmeck.

If you like, just before baking, use a knife to make
a long cut down the center of the batter so the cake
cracks open attractively as it bakes.

HOW TO MAKE A DECORATING CONE

All you need is a sheet of parchment paper and a pair
of scissors.

• Cut a rectangle and turn it so that one of the lengths
is facing you. From halfway along the bottom, cut a
right-angled triangle along the left.

• From this point, fold the triangle, bringing one side
over the other. Flatten to leave a crease along the
fold, and tightly roll the paper to shape a cone.

• Use the crease as a guideline. With the cone in one
hand, use the other to roll the cone along the rest of
the paper. Keep the tip firmly in place so it doesn't
unroll. Tuck the point of paper that's sticking out
over the top of the cone inside. Staple or tape it into
place so the cone doesn't unroll.

• Scoop the preparation into the cone as close to
the tip as possible. Fold the top over again to the
other side. For the opening, simply snip off the tip.
The hole should be small so that a thin line of your
decorative frosting comes out when you pipe.

RASPBERRY–ALMOND BRIOCHE SLICES
Bostock aux Framboises

Serves 6

Scant ½ cup (100 ml) water

¾ cup minus 1 teaspoon (5 oz. / 140 g) granulated sugar

2 tablespoons plus 2 teaspoons (15 g) ground almonds

1 drop bitter almond extract

1 tablespoon plus 1 scant tablespoon (15 g) confectioners' sugar,
plus more for dusting

1¾ oz. (50 g) raspberry purée

A 1-lb. (500-g) round brioche

7 oz. (200 g) raspberries

1 recipe Almond Cream (p. 15)

Sliced almonds for sprinkling

1. In a small saucepan, bring the water to a boil with the sugar, stirring, until the sugar dissolves. Remove from the heat and stir in the ground almonds, bitter almond extract, and confectioners' sugar. Stir in the raspberry purée and return to the heat. Bring to a boil, skimming the syrup. Whisk well, then pour into a medium bowl and let cool to lukewarm.

2. Preheat the oven to 400°F (200°C) convection. Cut slices of brioche 1½ inches (3 to 4 cm) thick.

3. Dip the slices in the syrup. Spread the almond cream on one side of each slice and press in the raspberries, hollow side down. Sprinkle with the sliced almonds.

4. Transfer to baking sheets. Bake for 10 to 15 minutes, until lightly browned, and serve warm. Dust with confectioners' sugar just before serving.

GRAPE–ALMOND BRIOCHE SLICES
Bostock aux Raisins

Serves 6

Scant ½ cup (100 ml) water

¾ cup minus 1 teaspoon (5 oz. / 140 g) granulated sugar

2 tablespoons plus 2 teaspoons (15 g) ground almonds

1 drop bitter almond extract

1 tablespoon plus 1 scant tablespoon (15 g) confectioners' sugar,
plus more for dusting

2 teaspoons (10 ml) orange flower water

7 oz. (200 g) green grapes

Sliced almonds

A 1-lb. (500-g) round brioche

1 recipe Almond Cream (see p. 15)

1. In a small saucepan, bring the water to a boil with the sugar, stirring until the sugar dissolves. Remove from the heat and stir in the ground almonds, bitter almond extract, and confectioners' sugar. Skim the syrup. Stir in the orange flower water, then pour into a medium bowl and let cool to lukewarm.

2. Preheat the oven to 400°F (200°C) convection. Cut slices of brioche 1½ inches (3 to 4 cm) thick. Dip them in the warm syrup.

3. Spread the almond cream on one side of each slice and press in the grapes, small hole down. Sprinkle with the sliced almonds and dust with confectioners' sugar.

4. Transfer to baking sheets. Bake for 10 to 15 minutes, until the almonds are lightly browned, and serve warm.

CHOCOLATE–ORANGE LOAF

Serves 8

Batter
1 stick plus 2 tablespoons (5¼ oz. / 150 g) unsalted butter,
softened, plus more for brushing
2¼ cups (7 oz. / 200 g) cake flour, plus more for dusting
1½ teaspoons (6 g) baking powder
¾ cup (5¼ oz. / 150 g) granulated sugar
3 eggs
Scant ½ cup (3 oz. / 80 g) chocolate chips
Finely grated zest of 2 oranges

Orange syrup and decoration
2 tablespoons (30 ml) orange juice
1 tablespoon plus 2 teaspoons (25 ml) water
1¼ teaspoons (5 g) granulated sugar
3½ oz. (100 g) Candied Orange Slices (p. 268)
Finely grated chocolate for sprinkling, optional

Equipment
A 3 by 9-inch (8 by 22-cm) loaf pan

BATTER

1. Preheat the oven to 340°F (170°C) convection. Brush the pan with butter and dust with flour. Sift the flour with the baking powder. In a large bowl, beat the butter with the sugar until very fluffy.

2. Gradually whisk in the eggs. Fold in the sifted ingredients, then the chocolate chips and orange zest. Spread in the loaf pan and bake for about 50 minutes, until a tester inserted into the center comes out clean.

ORANGE SYRUP AND DECORATION

3. Combine the orange juice and water with the sugar. Stir until the sugar dissolves.

4. As soon as the cake comes out of the oven, pour the syrup over the top, then let cool in the pan. Decorate with the orange slices and sprinkle with the grated chocolate, if desired.

Prep:
30 minutes

Chill:
30 minutes

Cook:
45 to 50 minutes

RASPBERRY FLORENTINES

Serves 8

Scant ⅓ cup (3½ oz. / 100 g) honey

½ cup (3½ oz. / 100 g) granulated sugar

Finely grated zest of 1 orange

6 tablespoons (3 oz. / 90 g) unsalted butter, diced

1 cup (3 ½ oz. (100 g) sliced almonds

10½ oz. (300 g) Sweet Almond Pastry (p. 10),
room temperature

9 oz. (250 g) Barely Sweet Raspberry Jam (p. 17),
warmed, for brushing

1. Line a baking sheet with parchment paper. In a medium saucepan, warm the honey with the sugar over medium heat, stirring until the sugar dissolves. Stir in the orange zest.

2. Using a wooden spoon, stir in the butter. Bring to a boil and let boil for 1 minute. Stir in the sliced almonds, coating them well.

3. Spread the almond praline on the baking sheet. Cover with a second sheet of parchment and roll out the praline ⅛ inch (3 mm) thick. Carefully transfer to the freezer and chill for 30 minutes.

4. Preheat the oven to 350°F (180°C) convection. Carefully peel off the top parchment and bake the praline for 10 to 15 minutes, until lightly browned. Let cool on the baking sheet. Leave the oven on.

5. On a lightly floured work surface, roll out the pastry into a rectangle the same size as the praline. Transfer to a baking sheet and bake for 20 minutes. Let cool slightly.

6. Brush the jam over the pastry about ⅛ inch (3 to 4 mm) thick and return to the oven for 10 minutes. Let cool. Invert the praline onto the pastry, peel off the parchment, and bake for 5 to 6 minutes. Let cool slightly, then using a large knife, cut into triangles.

GIANDUJA SANDWICH COOKIES

Makes 8 cookies

10½ oz. (300 g) Sweet Almond Pastry (p. 10),
room temperature

1 scant cup (5¾ oz. / 160 g) hazelnuts

1 generous cup (5¼ oz. / 150 g) confectioners' sugar

1 pinch fleur de sel

4½ oz. (130 g) 35% milk chocolate

¾ oz. (20 g) dark chocolate

1½ oz. (40 g) hazelnut paste, well softened, optional

Equipment

A 3-inch (7 cm) cookie cutter

A pastry bag fitted with a plain tip, optional

1. Preheat the oven to 320°F (160°C) convection. Line 2 baking sheets with Silpain® baking mats or other perforated mats to give the cookies a fine wafflelike texture. On a lightly floured work surface, roll out the pastry about ⅛ inch (3 to 4 mm) thick.

2. Cut out 16 rounds, transfer to the baking sheets, and bake for 20 to 25 minutes, until golden. Let cool on the baking mats. Leave the oven on.

3. Line a baking sheet with parchment paper. Spread the hazelnuts on the baking sheet and toast for 15 to 20 minutes. Let cool slightly. Rub the nuts between your hands to remove the skins. Peel as many as you can, but don't worry—perfectly peeled nuts are not essential.

4. In a food processor, grind the hazelnuts with the confectioners' sugar and fleur de sel until creamy and fairly smooth. Be patient. It can take up to 15 minutes to achieve the right texture. Let cool completely in the food processor.

5. Meanwhile, in a medium bowl set over a saucepan of simmering water, melt the two chocolates, stirring occasionally, until smooth. When the mixture is just warm to the touch, remove the bowl from the heat.

6. Add the melted chocolate and, if using, the hazelnut paste to the hazelnut butter and process briefly, until smooth.

7. Transfer the gianduja to a bowl and stir occasionally until room temperature. When it begins to thicken (the timing depends on the temperature of your kitchen), pipe or spread it over the centers of half the cookies, then sandwich with the plain cookies. Let firm up completely before serving.

Notes: If you prefer, you can use store-bought gianduja paste, milk or dark.

This recipe was created by Christophe Geistel.

Prep:
20 minutes

Rest:
20 minutes
+ 45 minutes

Cook:
35 to 45 minutes

SAFFRON BRIOCHE
Zopf

Serves 10

Brioche dough

1 oz. (30 g) fresh yeast

½ cup (3½ oz. / 100 g) granulated sugar, divided

1 cup (250 ml) whole milk, divided

1 stick plus 2 teaspoons (4½ oz. / 125 g) unsalted butter, diced, plus more for the baking sheet

½ teaspoon saffron threads

4 cups (1 lb. 2 oz. / 500 g) all-purpose flour, plus more for dredging

1 tablespoon vanilla sugar

1 pinch fine salt

1 egg

1 cup (3½ oz. / 100 g) almond flour

⅔ cup (3½ oz. / 100 g) raisins

Finish

1 egg, lightly beaten

¾ cup (3 oz. / 80 g) sliced almonds

3 tablespoons plus 1 teaspoon (50 ml) water

⅓ cup (2½ oz. / 70 g) granulated sugar

BRIOCHE DOUGH

1. In a small bowl, dissolve the yeast with 1 tablespoon plus 2 teaspoons (20 g) of the granulated sugar in a scant ¼ cup (50 ml) of the milk. Let stand for 20 minutes.

2. In a small saucepan, heat the remaining ¾ cup (200 ml) of the milk over medium-high heat until bubbles appear around the edge. Add the butter and stir until melted, then stir in the saffron. Remove from the heat.

3. In the bowl of a stand mixer fitted with the dough hook, combine the all-purpose flour with the remaining ½ cup minus 1 tablespoon (2¾ oz. / 80 g) granulated sugar, the vanilla sugar, salt, egg, yeast mixture, and almond flour. Knead, drizzling in the remaining ¾ cup (200 ml) milk, for at least 5 minutes.

4. Wash the raisins and pat dry. In a small bowl, dredge the raisins in a little all-purpose flour, then knead into the dough. Let rise in a warm place for about 30 minutes.

5. Divide the dough into 3 equal pieces. Shape into 3 long strands and place side by side on a baking sheet. Braid them, pinching the tips together. Let rise for 15 minutes.

FINISH

6. Preheat the oven to 340°F (170°C) convection. Brush the top with the beaten egg and sprinkle with the sliced almonds. Bake for 35 to 40 minutes.

7. In a small saucepan, bring the water to a boil with the sugar, stirring, until the sugar dissolves. Remove the pan from the heat. As soon as the brioche comes out of the oven, brush with the syrup. Let cool.

Note: This recipe is traditionally braided, but you can also use a ring mold.

RUSTIC WINE TART
Tarte Suisse

Serves 8

10½ oz. (300 g) Crisp Plain Pastry (p. 9), room temperature

Scant ⅔ cup (4 oz. / 120 g) granulated sugar

2 tablespoons (20 g) potato starch

1 tablespoon (8 g) cinnamon

1¼ cups (300 ml) dry white wine, such as Alsatian Pinot Gris

⅔ cup (150 ml) heavy cream

2 eggs

Equipment

A 9-inch (22-cm) tart ring or pan

1. Preheat the oven to 340°F (170°C) convection. If using a tart ring, line a baking sheet with parchment paper and place the ring in the center. On a lightly floured work surface, roll out the pastry ⅛ inch (3 mm) thick. Line the ring with the pastry. Cover the pastry with parchment paper and fill with baking beans.

2. Bake for 30 minutes, then carefully remove the paper with the beans. Increase the oven temperature to 425°F (220°C) convection.

3. In a large bowl, whisk the sugar with the potato starch and cinnamon. Whisk in the wine, cream, and eggs. Pour into a saucepan and cook over low heat, stirring constantly, until the mixture is smooth and creamy. Let cool slightly.

4. Spread the filling in the pastry shell and bake for 15 minutes.

5. Serve warm or cooled.

Note: You can also make individual versions of this tart.

SANDRINE'S COCONUT–RUM CAKE
Tourment d'Amour

Serves 10

Coconut-rum jam

1 vanilla bean

9 oz. (250 g) coconut jam

½ cup minus 1 tablespoon
(100 ml) white rum

¼ teaspoon cinnamon

3 drops bitter
almond extract

Pastry

Unsalted butter for brushing

All-purpose flour for dusting

10½ oz. (300 g) Crisp
Plain Pastry (p. 9), room
temperature

Cake batter and assembly

1 cup (4 oz. / 120 g)
all-purpose flour

1½ teaspoons (6 g)
baking powder

3 eggs, separated

Scant ⅔ cup (4 oz. / 120 g)
granulated sugar

1 stick plus 2 tablespoons
(5¼ oz. / 150 g) unsalted butter,
diced, softened

3 tablespoons plus 1 teaspoon
(50 ml) dark rum

Finely grated zest and
juice of 1 lime

Confectioners' sugar
for dusting

Lime wedges

Diced fresh coconut

Equipment

9-inch (22-cm)
springform pan

COCONUT–RUM JAM

1. Split the vanilla bean lengthwise and scrape out the seeds; reserve the bean for another use. In a medium saucepan, bring the coconut jam to a simmer over low heat with the white rum, cinnamon, vanilla seeds, and bitter almond extract. Remove from the heat and let cool.

PASTRY

2. Brush the pan with butter and dust with flour. On a lightly floured work surface, roll out the pastry ⅛ inch (3 mm) thick. Line the pan with the pastry. Prick the pastry with a fork and chill.

CAKE BATTER AND ASSEMBLY

3. Preheat the oven to 350°F (180°C) convection. Whisk the flour with the baking powder. In a medium bowl, whisk the egg whites until they hold a soft peak.

4. In a separate bowl, whisk the egg yolks with the sugar and butter. Whisk in the dark rum and lime zest and juice, then fold in the dry ingredients. Fold in the egg whites.

5. Spread the coconut-rum jam in the tart shell and cover with the cake batter.

6. Bake for 30 to 40 minutes. Let cool. Dust with confectioners' sugar and decorate with lime wedges and diced coconut. Dust again with confectioners' sugar.

Note: As an alternative garnish, you can decorate the cake with flaked coconut and candied lime peel as soon as it comes out of the oven.

WHOLE LEMON TART

Prep: 30 minutes   *Cool:* 1 hour   *Cook:* 20 minutes + 15 minutes

WHOLE LEMON TART

○○○○○○○○○○○○○○○○○○○○○○○

Serves 8

1 cup (250 ml) whole milk

7 oz. (200 g) lemon purée

7 tablespoons (3½ oz. / 100 g) unsalted butter, diced, room temperature

1 cup minus 3 tablespoons (5½ oz. / 160 g) granulated sugar, divided

5 eggs

2½ tablespoons (1 oz. / 25 g) cornstarch

10½ oz. (300 g) Crisp Plain Pastry (p. 9), room temperature

Equipment

An 8-inch (20-cm) tart ring or pan

1.   In a large saucepan, heat the milk with the lemon purée, butter, and ½ cup minus 1 tablespoon (2¾ oz. / 80 g) of the sugar over medium heat, stirring constantly, until smooth; remove from the heat. In a large bowl, whisk the eggs with the cornstarch and remaining ½ cup minus 1 tablespoon (2¾ oz. / 80 g) sugar. Whisk the milk-lemon mixture into the eggs, then return to the saucepan. Bring to a boil, stirring constantly, and simmer for 1 to 2 minutes.

2.   Preheat the oven to 350°F (180°C) convection. If using a tart ring, line a baking sheet with parchment paper and place the ring in the center. On a lightly floured work surface, roll out the pastry ⅛ inch (3 mm) thick. Line the ring with the pastry. Cover the pastry with parchment paper and fill with baking beans. Bake for 20 minutes. Carefully remove the paper with the beans and let cool to room temperature.

3.   Spread the lemon filling in the tart shell and let cool completely. Increase the oven heat to 375°F (190°C) convection and bake for 15 minutes.

Prep: 15 minutes   *Cook:* 20 to 25 minutes

THE BEST CHOCOLATE CAKE

○○○○○○○○○○○○○○○○○○○○○○○

Serves 8

1¾ sticks (7 oz. / 200 g) unsalted butter, diced, room temperature, plus more for brushing

¾ cup plus 2 tablespoons (3½ oz. / 100 g) all-purpose flour, plus more for dusting

7 oz. (200 g) 70% dark chocolate, such as Valrhona® Guanaja, chopped

4 eggs, separated

1 cup (7 oz. / 200 g) granulated sugar

1 pinch fine salt

Equipment

A 9-inch (22-cm) round cake pan

1.   Preheat the oven to 400°F (200°C) convection. Brush the cake pan with butter and dust with flour. In a medium bowl set over a saucepan of simmering water, melt the chocolate, stirring occasionally, until smooth. Remove from the heat and stir in the butter until smooth.

2.   Using an electric beater, whisk the egg yolks with the sugar for 4 minutes. Stir into the chocolate-butter mixture.

3.   In a medium bowl, whisk the egg whites with the salt until they hold a soft peak. Fold into the chocolate batter. Carefully fold in the flour.

4.   Spread the batter in the cake pan. Bake for 20 to 25 minutes, until the top begins to crack and a tester inserted into the cake comes out with moist crumbs. Let cool to room temperature.

THE BEST CHOCOLATE CAKE

LINZER COOKIES

Prep:
20 minutes

Cook:
20 minutes

Chill:
30 minutes

Prep:
20 minutes

Cook:
10 to 12 minutes

Chill:
1 hour, optional (see Note)

LINZER COOKIES

MADELEINES

Makes 20 sandwich cookies

Yolks of 2 hard-boiled eggs

1 stick plus 2 teaspoons (4½ oz. / 125 g) unsalted butter, diced, softened

½ cup (3½ oz. / 100 g) granulated sugar

Generous ¼ cup (25 g) almond flour

¼ teaspoon cinnamon

Finely grated zest of ¼ lemon

1 cup plus 2 tablespoons (5 oz. / 150 g) all-purpose flour

1 recipe Barely Sweet Raspberry Jam (p. 17)

Equipment

A pastry bag fitted with a plain tip, optional

Makes 20 madeleines

1¾ sticks (7 oz. / 200 g) unsalted butter, plus more for brushing

1⅔ cups (7 oz. / 200 g) all-purpose flour, plus more for dusting

2¾ teaspoons (10 g) baking powder

3 eggs

1 cup minus 3 tablespoons (5½ oz. / 160 g) granulated sugar

2 teaspoons orange flower water

3 tablespoons plus 1 teaspoon (50 ml) whole milk

1 pinch vanilla bean powder

½ teaspoon pure vanilla extract

Equipment

20 madeleine pans or mini muffin cups

A pastry bag, optional

1. Preheat the oven to 340°F (170°C) convection. Line 2 baking sheets with parchment paper (or bake in batches). Push the egg yolks through a fine sieve into a medium bowl. Beat in the butter, sugar, almond flour, cinnamon, and lemon zest.

2. Rub in the all-purpose flour. On a lightly floured work surface, roll out the dough ⅛ inch (3 mm) thick. Chill for 30 minutes. Using a large knife, cut into 40 squares.

3. Transfer to the baking sheets and bake for about 20 minutes, until evenly browned. Let cool slightly on the baking sheet, then transfer to a rack and let cool completely.

4. Pipe or spread the jam over half the cookies and sandwich with the plain cookies.

1. If not chilling the batter, preheat the oven to 410°F (210°C) convection. Brush the madeleine pans with butter and dust with flour. In a small saucepan, melt the butter over medium heat, then cook until it begins to brown and smells a little like hazelnuts. Strain the brown butter through a fine sieve. You'll need to use it while it's still warm.

2. Sift the flour with the baking powder. In a medium bowl, whisk the eggs with the sugar, orange flower water, milk, vanilla bean powder, and vanilla extract. Fold in the dry ingredients, then the brown butter. If possible, chill for 1 hour.

3. If the batter was chilled, heat the oven to 410°F (210°C) convection. Pipe or spoon the batter into the madeleine pans, filling three-quarters full. Place in the oven and reduce the temperature to 350°F (180°C) convection. Bake for 10 to 12 minutes, until well risen and golden. Let cool slightly in the pans, then turn them out carefully onto a rack.

Note: This recipe works very well even if you don't have time to chill the batter.

ALMOND–RASPBERRY CAKE

Serves 8

Cake

2 tablespoons plus 2 teaspoons (1 ½ oz. / 40 g) unsalted butter,
melted, plus more for brushing

½ cup minus 1 tablespoon (1¾ oz. / 50 g) all-purpose flour,
plus more for the pan

1½ teaspoons (5 g) potato starch

9 oz. (250 g) 50% almond paste, well softened

5 eggs

2 tablespoons raspberry liqueur

Pink glaze

1⅓ cups (6½ oz. / 180 g) confectioners' sugar, sifted

¾ oz. (20 g) raspberry purée

1 to 2 tablespoons raspberry liqueur

A little water

A few drops pink food coloring

Equipment

9-inch (22 cm) Bundt pan

CAKE

1. Brush the Bundt pan with butter and dust with flour. Sift the potato starch with the flour. Knead the almond paste to soften it further and place in the bowl of a stand mixer fitted with the paddle. Gradually beat in the eggs. Beat for 20 minutes, until pale and thick.

2. Preheat the oven to 340°F (170°C) convection. Using a wooden spoon or spatula, fold the dry ingredients into the almond mixture, then stir in the butter. Spread the batter in the pan and bake for 25 to 30 minutes, until a tester inserted into the center comes out clean. Immediately drizzle with the raspberry liqueur and let cool in the pan. Carefully turn out the cake onto a rack.

PINK GLAZE

3. In a medium bowl, whisk the confectioners' sugar with the raspberry purée, raspberry liqueur, water, and coloring. Brush the cooled cake with the glaze.

Note: If you prefer, you can color Fondant Icing (p. 17) and glaze the cake with that instead.

Friday

A day for fun, frivolity, and financiers, whose special taste comes from its distinctive ingredient, browned butter (beurre noisette). These little cakes (pgs. 200, 204) took off in the 19th century when a baker began making them for their financier clients, shaping them like gold bars.

Prep:
1 hour 30 minutes

Cook:
25 to 30 minutes

ALMOND MOUSSE LAYER CAKE
WITH RASPBERRIES

Serves 8

Breton Cake (p. 295)

8 oz. (250 g) raspberries, divided

1 tablespoon plus 1 teaspoon (20 ml) raspberry eau-de-vie

Almond mousse

3 sheets (6 g) 200 bloom gelatin

½ cup minus 1 tablespoon (100 ml) whole milk

¼ vanilla bean, split lengthwise and seeds scraped

1⅓ cups (315 ml) heavy cream, divided

2 egg yolks

1 tablespoon plus 2 teaspoons (20 g) granulated sugar

A few drops bitter almond extract

Assembly

Barely Sweet Raspberry Jam (p. 17), warmed, for brushing

A few drops pure vanilla extract

A little vanilla bean powder

Equipment

A 10-inch (24-cm) cake ring, 1¼ cm (3 cm) deep, or springform pan

A pastry bag fitted with a ⅓-inch (8-mm) plain tip, optional

BRETON CAKE

1. Follow steps 1 to 4 of Breton Cake (p. 295). Pipe or spoon the batter into the ring. Press some of the raspberries into the batter. Bake for 25 to 30 minutes, until lightly browned and crisp on the outside. Drizzle the top with the eau-de-vie.

ALMOND MOUSSE

2. In a medium bowl of very cold water, soften the gelatin.

3. In a medium saucepan, heat the milk with the vanilla bean and seeds and 1 tablespoon (15 ml) of the cream over medium-high heat until bubbles appear around the edge; remove from the heat. In a medium bowl, whisk the egg yolks with the sugar until pale and thick.

4. Whisk the yolk-sugar mixture into the hot milk mixture. Reduce the heat to low and cook, whisking constantly, until the mixture thickens; do not let boil. Remove from the heat. Remove the vanilla bean. Squeeze the gelatin dry and whisk in until completely dissolved.

5. Scrape the mousse into a separate bowl and let cool. Meanwhile, in a separate bowl, whip the remaining 1¼ cups (300 ml) cream until it holds a soft peak. Stir the bitter almond extract into the mousse and fold in the whipped cream. Chill until lightly set.

ASSEMBLY

6. Brush a thin layer of the raspberry jam on the Breton cake. Arrange the remaining raspberries on top, leaving a 1-inch (3-cm) border. Pipe or spoon the almond mousse on top. Freeze the cake for a few minutes, until the mousse sets, then pipe or spread the remaining mousse over the top, making dollops or wavy shapes.

7. Chill until set. Combine a little vanilla extract with the vanilla bean powder and drizzle a line across the top of the mousse.

Prep:
30 minutes

Rest and Chill:
12 hours + 2 hours

Cook:
25 to 30 minutes

CINNAMON–NUT BRIOCHE
Ropfküche

Serves 10

Brioche dough

⅓ oz. (10 g) fresh yeast

½ cup minus 1 tablespoon
(100 ml) whole milk, divided

2 cups (9 oz. / 250 g)
all-purpose flour

1 medium egg

3 tablespoons (1¼ oz. / 35 g)
granulated sugar

1 teaspoon (5 g) fine salt

6 tablespoons (3 oz. / 90 g)
unsalted butter, diced, room
temperature

Nut cream

½ cup minus 1 tablespoon
(100 ml) crème fraîche

⅓ cup (2½ oz. / 75 g)
granulated sugar

1 heaping tablespoon
(1 oz. / 25 g) honey

¼ cup (1¼ oz. / 35 g) hazelnuts

¼ cup (1¼ oz. / 35 g)
natural almonds

Generous ¼ cup (1¼ oz. / 35 g)
walnuts

¾ teaspoon (2 g) cinnamon

Equipment

A 10-inch (26-cm)
cake ring or pan

BRIOCHE DOUGH

1. In a small bowl, dissolve the yeast in a little of the milk. In the bowl of a stand mixer fitted with the paddle, combine the yeast mixture with the flour, egg, remaining milk, sugar, and salt. Knead at low speed until smooth, then increase the speed and knead until the dough pulls away from the sides of the bowl. Gradually knead in the butter. Knead for 10 minutes, until the dough pulls away easily from the side of the bowl.

2. Cover the bowl with a cloth and chill for at least 2 hours or, even better, 12 hours.

NUT CREAM

3. In a medium bowl, combine the crème fraîche with the sugar, honey, hazelnuts, almonds, walnuts, and cinnamon.

4. If using a cake ring, line a baking sheet with parchment paper and place the ring in the center. Pat 1 lb. 2 oz. (500 g) of the dough in the cake ring. Spread a ¼-inch (5 to 6-mm) layer of nut cream on top. Let rise for 2 hours.

5. Preheat the oven to 400°F (200°C) convection. Place the brioche in the oven and immediately reduce the oven temperature to 350°F (180°C) convection. Bake for 25 to 30 minutes, until well risen and lightly browned. Let cool slightly in the ring, then transfer to a rack and let cool completely.

Prep:
15 minutes

Cook:
10 to 15 minutes

Chill:
12 hours

GRAPEFRUIT AMARETTI

Prep:
10 minutes

Cook:
about 5 minutes per batch

Rest:
40 to 60 minutes

Makes about 30 amaretti

1 cup plus scant ½ cup (4¾ oz. / 135 g) almond flour

1 cup plus 3 tablespoons (8 oz. / 225 g)
granulated sugar, divided

1¾ oz. (50 g) candied grapefruit peel, finely chopped

4 egg whites

Confectioners' sugar for dusting

Equipment

A pastry bag fitted with a ⅓-inch (8-mm)
plain tip, optional

BLINIS

Serves 8 to 10

2 cups (9 oz. / 250 g) all-purpose flour

3 eggs, separated

1 tablespoon (15 ml) neutral oil

1 cup (250 ml) whole milk

½ oz. (15 g) fresh yeast

1 teaspoon (5 g) fine salt

4 tablespoons (2 oz. / 60 g) unsalted butter,
melted and cooled

1 heaping tablespoon (15 g) granulated sugar

Equipment

Cast-iron blini or pancake molds, or a small skillet

1. In a food processor, finely grind the almond flour with 1 cup minus 2 tablespoons (6 oz. / 175 g) of the granulated sugar, the grapefruit peel, and 2 of the egg whites until a paste forms. Transfer to a medium bowl.

2. In a separate medium bowl, whisk the remaining 2 egg whites, gradually adding the remaining ¼ cup (1¾ oz. / 50 g) granulated sugar, until they hold a firm peak.

3. Fold the meringue into the grapefruit peel paste. Line a baking sheet with parchment paper. Pipe or spoon small balls of the batter on the baking sheet. Dust with confectioners' sugar. Let dry out, uncovered, for 12 hours.

4. Preheat the oven to 340°F (170°C) convection. Pinch the tops of the amaretti to create cracks in the tops. Bake for 10 to 15 minutes, watching them carefully, until lightly colored. Drizzle a little water beneath the parchment paper to make it easier to peel off the amaretti when they cool.

5. Let rest for 15 minutes. While still warm and sticky, peel off like-size pairs and sandwich them, flat ends together. Let dry out for at least 1 hour.

Note: The amaretti can be wrapped and stored in an airtight container in a dry place.

1. Sift the flour. In a medium bowl, combine the egg yolks with the oil. Pour in the milk and crumble in the yeast. Stir until smooth.

2. Stir in the salt and the melted butter, then fold in the flour.

3. Let rise at room temperature for 40 to 60 minutes. In a medium bowl, whisk the egg whites with the sugar until they hold a soft peak and carefully fold into the batter.

4. Working in batches, spoon the batter into the molds and cook over low heat, until lightly browned on the bottom, then turn to brown the other side.

Note: The blinis are delicious with berries and maple syrup. They're also terrific with savory toppings like smoked salmon or ham.

BLINIS

ALMOND PETITS FOURS

Prep:
20 minutes

Cook:
25 to 30 minutes

CHESTNUT MADELEINES

⚬⚬⚬⚬⚬⚬⚬⚬⚬⚬⚬⚬⚬⚬⚬⚬⚬⚬⚬⚬⚬⚬⚬⚬⚬⚬⚬⚬⚬⚬

Makes 20 madeleines

1¾ sticks (7 oz. / 200 g) unsalted butter,
plus more for brushing

1⅔ cups (7 oz. / 200 g) all-purpose flour,
plus more for dusting

2¾ teaspoons (10 g) baking powder

3 eggs

⅔ cup (4½ oz. / 130 g) granulated sugar

3 tablespoons (2 oz. / 60 g) pine honey
or other flavorful honey

¼ cup (60 ml) whole milk

1 teaspoon pure vanilla extract

9 oz. (260 g) chestnut spread (*crème de marrons*),
warmed slightly until runny, plus more for decorating

Equipment
20 nonstick madeleine pans or financier pans
(as shown in the photo)

A pastry bag, optional

1. Preheat the oven to 410°F (210°C) convection.
Brush the madeleine pans with butter and dust
with flour. In a small saucepan, melt the butter
over medium heat, then cook until it begins to
brown and smells a little like hazelnuts. Strain the
brown butter through a fine sieve. You'll need to
use it while it's still warm.

2. Sift the flour with the baking powder. In a large
bowl, whisk the eggs with the sugar, honey, milk,
and vanilla. Fold in the dry ingredients, then the
brown butter and chestnut spread.

3. Pipe or spoon the batter into the madeleine
pans, filling three-quarters full.

4. Bake for 25 to 30 minutes. Let cool slightly
in the pans, then carefully turn out onto a rack.
Decorate with a swoosh of chestnut spread.

Prep:
30 minutes

Cook:
4 to 5 minutes

Rest:
12 hours

ALMOND PETITS FOURS

⚬⚬⚬⚬⚬⚬⚬⚬⚬⚬⚬⚬⚬⚬⚬⚬⚬⚬⚬⚬⚬⚬⚬⚬⚬⚬⚬⚬⚬⚬

Makes about 40 petits fours

1 lb. 2 oz. (500 g) 50% almond paste,
well softened (see Note)

½ egg white

2 tablespoons plus 1 teaspoon (1¾ oz. / 50 g) glucose

3 tablespoons (1¾ oz. / 50 g) apricot purée

3½ oz. (100 g) candied cherries, halved

Equipment
A pastry bag fitted with a thinly fluted
3/8-inch (1-cm) tip, optional

1. In the bowl of a stand mixer fitted with the
paddle, beat the almond paste with the egg white.
In a small saucepan, combine the glucose and
apricot purée and heat to 113°F (45°C), then stir
into the almond paste mixture.

2. Line 2 baking sheets with parchment paper.
Pipe or spoon rosettes of the batter on the baking
sheets and decorate with a cherry half.

3. Let the petits fours dry out, uncovered, for
a few hours or up to 12 hours. They're ready for
baking when the crust feels a little dry.

4. Preheat the oven to 450°F (230°C)
convection. Bake for 4 to 5 minutes, rotating the
pans halfway through and watching petits fours
carefully so they don't darken. Let cool slightly on
the baking sheet, then transfer to a rack and let
cool completely.

Notes: The percentage of almonds in the almond
paste is important so you get the right texture
and balance of almond flavor and sweetness.

These petits fours can be stored in an airtight
container or ziplock bag.

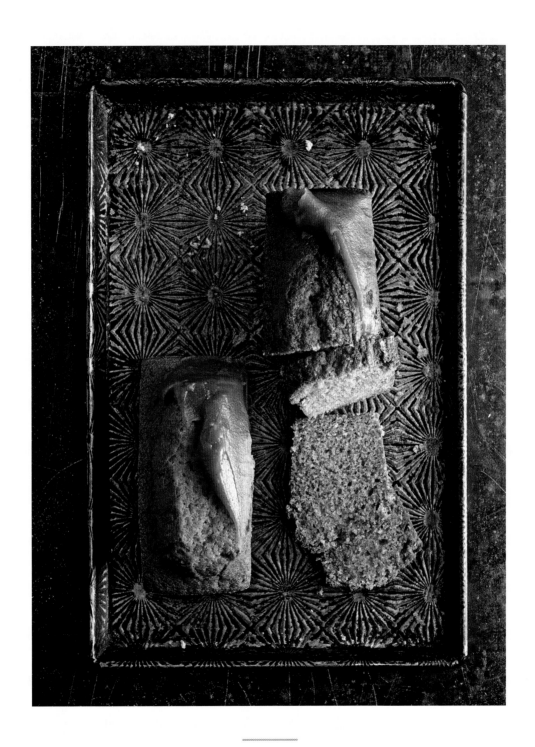

CHESTNUT MADELEINES

UPSIDE–DOWN CHERRY CAKE

Serves 8

Cherry topping

8 oz. (250 g) frozen thawed sour cherries

2 tablespoons (1 oz. / 25 g) granulated sugar

Cake

1 stick (4 oz. / 120 g) unsalted butter, softened,
plus more for brushing

½ cup (3½ oz. / 100 g) granulated sugar,
plus more for sprinkling

1 cup plus 2 tablespoons (5 oz. / 150 g) all-purpose flour

2 teaspoons (8 g) baking powder

2 eggs

Equipment

An 8-inch (20-cm) cake pan

CHERRY TOPPING

1. Preheat the oven to 350°F (180°C) convection. In a shallow baking dish, toss the sour cherries with the sugar. Place in the oven for 15 to 20 minutes, until juicy. Leave the oven on.

2. Let the cherries cool. Transfer to a colander set over a bowl and drain for a few minutes. Reserve the juice.

CAKE

3. Brush the cake pan with butter and sprinkle with sugar. Sift the flour with the baking powder.

4. In a medium bowl, cream the butter with the sugar. Gradually beat in the eggs, then fold in the dry ingredients. Stir in 3 tablespoons of the reserved cherry juice.

5. Spread the cherries in the cake pan and pour in the batter. Bake for 20 to 25 minutes, until golden. Let cool in the pan, then invert onto a serving platter.

Note: If you like, dust the cake with confectioners' sugar before serving.

GLUTEN–FREE APRICOT CAKE

Serves 8

Streusel topping

¼ cup (1½ oz. / 40 g) rice flour

3½ tablespoons (1½ oz. / 40 g) granulated sugar

Scant ½ cup (1½ oz. / 40 g) ground almonds

2 tablespoons plus 2 teaspoons (1½ oz. / 40 g) unsalted butter, diced

Sautéed apricots

7 oz. (200 g) apricots

2½ teaspoons (10 g) granulated sugar

1 tablespoon plus 1 teaspoon (20 g) unsalted butter

Cake

1 stick plus 2 tablespoons (5 oz. / 140 g) unsalted butter, plus more for brushing

Generous ½ cup (3 oz. / 90 g) rice flour, plus more for dusting

Scant ⅔ cup (2 oz. / 60 g) almond flour

½ cup plus 3 tablespoons (4¾ oz. / 135 g) granulated sugar, divided

4 eggs, separated

Decoration

Confectioners' sugar for dusting

Apricots, quartered

Equipment

A 2 by 9-inch (5 by 22-cm) pan

STREUSEL TOPPING

1. In a medium bowl, whisk the rice flour with the granulated sugar and ground almonds. Squeeze in the butter until the dough forms large crumbs. Chill until needed.

SAUTÉED APRICOTS

2. Quarter and pit the apricots. In a medium skillet, cook with the sugar and butter, stirring occasionally, until softened.

CAKE

3. Preheat the oven to 350°F (180°C) convection. Brush the loaf pan generously with butter and dust with rice flour.

4. In a small saucepan, melt the butter and let cool slightly—it needs to be barely warm when incorporated. In a medium bowl, whisk the rice flour with the almond flour and 3½ tablespoons (1½ oz. / 40 g) of the sugar.

5. In a large bowl, whisk the egg whites until they hold a soft peak. Gradually whisk in the remaining scant ½ cup (3½ oz. / 95 g) sugar until the egg whites are firm and glossy. Stir the egg yolks into the meringue, then the dry ingredients. Stir in the melted butter.

6. Spread a layer of batter in the pan ¾ inch (2 cm) deep. Arrange the sautéed apricots down the center of the pan. Spread the remaining batter in the pan and sprinkle with the streusel topping. Bake for about 30 minutes, until a tester inserted into the center comes out clean. Let the loaf cool slightly in the pan, then transfer to a rack and let cool completely. Dust with confectioners' sugar and decorate with the quartered apricots.

MAGGIE'S APPLE CHEESECAKE

Serves 10

5 Granny Smith apples

1 heaping cup (6 oz. / 170 g) brown sugar, divided

5 tablespoons (2½ oz. / 75 g) unsalted butter, divided, plus more for brushing

2½ teaspoons (13 ml) pure vanilla extract, divided

7 oz. (200 g) gingersnaps, digestive biscuits, or speculaas

1 lb. 8 oz. (675 g) cream cheese

2½ eggs, lightly beaten

1¾ oz. (50 g) apple or apricot jelly, warmed, for brushing

Equipment

A 10-inch (24-cm) springform pan

1. Peel, core, and quarter the apples, then slice lengthwise just under ½ inch (1 cm) thick. In a large bowl, toss with ⅓ cup (1¾ oz. / 50 g) of the brown sugar.

2. In a large saucepan, melt 1 tablespoon (15 g) of the butter over medium heat and stir in 1 teaspoon (5 ml) of the vanilla. Add the apples and cook over medium heat, stirring often, until light golden and tender. Remove from the heat and let cool.

3. Preheat the oven to 345°F (175°C) convection. Line the base of the springform pan with parchment paper and brush the base and side with butter.

4. In a small saucepan, melt the remaining 4 tablespoons (4 oz. / 60 g) butter. In a medium bowl, finely crush the digestive biscuits and toss with the melted butter. Spread two-thirds of this mixture evenly in the base of the pan, packing it down. Carefully pat the rim of the pan with the remaining third of the biscuit mixture. This can be a tricky operation, so work slowly. You don't need a thick rim of crumbs; just the right amount will naturally stick to the buttered rim.

5. Bake the tart shell for 10 to 15 minutes, until light golden. Let cool completely in the pan.

6. In the bowl of a stand mixer fitted with the paddle, beat the cream cheese with the remaining 1 cup minus 3 tablespoons (4¼ oz. / 120 g) brown sugar and 1½ teaspoons (8 ml) vanilla at medium speed until smooth. Add the eggs in several additions, incorporating each thoroughly.

7. Spread the cream cheese mixture in the tart shell. Arrange the apples in concentric circles on top. Bake for 1 hour.

8. Let the cake cool to room temperature in the pan set on a rack, then chill for a few hours. Run a knife around the inside of the pan and remove the side. Brush the top with jelly.

Note: All the ingredients should be at room temperature before starting the recipe.

GLUTEN–FREE FINANCIERS

Serves 6 to 8

1 stick plus 2 tablespoons (5¼ oz. / 150 g) unsalted butter,
plus more for brushing

⅓ cup (1¾ oz. / 50 g) rice flour or cornstarch, plus more for dusting

¾ cup (2½ oz. / 70 g) almond flour

Generous ⅓ cup (1 oz. / 30 g) ground hazelnuts

1⅓ cups (6 oz. / 170 g) confectioners' sugar

5 egg whites

1 tablespoon (20 g) apricot purée

Equipment

7 by 9-inch (18 by 23-cm)

A pastry bag fitted with a plain ⅓-inch (8 mm) tip, optional

1. Preheat the oven to 340°F (170°C) convection. Brush the cake pan with butter and dust with rice flour.

2. In a small saucepan, melt the butter over medium heat, then cook until it begins to brown and smells a little like hazelnuts. Strain the brown butter through a fine sieve. You'll need to use it while it's still warm.

3. Sift the almond flour with the ground hazelnuts, confectioners' sugar, and rice flour into a medium bowl.

4. Stir in the egg whites. Whisk in the brown butter and apricot purée.

5. Spread the batter in the cake pan, filling three-quarters full. Bake for 30 to 40 minutes, until a tester inserted into the center comes out clean. Immediately turn out the financier onto a rack and let cool to room temperature. Cut into triangles, rectangles, or squares.

Note: For a crisp crust, use a metal pan. You get better results with metal than silicone, which is why most professional pastry chefs use metal pans to make this type of cake.

Prep:
1 hour

Cook:
20 to 25 minutes

Chill:
1 hour

PINEAPPLE–ALMOND MERINGUE LAYER CAKE
Succès à l'Ananas

Serves 8

Almond meringue

¾ cup (2½ oz. / 70 g) almond flour

Scant ⅔ cup (3 oz. / 90 g) confectioners' sugar

¼ cup (1¼ oz. / 35 g) all-purpose flour

4 egg whites

Scant ½ cup (3 oz. / 95 g) granulated sugar

Pineapple cream

5¼ oz. (150 g) pineapple purée

⅔ cup (150 ml) whole milk

3½ egg yolks

½ cup minus 1 tablespoon (2¾ oz. / 80 g) granulated sugar

2½ tablespoons (1 oz. / 25 g) cornstarch

1 stick plus 2 tablespoons (5¼ oz. / 150 g) unsalted butter, softened, divided

⅔ cup (155 ml) heavy cream

Sautéed pineapple

7 oz. (200 g) diced pineapple

5¼ oz. (150 g) sliced pineapple

1 drop dark rum

Juice of ½ lime

Assembly

Unsweetened shredded coconut, toasted at 320°F (160°C) convection for 20 minutes

Confectioners' sugar for dusting

Equipment

A pastry bag fitted with a plain ⅓ or ⅜-inch (8 or 10-mm) tip, optional

A 9-inch (22-cm) cake ring, 1½ inches (4 cm) deep

ALMOND MERINGUE

1. Preheat the oven to 375°F (190°C) convection. Line a baking sheet with parchment paper. Draw two 9-inch (22-cm) circles on the paper and turn it over. Sift the almond flour with the confectioners' sugar and all-purpose flour. In a medium bowl, whisk the egg whites with the granulated sugar until they hold a soft peak. Carefully fold in the dry ingredients.

2. Using the circles as a guide, pipe or spread almond meringue disks on the baking sheet. Bake for 20 to 25 minutes, until a thin crust forms and the disks are springy to the touch.

PINEAPPLE CREAM

3. In a medium saucepan, heat the pineapple purée with the milk over medium-high heat until bubbles appear around the edge; remove from the heat. In a medium bowl, whisk the egg yolks with the sugar and cornstarch. Gradually whisk in the hot pineapple-milk mixture.

4. Return the egg-pineapple mixture to the pan and cook over medium heat, whisking constantly, until thickened. Remove from the heat, stir in 3 tablespoons plus 1 teaspoon (1¾ oz. /50 g) of the butter, and let cool.

5. In a medium bowl, whip the remaining 7 tablespoons (3½ oz. / 100 g) butter until very light and gradually fold into the pastry cream. In a separate bowl, whip the cream until it holds a soft peak and fold into the pastry cream.

SAUTÉED PINEAPPLE

6. In a large skillet, combine the diced and sliced pineapple with the rum and lime juice and cook, stirring, for 2 to 3 minutes, then chill.

ASSEMBLY

7. Line a baking sheet with parchment paper and place the cake ring in the center. Place one of the meringue disks in the cake ring. Spread with some of the pineapple cream and arrange the pineapple cubes on top. Spread with the remaining pineapple cream and cover with the second meringue disk. Chill for 1 hour.

8. At least 30 minutes before serving, remove the cake from the refrigerator. Decorate the top with the pineapple slices. Pat the shredded coconut around the side of the cake. Dust the rim with confectioners' sugar.

ALMOND FINANCIERS

Makes 20 financiers

1¼ sticks (5¼ oz. / 150 g) unsalted butter, plus more for brushing

½ cup (2 oz. / 55 g) all-purpose flour, plus more for dusting

¾ cup (2½ oz. / 70 g) almond flour

Generous ⅓ cup (1 oz. / 30 g) ground hazelnuts

1 pinch vanilla bean powder

1⅓ cups (6 oz. / 170 g) confectioners' sugar

5 egg whites

1 tablespoon (20 g) apricot purée

Sliced almonds for decorating

Equipment

20 metal financier pans, nonstick if you like, or mini muffin pans

A pastry bag, optional

1. Preheat the oven to 350°F (180°C) convection. Brush the financier pans with butter and dust with all-purpose flour. In a small saucepan, melt the butter over medium heat, then cook until it begins to brown and smells a little like hazelnuts. Strain the brown butter through a fine sieve. You'll need to use it while it's still warm.

2. Sift the almond flour with the ground hazelnuts, vanilla bean powder, confectioners' sugar, and all-purpose flour into a large bowl.

3. Whisk the egg whites into the dry ingredients, then whisk in the brown butter and apricot purée.

4. Pipe or spoon the batter into the pans, filling three-quarters full. Decorate with sliced almonds and bake for at least 12 minutes.

5. Immediately turn the financiers out of the pans and serve warm or at room temperature.

Notes: For a crisp crust, use metal pans. You get better results with metal than silicone, which is why most professional pastry chefs use metal pans to make this type of cake.

I used to make this recipe when I was pastry chef at the Hôtel de Crillon.

PRALINE–CHOCOLATE TART

Serves 8

10½ oz. (300 g) Breton Hazelnut Pastry (p. 13),
room temperature

7 oz. (200 g) 66% dark chocolate

1 cup (250 ml) heavy cream

5½ oz. (160 g) Pure Hazelnut Praline Paste (p. 16), warmed

2 tablespoons plus 2 teaspoons (1 ½ oz. / 40 g)
unsalted butter, softened

Scant ¼ cup (2 oz. / 50 g) caramelized hazelnuts
(see Sweet and Salty Caramelized Peanuts, p. 9)

Equipment

A fluted 9-inch (22-cm) tart pan,
preferably with a removable bottom

1. Preheat the oven to 340°F (170°C) convection. On a lightly floured work surface, roll out the pastry ⅛ inch (4 mm) thick. Line the tart pan with the pastry. Bake for about 30 minutes, until golden. Let cool.

2. In a food processor or using a knife, finely chop the chocolate. In a medium saucepan, heat the cream over medium-high heat until bubbles appear around the edge. Stir in the chocolate in 2 additions until smooth. Stir in 2 oz. (60 g) of the hazelnut paste and the butter.

3. Spread the remaining 3½ oz. (100 g) praline paste on the hazelnut pastry in a thin layer. Spread the ganache on top and let set at room temperature. If you're making this tart in summer, chill it briefly, until set.

4. Decorate with the caramelized hazelnuts. Serve at room temperature.

Prep:
30 minutes

Chill:
30 minutes

CHOCOLATE MOUSSE IN COCONUT SHELLS

Serves 6

5¼ oz. (150 g) dark chocolate, chopped
1 tablespoon plus 2 teaspoons (1 oz. / 25 g) unsalted butter
4 eggs, separated
½ egg white
Scant ½ cup (3 oz. / 85 g) granulated sugar
3 small coconuts
Chocolate shavings, made by scraping a chocolate slab
with a serrated knife, for decorating

Equipment
A pastry bag, optional

1. In a medium bowl set over a saucepan of simmering water, melt the chocolate with the butter, stirring until smooth. Heat to 105°F (40°C).

2. In a separate bowl, whisk the 4½ egg whites with the sugar until they hold a firm peak.

3. In a small bowl, lightly beat 3½ of the egg yolks. Using a silicone spatula, fold into the meringue, then fold in the chocolate-butter mixture.

4. Using a sturdy knife, pierce the three "eyes" at the stem of each coconut. Invert the coconuts and pour the water into a small bowl; reserve the coconut water for another use. To split each coconut cleanly in half, hold it in one hand and take the knife in the other. Rap the blunt edge of the knife around the circumference of the coconut, continuing until it opens.

5. Place each coconut half cut side up in a bowl. If you like, you can smooth the top using a fine grater.

6. Pipe or spoon the chocolate mousse into the coconut halves and chill for at least 30 minutes. Before serving, decorate with the chocolate shavings.

Notes: There's an extra ½ egg yolk leftover after making the chocolate mousse. Cover and refrigerate it and add to an omelet or scrambled eggs, or beat it lightly and use it to brush the top of bread before baking. Please note that the eggs are not cooked in this recipe.

RASPBERRY BLACK FOREST CAKE

Serves 8 to 10

Chocolate sponge cake

Unsalted butter for brushing

1 cup plus 2 teaspoons
(4½ oz. / 130 g) all-purpose
flour, plus more for dusting

¼ cup (1 oz. / 30 g)
unsweetened cocoa powder

2 tablespoons (20 g) cornstarch

6 eggs

1 cup (2½ oz. / 70 g)
granulated sugar

Raspberry syrup

3 tablespoons plus 1 teaspoon
(50 ml) water

1 cup minus 2½ tablespoons
(6 oz. / 170 g) granulated sugar

5 oz. (150 g) raspberries

3 tablespoons plus 1 teaspoon
(50 ml) kirsch

Assembly

14 oz. (400 g) Set Vanilla Cream
(p. 16)

3½ oz. (100 g) Barely Sweet

Raspberry Jam (p. 17),
warmed, for brushing

14 oz. (400 g) raspberries

Unsweetened cocoa powder
for dusting

A few small tuile cookies or
other thin crisp cookies

Equipment

A 10-inch (24-cm) cake pan

A pastry bag fitted with a
⅓-inch (8-mm) plain or fluted
tip, optional

CHOCOLATE SPONGE CAKE

1. Preheat the oven to 400°F (200°C) convection. Brush the cake pan with butter and dust with flour. Sift the flour with the cocoa powder and cornstarch.

2. In a medium bowl, using an electric beater, lightly whisk the eggs with the sugar. Place the bowl over a saucepan of simmering water and whisk for 2 to 3 minutes. Remove the bowl from the heat and beat for 10 to 15 minutes, until airy and light.

3. Using a wooden spoon or silicone spatula, carefully fold in the dry ingredients. Spread the batter in the pan and bake for 10 minutes. Reduce the oven temperature to 350°F (180°C) convection and bake for 20 to 25 minutes, until a tester inserted into the center comes out clean. Let the cake cool slightly in the pan, then turn out onto a rack and let cool completely.

RASPBERRY SYRUP

4. In a small saucepan, bring the water to a boil with the sugar and raspberries, stirring, until the sugar dissolves and the raspberries soften. Strain through a fine sieve into a small bowl. Let cool and stir in the kirsch.

ASSEMBLY

5. Using a long serrated knife, cut the cake horizontally in half. Place the bottom cake half on a flat dish, cut side up. Brush with the syrup to moisten well. Brush the raspberry jam thinly on top. Pipe or spoon dollops of the vanilla cream over the entire surface. Press the raspberries into the cream, packing in as many as possible but reserving a few for decoration. Place the top cake half on a large flat paper plate, cut side up. Brush well with the syrup and invert onto the raspberries. Dust the top with the cocoa powder.

6. Cut the reserved raspberries in half crosswise. Using a spoon, drop a few small mounds of jam on the cake and glue in the raspberry halves. Dust the cookies with the cocoa powder and glue them on using a little raspberry jam.

Prep:
40 minutes

Cook:
35 to 40 minutes

Chill:
1 hour

CHOCOLATE CUBE CAKE WITH GANACHE

Serves 8

Chocolate cake

4 tablespoons (2 oz. / 60 g) unsalted butter, melted, plus more for brushing

1 cup plus 2 teaspoons (4½ oz. / 130 g) all-purpose flour, plus more for dusting

¼ cup (1 oz. / 30 g) unsweetened cocoa powder

1¼ teaspoons (5 g) baking powder

1½ oz. (40 g) dark chocolate

3 eggs

1⅔ cups (7½ oz. / 210 g) confectioners' sugar

Generous ⅓ cup (90 ml) heavy cream

¾ oz. (20 g) pailletés fin chocolate (at specialty stores or online) or dark chocolate chips

Ganache

¾ cup (200 ml) heavy cream

Finely grated zest of ¼ orange

2 star anise pods

1 oz. (25 g) milk chocolate

5½ oz. (160 g) 64% dark chocolate

¾ oz. (20 g) trimoline or granulated sugar

5 tablespoons (2½ oz. / 75 g) unsalted butter, diced, room temperature

Cocoa syrup

2 tablespoons plus 2 teaspoons (40 ml) water

3½ tablespoons (1 oz. / 25 g) unsweetened cocoa powder

2 tablespoons (1 oz. / 25 g) granulated sugar

1 tablespoon pure vanilla syrup

Assembly

Chocolate shavings, made by scraping a chocolate slab with a serrated knife, for sprinkling

Equipment

A cube-shaped mold

CHOCOLATE CAKE

1. Preheat the oven to 340°F (170°C) convection. Brush the mold with butter and dust with flour. Sift the flour with the cocoa powder and baking powder.

2. In a small bowl set over a saucepan of simmering water, melt the chocolate, stirring until smooth. Remove the bowl from the heat.

3. In a medium bowl, whisk the eggs with the confectioners' sugar and cream. Whisk in the dry ingredients. Stir in the melted chocolate, then the pailletés. Stir in the melted butter.

4. Spread the batter in the mold and bake for 35 to 40 minutes, until a tester inserted into the center comes out clean. Turn out onto a rack and let cool completely. Wash and dry the mold.

GANACHE

5. In a small saucepan, heat the cream with the orange zest and star anise until bubbles appear around the edge. Remove from the heat and let

infuse for a few minutes; remove the star anise. Place the two chocolates in a medium bowl and pour in the cream. Stir in the trimoline. Beat in the butter.

COCOA SYRUP

6. In a small saucepan, bring the water to a boil with the cocoa powder, granulated sugar, and vanilla syrup, stirring, until the sugar dissolves.

ASSEMBLY

7. Slice the cake. Place the first slice in the base of the mold. Brush lightly with the syrup and spread with ganache. Continue making layers of moistened chocolate cake and ganache, reserving enough ganache to cover all sides of the cake. Chill for 1 hour.

8. Turn the cake out of the mold and spread 5 sides with the remaining ganache. Sprinkle with the chocolate shavings.

Prep:
20 minutes

Chill:
2 hours

Cook:
12 minutes

LEMON–BASIL MADELEINES

Makes 20 madeleines

Madeleines

2 sticks plus 3 tablespoons
(9¾ oz. / 275 g) unsalted butter,
plus more for brushing

2¾ cups (9 oz. / 250 g) cake
flour, plus more for dusting

2¾ teaspoons (10 g) baking
powder

4 eggs

1 cup (7 oz. / 200 g)
granulated sugar

⅓ cup (80 ml) whole milk

½ teaspoon pure vanilla extract

Finely grated zest of ½ lemon

Finely grated zest of ½ lime

10 leaves basil, finely chopped

⅓ cup (3½ oz. / 100 g) smooth
apricot jam

Lemon-basil glaze

1⅓ cups (6½ oz. / 180 g)
confectioners' sugar

Finely grated zest and juice
of ½ lemon

Finely grated zest and juice
of ½ lime

2 basil leaves, finely chopped

Equipment

20 madeleine pans or mini
muffin cups

A pastry bag, optional

MADELEINES

1. Preheat the oven to 410°F (210°C) convection. Brush the madeleine pans with butter and dust with flour. In a small saucepan, melt the butter over medium heat and let cool to lukewarm.

2. Sift the flour with the baking powder. In a large bowl, whisk the eggs with the sugar, milk, vanilla, and lemon and lime zest. Fold in the dry ingredients, then the melted butter and chopped basil.

3. Pipe or spoon the batter into the madeleine pans, filling three-quarters full. Place in the oven and immediately reduce the temperature to 350°F (180°C) convection. Bake for 10 to 12 minutes, until well-risen and golden. Let cool slightly in the pans then turn out onto a rack and let cool completely. For the final step, the oven must be off but still warm.

4. Meanwhile, in a small saucepan, heat the apricot jam over low heat, stirring, until warm and spreadable.

LEMON–BASIL GLAZE

5. In a medium bowl, sift the confectioners' sugar and stir in the lemon and lime zest and juice and basil. The glaze should be creamy and not too runny, so adjust if needed by adding confectioners' sugar or lemon or lime juice.

6. Set a rack on a rimmed baking sheet. Brush the fluted side of the madeleines with the apricot jam. Dip the same side into the glaze and let the excess drip off for a few moments.

7. Return the madeleines to the pans and warm in the oven for about 30 seconds to dry the glaze. Serve at room temperature.

DUNDEE CAKE

~~~~~~

Serves 8 to 10

Cake

1 stick plus 2 teaspoons (4½ oz. / 125 g) unsalted butter,
room temperature, plus more for brushing

1¼ cups (5½ oz. / 160 g) all-purpose flour

½ teaspoon (2 g) baking powder

⅔ cup (4½ oz. / 125 g) granulated sugar

3 eggs

2½ tablespoons (15 g) almond flour

1⅓ cups (7 oz. / 200 g) raisins

1¼ oz. (40 g) candied orange peel, diced

1 teaspoon (5 ml) dark rum

1 teaspoon (5 ml) caramel sauce

1 heaping cup (5¼ oz. / 150 g) natural almonds, halved lengthwise

Finish

3 tablespoons plus 1 teaspoon (50 ml) hot water

¼ cup (1¾ oz. / 50 g) granulated sugar

Finely grated zest of ½ lemon

Seeds of ½ vanilla bean

Confectioners' sugar for dusting

Equipment

An 8- to 9-inch (20- to 22-cm) cake ring or springform pan

CAKE

1. Preheat the oven to 340°F (170°C) convection. If using a cake ring, line a baking sheet with parchment paper and place the ring in the center. Brush the cake ring with butter and line with parchment paper. Sift the flour with the baking powder.

2. In a large bowl, whisk the butter until soft, then whisk in the sugar. Gradually whisk in the eggs until creamy.

3. Fold in the dry ingredients; do not overmix. Fold in the almond flour, raisins, candied orange peel, rum, and caramel.

4. Spread the batter in the cake ring and decorate the top with concentric circles of the almond halves. Bake for 40 minutes.

FINISH

5. Meanwhile, in a small saucepan, bring the water to a boil with the granulated sugar, lemon zest, and vanilla seeds, stirring, until the sugar dissolves.

6. When the cake comes out of the oven, pour over the syrup. Let cool completely. Dust with confectioners' sugar.

ALMOND MERINGUE CAKE
WITH BERRIES
Dacquoise aux Framboises et Fraises

Serves 8

1 teaspoon green aniseed

10 oz. (300 g) Light Pistachio Pastry Cream (p. 15)

Almond Meringue Base (p. 10)

14 oz. (400 g) strawberries

7 oz. (200 g) raspberries

Basil or mint leaves

⅓ cup (1¾ oz. / 50 g) whole peeled pistachios

1. Crush the aniseeds and beat into the pastry cream.

2. Spread the pastry cream over the almond meringue and arrange the berries on top. Decorate with the basil leaves and sprinkle with the pistachios.

COCONUT MERINGUE CAKE
WITH PINEAPPLE
Dacquoise à l'Ananas

Serves 8

10 oz. (300 g) Light Coconut Pastry Cream (p. 15)

Almond Meringue Base (p. 10)

Finely grated zest and juice of 1 lime

14 oz. (400 g) sliced pineapple

Fruity Glaze (p. 18)

1. Spread the pastry cream over the almond meringue. Sprinkle with some of the lime zest.

2. Arrange the pineapple slices on top and drizzle with the lime juice. Brush with the glaze and sprinkle with the remaining lime zest.

FLORENTINE SHORTBREAD COOKIES

Makes about 30 cookies

10½ oz. (300 g) Sweet Almond Pastry (p. 10), room temperature

1¾ oz. (50 g) apricot jam, warmed, for brushing

6 tablespoons (3 oz. / 90 g) unsalted butter

⅔ cup (4½ oz. / 125 g) granulated sugar

1 tablespoon plus 2 teaspoons (25 ml) crème fraîche

2 oz. (55 g) candied orange and lemon peel, cut in ¼-inch (5-mm) cubes

Finely grated zest of 1 orange

1¼ cups (4½ oz. / 125 g) sliced almonds

Equipment

An 8 by 12-inch (20 by 30-cm) confectionery frame or brownie pan

1. Preheat the oven to 350°F (180°C) convection. Position the baking rack in the upper third of the oven. If using a confectionery frame, line a baking sheet with parchment paper and place the frame in the center. Or line a brownie pan with parchment paper. On a lightly floured work surface, roll out the pastry ⅛ inch (3 mm) thick. Line the frame with the pastry. Bake for about 15 minutes, until golden. Let cool in the pan and brush with the apricot jam. Leave the oven on.

2. In a medium saucepan, bring the butter to a boil over medium heat with the sugar, crème fraiche, candied peel, and orange zest. Immediately remove from the heat and stir in the sliced almonds, taking care not to break them.

3. Spread the citrus mixture over the pastry and bake for 15 to 20 minutes, until the topping is lightly golden and beginning to bubble.

4. Let cool in the pan and cut into 1¼-inch (4 cm) squares or whatever size you like.

Note: This is absolutely delicious, and it's very easy to make!

APRICOT-PRALINE BROWNIES

Makes 25 2-inch (5-cm) brownies

Hazelnut praline cream

1 cup (250 ml) heavy cream, well chilled

2¾ oz. (80 g) 60% hazelnut praline, well softened but not warmed

Sautéed apricots

5 apricots

2½ tablespoons (1 oz. / 30 g) vanilla sugar

1 tablespoon plus 1 teaspoon (20 g) unsalted butter

Finely grated zest and juice of 1 lime, plus more zest for decorating

Brownies

1 stick plus 4 tablespoons (6 oz. / 170 g) unsalted butter, plus more for brushing

⅓ cup (1½ oz. / 40 g) all-purpose flour, plus more for dusting

1½ tablespoons (10 g) unsweetened cocoa powder

3 oz. (90 g) 60-70% dark chocolate

3 eggs, separated

½ cup plus 2 tablespoons (4 oz. / 115 g) light brown sugar

½ cup plus 2 tablespoons (4 oz. / 115 g) granulated sugar

⅔ cup (2½ oz. / 75 g) chopped walnuts

⅓ cup (1¾ oz. / 50 g) toasted hazelnuts plus ¼ cup (1 oz. / 30 g) toasted hazelnuts, halved

Equipment

A 10-inch (25-cm) square pan

HAZELNUT PRALINE CREAM

1. In a well-chilled bowl, whisk the cream until it holds a soft peak. Using a silicone spatula, fold in the praline. Chill.

SAUTÉED APRICOTS

2. Cut each apricot into 8 pieces. In a medium skillet, melt the sugar, stirring, over medium-high heat. Add the apricots and cook for a few minutes, then stir in the butter. Remove from the heat, stir in the lime zest, and drizzle with the lime juice. Let cool.

BROWNIES

3. Preheat the oven to 340°F (170°C) convection. Brush the pan with butter and dust with flour. Sift the flour with the cocoa powder.

4. In a medium bowl, whisk the egg whites until they hold a very soft peak. In a medium bowl set over a saucepan of simmering water, melt the chocolate, stirring occasionally, until smooth, then add the butter. Stir until smooth and lukewarm. Whisk in the egg yolks, brown sugar, and granulated sugar.

5. Fold the dry ingredients, walnuts, and the ⅓ cup (1¾ oz. / 50 g) of hazelnuts into the chocolate mixture, then fold in the egg whites.

6. Spread the batter in the pan. Bake for 25 minutes, until a cake tester inserted into the center comes out dry. Let cool in the pan.

Decorate the brownies with the hazelnut praline cream, sautéed apricots, halved hazelnuts, and a little lime zest.

Saturday

Anything goes! Why not start
the weekend by adding some
luscious Chantilly Cream
(p. 262) to your fruits,
cakes, or ice cream?

Prep:

1 hour

Chill:

2 hours

Cook:

10 to 15 minutes

VANILLA–CHOCOLATE CHARLOTTE

Serves 12

Vanilla Bavarian cream

2½ sheets (5 g) 200 bloom gelatin

¾ cup (200 ml) heavy cream, well chilled

1 vanilla bean

1 cup (250 ml) whole milk

3 egg yolks

Scant ⅓ cup (2 oz. / 60 g) granulated sugar

Chocolate mousse

1 cup (250 ml) heavy cream, well chilled

5¾ oz. (160 g) 70% dark chocolate, such as Valrhona® Guanaja

3 tablespoons (40 ml) water

⅔ cup (5 oz. / 150 g) granulated sugar, divided

1 teaspoon pure vanilla extract

1 whole egg

3 egg yolks

Moistening syrup

⅓ cup (75 ml) water

⅓ cup (2½ oz. / 75 g) sugar

1 teaspoon pure vanilla extract

Assembly

1 recipe Chocolate Ladyfinger Sponge Cake (p. 11),
biscuits plus two 9-inch (20-cm) disks

3½ oz. (100 g) chocolate of your choice

Equipment

A 10-inch (24-cm) dessert ring

A 2-inch (5-cm) or smaller plastic cookie cutter

VANILLA–CHOCOLATE CHARLOTTE

VANILLA–CHOCOLATE MOUSSE

1. An hour ahead, place 2 large bowls, preferably metal, in the freezer. You'll need them to whip the cream for the Bavarian cream and the mousse.

VANILLA BAVARIAN CREAM

2. In a medium bowl of very cold water, soften the gelatin.

3. In one of the chilled bowls, whip the cream until it holds a firm peak. Chill.

4. Split the vanilla bean lengthwise and scrape out the seeds. In a medium saucepan, heat the milk with the vanilla bean and seeds over medium-high heat until bubbles appear around the edge; remove from the heat. Remove the vanilla bean.

5. Have ready a large bowl of cold water. In a medium bowl, whisk the egg yolks with the sugar until blended. Drizzle in the hot milk, whisking constantly. Return the mixture to the saucepan and whisk constantly over low heat until the temperature reaches 175°F (80°C). Immediately dip the base of the pan in the cold water to stop the cooking.

6. Squeeze the gelatin dry and whisk it into the custard. Scrape the Bavarian cream into a large bowl and let cool completely, but don't let it set. Fold in the whipped cream and let stand at room temperature.

CHOCOLATE MOUSSE

7. In the second chilled bowl, whisk the cream until it holds a firm peak. Chill.

8. In a medium bowl set over a saucepan of simmering water, melt the chocolate, stirring occasionally, until smooth and the temperature reaches 115°F (45°C).

9. In a small saucepan, bring the water to a boil with ⅓ cup (2½ oz. / 75 g) of the sugar, stirring until the sugar dissolves. Stir in the vanilla. Keep at a low simmer.

10. In a large bowl, using an electric beater, whisk the whole egg and egg yolks with the remaining ⅓ cup (2½ oz. / 70 g) sugar until blended. Drizzle in the simmering syrup, whisking constantly, until the mixture is light and creamy. Whisk in the melted chocolate, then fold in the whipped cream. Let stand at room temperature.

ASSEMBLY

11. Heat the water with the sugar, stirring just until dissolved. Remove from the heat and stir in the vanilla extract.

12. Line a baking sheet with parchment paper and place the cake ring in the center. Lightly brush the biscuits with the syrup. Stand the biscuits around the rim, smooth side out.

13. Place 1 biscuit disk in the ring and brush lightly with the vanilla syrup. Spread the Bavarian cream in the ring, filling halfway. Place the second biscuit disk in the ring and brush lightly with the syrup. Fill to the top with the chocolate mousse. Chill for 2 hours.

14. Place a separate baking sheet in the freezer. In a medium bowl set over a saucepan of simmering water, melt the chocolate, stirring occasionally, until smooth. Remove the bowl from the heat and let the chocolate cool until syrupy. Spread in a thin layer over the baking sheet. Before the chocolate sets fully, scrape the chocolate with the plastic cookie cutter, working from top to bottom, to make wavy round shavings. Decorate the top of the charlotte with the shavings.

Note: The technique for making this chocolate mousse is based on the classic *pâte à bombe* method. It may take some practice blending the different components into a perfectly smooth mixture.

Prep:
25 minutes

Cook:
about 1 hour

Chill:
30 minutes

GRANNY SMITH APPLE TART

Serves 8

Light brown sugar for sprinkling
9 oz. (250 g) Quick Puff Pastry (p. 12), chilled
8 to 10 Granny Smith apples
½ cup minus 1 tablespoon (2¾ oz. / 80 g) granulated sugar
5 oz. (150 g) Almond Cream (p. 15)
4 tablespoons (2 oz. / 60 g) unsalted butter, diced

Equipment
A 10-inch (24-cm) tart ring or pan

1. Sprinkle a work surface with the light brown sugar and roll out the pastry to make an 11-inch (28-cm) disk. Prick the pastry with a fork. If using a tart ring, line a baking sheet with parchment paper and place the ring in the center. Line the tart ring with the pastry and chill for 30 minutes.

2. Peel, core, and quarter the apples.

3. In a small saucepan, cook half of the sugar over medium heat until lightly colored. Gradually add the remaining sugar, cooking until it's a lovely caramel color. If it darkens too much, dip the base in a bowl of cold water for 2 to 3 seconds to stop the cooking. However, keep the caramel barely warm to brush over the apples as they bake.

4. Preheat the oven to 400°F (200°C) convection. Spread the Almond Cream in the tart shell and arrange the apple quarters on top, packing them as tightly as possible.

5. Bake the tart for up to 1 hour, brushing the top with the caramel and adding the butter occasionally to soften and caramelize the apples.

Note: As simple as this recipe is, the result depends mainly on how it's baked and, even more importantly, on the taste of the apples.

BAKED CHOCOLATE MOUSSE CAKE

<hr>

Serves 8

Salted caramel spread

½ cup (3½ oz. / 100 g)
granulated sugar

2 teaspoons (15 g) glucose

½ vanilla bean

3 tablespoons plus 1 teaspoon
(50 ml) heavy cream

5 tablespoons (3 oz. / 80 g)
unsalted butter, room
temperature, diced

½ teaspoon (2 g) fleur de sel

Baked chocolate mousse cake

1 stick plus 2 tablespoons
(5 oz. / 140 g) unsalted butter,
diced, room temperature, plus
more for brushing

All-purpose flour for dusting

6 oz. (175 g) 70% dark chocolate,
preferably Valrhona® Guanaja

7 eggs, separated

1 cup plus 1 tablespoon
(7 ½ oz. / 210 g) granulated
sugar, divided

¼ cup plus 1 tablespoon
(1¼ oz. / 35 g) unsweetened
cocoa powder

Chocolate disks or shavings,
or chopped chocolate

Equipment

A 10- to 11-inch (24- to 26-cm)
cake pan

A pastry bag fitted with a plain
¼-inch (6-mm) tip, optional

SALTED CARAMEL SPREAD

1. A day ahead, in a small saucepan, melt the sugar with the glucose over medium heat until it's a light caramel color.

2. Split the vanilla bean lengthwise and scrape out the seeds; reserve the bean for a separate use. In a small saucepan over medium heat, or in the microwave oven, heat the cream with the vanilla seeds to lukewarm. Using a wooden spoon, stir into the caramel in 3 additions.

3. Stir in the butter and fleur de sel, then return the saucepan to medium heat for about 10 seconds, stirring until the caramel is smooth.

4. Using an immersion blender and inserting it below the surface of the caramel (you don't want bubbles), mix the caramel until very smooth. Let stand at room temperature.

BAKED CHOCOLATE MOUSSE CAKE

5. Preheat the oven to 400°F (200°C) convection. Brush the cake pan with butter and dust with flour. In a large bowl set over a saucepan of simmering water, melt the chocolate, stirring occasionally, until

smooth. Add the butter and stir until smooth and lukewarm. Remove the bowl from the heat.

6. In a medium bowl, whisk the egg yolks with ¾ cup (5¼ oz. / 150 g) of the sugar until pale and thick, then stir into the chocolate-butter mixture. Stir in the cocoa powder.

7. In a separate large bowl, whisk the egg whites with the remaining scant ⅓ cup (2 oz. / 60 g) sugar until they hold a soft peak. Fold into the chocolate-egg yolk mixture in 3 additions.

8. Pour the batter into the pan, stopping ¾ inch (2 cm) below the rim, and bake for 15 to 20 minutes. The center should remain molten.

9. You can serve the cake directly from the mold— it's even more delicious this way! When cool enough to decorate, pipe or drizzle swirls of caramel over the top. Decorate with the chocolate disks.

Notes: You'll notice there's no flour in this recipe. Don't worry. There's nothing missing. The large number of eggs binds the mixture as it cooks. This incredible dessert has the texture of a molten cake. I recommend the Bamix® immersion blender, because it doesn't create bubbles.

ALMOND CREAM–PRALINE TARTLETS

Makes 10 tartlets

7 oz. (200 g) Sweet Almond Pastry, room temperature (p. 10)
7 oz. (200 g) Almond Cream (p. 15)
1¾ oz. (50 g) cocoa butter
12¼ oz. (350 g) hazelnut praline
1¼ oz. (35 g) dark chocolate
½ oz. (15 g) trimoline or 2 teaspoons (15 g) acacia honey
10 oz. (300 g) Chocolate Fondant Icing (p. 17), heated to 95°F (35°C)

Equipment
Ten 3-inch (8-cm) tartlet pans
A paper decorating cone (p. 157)

1. Preheat the oven to 350°F (180°C) convection. On a lightly floured work surface, roll out the pastry about ⅛ inch (4 mm) thick. Line the tartlet pans with the pastry. Bake for 10 minutes. Spread the Almond Cream in the tart shells, filling halfway. Return to the oven and bake for 15 minutes.

2. In a medium bowl set over a saucepan of simmering water, melt the cocoa butter, stirring occasionally, until smooth. Remove the bowl from the heat and stir in the hazelnut praline. In a separate medium bowl set over a saucepan of simmering water, melt the chocolate, stirring occasionally, until smooth, then stir into the cocoa butter-praline mixture. Stir in the trimoline.

3. Mound the praline filling in the tartlets. Chill until set.

4. Dip the tartlets, praline side down, in the fondant. Turn right side up and remove any excess. Let set.

5. Using a paper cone filled with the fondant, draw decorative lines across the top.

Notes: These tartlets, which we call Saphos, are one of the specialties at our pastry shop.

This dessert can also be prepared in a large format, using an 8-inch (20-cm) tart pan.

CHRISTOPHE'S PINEAPPLE–COCONUT CREAM TART

Serves 8

Pineapple-coconut cream tart

4 cored pineapple slices, diced

½ cup minus 1 tablespoon (100 ml) whole milk

1 cup plus generous ¼ cup (4½ oz. / 125 g) almond flour

1 cup (4½ oz. / 125 g) confectioners' sugar

1⅓ cups (3½ oz. / 100 g) unsweetened shredded coconut

2 whole eggs

2 egg yolks

14 oz. (400 g) Pastry Cream (p. 14)

9 oz. (250 g) Sweet Almond Pastry (p. 10), room temperature

1 tablespoon (15 ml) dark rum

Decoration

Fondant Icing (p. 17), heated to 95°F (35°C) and colored green

1 oz. (30 g) dark chocolate, melted

2 tablespoons (20 g) natural almonds

Equipment

A 9-inch (22-cm) cake ring or pan, 1¼ inches (3 cm) deep, preferably with a removable bottom

A paper decorating cone (p. 157)

PINEAPPLE–COCONUT CREAM TART

1. Preheat the oven to 340°F (170°C) convection. Cut the pineapple dice into thin strips and drain well on paper towels.

2. In a medium bowl, combine the milk with the almond flour, confectioners' sugar, and shredded coconut. Whisk in the whole eggs and egg yolks.

3. In a separate bowl, whisk the Pastry Cream until light and smooth and fold into the almond-coconut mixture. Stir in the pineapple strips.

4. Preheat the oven to 320°F (160°C) convection. If using a cake ring, line a baking sheet with parchment paper and place the ring in the center. On a lightly floured work surface, roll out the pastry ⅛ inch (4 mm) thick. Line the cake ring with the pastry.

5. Spread the cream mixture in the tart shell and bake for 50 to 60 minutes. Immediately drizzle the cake with the rum. The alcohol evaporates, and you're left with the delicious taste of dark rum. Let cool.

DECORATION

6. Pour the fondant on top of the tart and smooth with a metal spatula. Remove any excess from the side. Using a small paper cone, draw lines of melted chocolate over the tart, letting them drizzle down the side. Decorate with the almonds.

Prep: 40 minutes

Cook: 25 minutes

Chill: 10 minutes + 1 hour

CHOUX PUFFS WITH VANILLA PASTRY CREAM

Makes 25 choux puffs

½ recipe Choux Pastry (p. 12)

1 vanilla bean

1⅔ cups (400 ml) whole milk

1¼ cups (300 ml) heavy cream, divided

6 egg yolks

Scant ⅔ cup (4 oz. / 120 g) granulated sugar

⅓ cup (1¾ oz. / 50 g) cornstarch

3 tablespoons plus 1 teaspoon (1¾ oz. / 50 g) unsalted butter, diced, room temperature

Confectioners' sugar for dusting

Equipment

A pastry bag fitted with a small, plain tip

1. Following the instructions for Choux Pastry but halving the quantities, make Chouquettes with Pearl Sugar (p. 12).

2. Split the vanilla bean lengthwise and scrape out the seeds. In a medium saucepan, heat the milk with ½ cup minus 1 tablespoon (100 ml) of the cream and the vanilla bean and seeds over medium-high heat until bubbles appear around the edge. Remove from the heat, cover, and let infuse for 1 hour.

3. In a medium bowl, whisk the egg yolks with the granulated sugar and cornstarch until well combined; do not let the mixture become pale.

4. Remove the vanilla bean from the milk-cream infusion. Return the saucepan to the heat and bring to a boil. Drizzle one-third of the milk-cream infusion into the yolk mixture, whisking constantly.

5. Return this mixture to the saucepan and cook over high heat, whisking constantly, until the pastry cream thickens, then immediately remove

from the heat. Whisk in the butter until completely incorporated.

6. Line a baking sheet with plastic wrap, letting the plastic wrap hang generously over the two short sides. Spread the pastry cream over it. Fold the wrap to cover the pastry cream completely so it doesn't dry out. Place in the freezer for 10 minutes, then transfer to the refrigerator for 1 hour.

7. In a medium bowl. whisk the remaining ¾ cup (200 ml) heavy cream until it holds a soft peak. Transfer the pastry cream to a large bowl and whisk briskly to soften it. Fold the whipped cream into the pastry cream.

8. Using the pastry tip, make a hole in the base of each choux puff. Pipe enough pastry cream through the small hole to fill. Dust with confectioners' sugar.

UPSIDE-DOWN CLEMENTINE CAKE

Serves 8

1 stick plus 1 teaspoon (4¼ oz. / 120 g) unsalted butter,
room temperature, plus more for brushing
⅓ cup (2½ oz. / 70 g) granulated sugar, plus more for sprinkling
1½ tablespoons (1 oz. / 30 g) honey, preferably lavender
2 eggs, room temperature
5 clementines
1 cup plus 2 tablespoons (5 oz. / 150 g) all-purpose flour
2 teaspoons (8 g) baking powder
Confectioners' sugar for dusting

Equipment
An 8-inch (20-cm) cake pan

1. Preheat the oven to 350°F (180°C) convection. Brush the cake pan with butter and sprinkle with granulated sugar. In a large bowl, cream the butter with the granulated sugar and honey. Beat in the eggs, one by one.

2. Using a fine grater, zest the clementines. Stir the zest into the batter. Squeeze 2 of the clementines and stir the juice into the batter.

3. Peel the remaining 3 clementines and cut crosswise into slices just under ½ inch (1 cm) thick. Arrange the clementine slices in the pan and pour in the batter.

4. Bake for 25 to 30 minutes. Let the cake cool to room temperature in the pan, then turn out and dust with confectioners' sugar.

Note: Eggs are more easily incorporated into any batter if they're at room temperature rather than cold out of the refrigerator.

VANILLA PAVLOVA
WITH CITRUS CREAM, PEACHES, AND APRICOTS

Serves 8

4 egg whites

Scant ⅔ cup (4 oz. / 120 g) granulated sugar, divided

Scant cup (4 oz. / 120 g) confectioners' sugar, plus more for dusting

1 orange, zest finely grated and peeled

12 oz. (350 g) Light Pastry Cream (p. 15)

2 large passion fruit

2 yellow peaches

3 apricots

Lemon juice for drizzling

Equipment

2 pastry bags fitted with a wide fluted tip, optional

1. Preheat the oven to 285°F (140°C) convection. Line a baking sheet with parchment paper. Draw an 8-inch (20-cm) circle on the paper and turn it over.

2. In the bowl of a stand mixer fitted with the whisk, whip the egg whites with a little granulated sugar at high speed until they hold a soft peak.

3. Gradually add the remaining granulated sugar, whipping for at least 10 minutes, until the meringue holds a firm peak. Sift the confectioners' sugar over the meringue and fold in using a silicone spatula.

4. Using the circle as a guide, pipe overlapping concentric circles of meringue rosettes on the baking sheet. Or use a spoon to spread the meringue, making a hollow in the center. Dust with confectioners' sugar.

5. Bake for 10 minutes, then reduce the oven temperature to between 210 and 230°F (100 to 110°C) convection. Bake for about 2 hours, until dry inside. Let cool completely.

6. Beat the orange zest into the pastry cream until smooth. Pipe or mound the pastry cream in the center of the meringue, leaving a border. Scoop out the seeds and pulp of the passion fruit and spoon on the cream. Using a small, sharp knife, cut in between the membranes of the orange to release the segments and drain on paper towels. Slice the peaches and apricots. Arrange the orange, peaches and apricots in the center of the pavlova.

7. Drizzle the fruit with the lemon juice. Serve well chilled.

Notes: I prefer meringue that's very lightly browned, because it's tastier and seems a little less sweet.

Instead of peaches and apricots, substitute ripe mangoes at the peak of their perfection if you can.

Christelle's Mandelbari

Mandelbari means "mount of almonds" in the dialect we speak
in Alsace. It's a specialty that's found only in a few villages
in the center of the region, near Ebersmunster, Muttersholtz,
and Ebersheim, where my father was born. To make it, we
stack almond-meringue topped cookies to form a cone. It's
traditionally served along with coffee, after dessert—often a
vacherin, a luscious meringue-ice cream concoction. You can
buy mandelbari at bakeries and pastry shops in these villages,
but it's mainly made at home, using a recipe that's handed down
over generations, for family celebrations.

I'm always delighted to show off this cake. It's little known,
even in Alsace. It's particularly good when made with excellent
ingredients. Some of my friends even prefer it to macarons, and
that's saying something. Here, I've brought a new twist to
my family recipe and have developed three original versions
exclusively for Christophe and Camille.

I wish you bon appétit.

Prep:
30 minutes

Chill:
1 hour

Cook:
1 hour 20 minutes

STACKED COFFEE–HAZELNUT COOKIE CAKE
Mandelbari Café-Noisette

∞∞∞∞∞∞∞∞∞∞∞∞∞∞∞∞∞∞∞∞∞∞∞

Serves 6

Coffee-hazelnut cookies

Scant ⅔ cup (3 oz. / 80 g)
hazelnuts, plus a few
for decorating

1 cup (4 oz. / 120 g)
all-purpose flour

½ teaspoon (2 g)
baking p owder

3½ tablespoons (1½ oz. / 40 g)
granulated sugar

1½ tablespoons (20 g)
muscovado sugar,
finely ground

1 egg yolk

2 teaspoons coffee extract

1 teaspoon ground coffee

Seeds of ½ vanilla bean

1 stick plus 2 teaspoons
(4½ oz. / 125 g) unsalted butter,
diced, room temperature

Meringue

3 egg whites

1 cup plus 1 tablespoon (7½ oz. /
210 g) granulated sugar

1 teaspoon coffee extract

Seeds of ½ vanilla bean

Decoration

A few hazelnuts

Finely ground coffee

Confectioners' sugar for
dusting

Equipment

A set of graduated round
cookie cutters

A pastry bag fitted with a fluted
¾-inch (18-mm) tip, optional

STACKED COFFEE–HAZELNUT COOKIE CAKE

COFFEE–HAZELNUT COOKIES

1. Preheat the oven to 340°F (170°C) convection. Spread all the hazelnuts (for the cookies and for decoration) on a baking sheet and toast for about 10 minutes, then let cool. Transfer to a kitchen towel and rub off the skin; the nuts don't have to be perfectly skinned. In a food processor, finely grind ⅔ cup (3 oz. / 80 g) of the hazelnuts until a powder forms. Cut the remaining hazelnuts into halves and reserve for decorating.

2. In a large bowl, sift the flour with the baking powder. Whisk in the granulated sugar, muscovado sugar, egg yolk, coffee extract, ground coffee, and vanilla seeds. Rub in the butter until smooth. Or use a stand mixer fitted with the dough hook.

3. Shape the dough into a disk, cover with plastic wrap, and chill for at least 1 hour.

4. Preheat the oven to 320°F (160°C) convection. Bring the dough to room temperature. Line at least 2 baking sheets with parchment paper. On a lightly floured work surface, roll out the dough ⅛ inch (4 mm) thick. Beginning with the largest cookie cutter plus a size that enables you to cut out a disk to form a ring, cut out a cookie ring.

5. Using the next size down, cut out a cookie ring. Continue to cut out increasingly smaller rings. Place on the baking sheets.

6. Bake for about 20 minutes, rotating the pans halfway through, until nicely colored. Let cool on the baking sheets.

MERINGUE

7. Reduce the oven temperature to 195°F (90°C) convection. In the bowl of a stand mixer fitted with the whisk, whip the egg whites until frothy. Add a little of the sugar and whip at medium-high speed until they hold a firm peak. Gradually add the remaining sugar, then whip for 10 minutes, until the egg whites hold a firm glossy peak. Reduce the speed of the stand mixer and add the coffee extract and vanilla seeds. Whip for 1 minute.

8. Pipe or spoon equal dollops of meringue on the cookies. Decorate each meringue with a hazelnut half and a pinch of ground coffee.

9. Bake for 1 hour, then let cool completely.

10. Just before serving, dust the cookies with confectioners' sugar. Stack them, from largest to smallest, to create the mandelbari.

Note: I love the sophisticated combination of coffee and roasted hazelnuts. This mandelbari would be wonderful with an excellent espresso.

Prep:
1 hour

Chill:
1 hour

Cook:
10 to 15 minutes

LEMON–STRAWBERRY LAYER CAKE

Serves 10 using half the sponge cake

Lemon cream

Finely grated zest of 4 lemons

½ cup minus 1 tablespoon (110 ml) lemon juice

Scant ½ cup (4 oz. / 120 g) granulated sugar

3 eggs

1 stick plus 2 teaspoons (4½ oz. / 125 g) unsalted butter, diced, room temperature

Lemon syrup

3 tablespoons plus 1 teaspoon (50 ml) water

¼ cup (1¾ oz. / 50 g) granulated sugar

1 tablespoon plus 1 teaspoon (20 ml) lemon juice

Pistachio sponge cake

3 tablespoons plus 1 teaspoon (1¾ oz. / 50 g) unsalted butter

1 cup plus 1 tablespoon (5 oz. / 140 g) all-purpose flour

1¼ cups (8½ oz. / 240 g) granulated sugar, divided

7 egg whites

¾ oz. (20 g) pistachio paste, well softened

Lemon mousse

7 sheets (14 g) 200 bloom gelatin (see Note)

½ cup minus 1 tablespoon (110 ml) lemon juice

Finely grated zest of 2 lemons

Lemon Cream (from above)

2 cups (500 g) heavy cream, well chilled

Assembly

Assorted fruit, such as halved strawberries and halved yellow cherries

A little Fruity Glaze (p. 18), optional

LEMON CREAM

1. In a medium saucepan, combine the lemon zest and juice with the sugar and eggs. Bring to a boil, then immediately remove from the heat. Stir in the butter. Strain through a fine sieve into a medium bowl. Process with an immersion blender for 1 minute, then chill.

LEMON SYRUP

2. In a small saucepan, bring the water to a boil with the sugar, stirring, until the sugar dissolves. Remove from the heat and stir in the lemon juice. Let cool.

PISTACHIO SPONGE CAKE

3. Preheat the oven to 375°F (190°C) convection. Line a 12 by 16-inch (30 by 40-cm) baking sheet with parchment paper. In a small saucepan, melt the butter and let cool to lukewarm. Whisk the flour with a scant ½ cup (4 oz. / 120 g) of the sugar.

4. In the bowl of a stand mixer fitted with the whisk, whip the egg whites with the remaining scant ½ cup (4 oz. / 120 g) sugar until they hold a firm peak. Gradually fold in the dry ingredients, then gently fold in the melted butter and pistachio paste.

5. Spread the batter on the baking sheet in a layer just under ½ inch (1 cm) thick. Bake for 10 to 15 minutes, until barely colored and springy.

6. Invert the cake onto a rack and let cool. Carefully peel off the parchment paper.

LEMON MOUSSE

7. In a medium bowl of very cold water, soften the gelatin. Squeeze the gelatin dry. In a small saucepan, warm the gelatin over low heat with the lemon juice, stirring until dissolved. Transfer to a large bowl. In a medium bowl, whip the cream until it holds a soft peak. Stir the lemon zest and lemon cream into the gelatin-lemon juice mixture and whisk briskly to combine. Carefully fold in the whipped cream.

Assembly

8. Trim the edges of the pistachio sponge cake. Brush the cake with the lemon syrup. Spread the lemon mousse over the top. Place in the freezer for 1 hour, until set.

9. Cut the cake crosswise in half. Cover one half with plastic wrap and freeze for another occasion. It'll keep well for a few weeks.

10. Decorate the other half with the fruit, covering the lemon mousse. If you like, drizzle the fruit with some Fruity Glaze.

Notes: It's hard to make a smaller quantity of this particular sponge cake, known as a Lorrain, which is why we suggest freezing half. Depending on the texture you prefer for your mousse, you can decrease or increase the quantity of gelatin.

Prep:
1 hour

Cook:
30 minutes

Chill:
12 hours

CHOCOLATE LAYER CAKE

∞∞∞∞∞∞∞∞∞∞∞∞∞∞∞∞∞∞∞∞∞∞∞∞∞∞∞∞∞∞∞

Serves 8

Chocolate sponge cake

1 tablespoon (15 g) unsalted butter, melted, plus more for brushing

Generous ½ cup (2¼ oz. / 65 g) all-purpose flour, plus more for dusting

2 tablespoons (15 g) unsweetened cocoa powder, plus more for dusting

1 tablespoon (10 g) potato starch

3 eggs

Scant ½ cup (3 oz. / 90 g) granulated sugar

Chocolate whipped cream

2½ cups (600 ml) heavy cream

7¾ oz. (220 g) 70% dark chocolate

½ cup (120 ml) whole milk

Scant ¼ cup (1½ oz. / 45 g) granulated sugar

Crispy praline

3½ oz. (100 g) praline milk chocolate

A 4.41-oz. (125 g) packet of plain Gavottes® cookies or other crispy cookies, such as wafers

Equipment

A 10-inch (24-cm) nonstick cake pan

A 10-inch (24-cm) dessert ring, 1¼ inches (3 cm) deep

CHOCOLATE SPONGE CAKE

1. Preheat the oven to 410°F (210°C) convection. Brush the cake pan with butter and dust with flour. Sift the flour with the cocoa powder and potato starch.

2. In a medium bowl, lightly whisk the eggs with the sugar until dissolved. Set over a saucepan of simmering water and whisk for 2 to 3 minutes, until slightly warmed but not hot.

3. Remove the bowl from the heat and, using an electric beater, whisk until the mixture cools to room temperature and forms a slowly dissolving ribbon when the whisk is lifted.

4. Using a silicone spatula, carefully fold in the dry ingredients. Fold in the butter.

5. Immediately spread the batter in the cake pan and bake for 10 minutes. Reduce the oven temperature to 350°F (180°C) convection and bake for 20 minutes. Let the cake cool to lukewarm in the pan, then turn out onto a rack and let cool completely.

CHOCOLATE WHIPPED CREAM

6. At least 10 minutes ahead, place a large bowl, preferably metal, in the freezer. You'll need it to whip the cream. Whip the cream until it holds between the wires of the whisk and has doubled in volume, then chill.

7. Chop the chocolate. In a large bowl set over a saucepan of simmering water, melt the chocolate, stirring occasionally, until smooth. Remove the bowl from the heat.

8. In a medium saucepan, heat the milk with the sugar over medium-high heat, stirring, until bubbles appear around the edge and the sugar dissolves. Pour into the chocolate and stir until smooth. Let cool to lukewarm, then fold in the whipped cream.

CRISPY PRALINE

9. In a medium bowl set over a saucepan of simmering water, melt the praline chocolate, stirring occasionally, until smooth. Remove from the heat. Leaving the cookies in their plastic packet, crush them well. Stir the crumbs into the melted chocolate.

ASSEMBLY

10. Using a long serrated knife, cut the sponge cake horizontally in half. Set the dessert ring on a large, flat platter. Place the bottom cake half in the ring and spread with half of the crispy praline, then half of the chocolate whipped cream. Smooth the top with a large knife and a metal spatula. Repeat with the top cake half and the remaining crispy praline and chocolate whipped cream.

11. Chill for 12 hours, until set. Before serving, dust with cocoa powder.

ALMOND MERINGUE CAKE
WITH APPLES AND CHIBOUST CREAM
Dacquoise Pomme Chiboust

Serves 8

Apple compote

6½ oz. (180 g) Belle de Boskoop or other baking apples

2 teaspoons (10 g) unsalted butter

¾ oz. (20 g) granulated sugar (see Note)

1 pinch cinnamon

Flambéed apples

1 tablespoon plus 1 teaspoon (20 g) unsalted butter

2 Belle de Boskoop or other baking apples

Brown sugar for sprinkling

1 tablespoon (15 ml) Calvados or other apple brandy

Caramel powder

½ cup (3½ oz. / 100 g) granulated sugar

2 tablespoons plus 2 teaspoons (40 ml) water

Vanilla Chiboust cream

2 sheets (4 g) 200 bloom gelatin

4 whole eggs, separated

1 egg yolk

6 tablespoons (2½ oz. / 70 g) granulated sugar, divided

2 tablespoons (20 g) cornstarch

¾ cup plus 2 tablespoons (210 ml) whole milk

1 vanilla bean, split lengthwise and seeds scraped

Assembly

Almond Meringue Base (p. 10)

A few caramel shards

2 oz. (50 g) Fruity Glaze (p. 18)

Equipment

A 10-inch (24-cm) cake ring

A 2-inch (5-cm) strip food-safe acetate

Almond Meringue Cake
with Apples and Chiboust Cream

Apple Compote

1. Preheat the oven to 400°F (200°C) convection. Peel, core, and cut the apples into large chunks and place in an ovenproof dish. Dot with the butter.

2. In a small heavy saucepan, cook half of the sugar over medium heat, stirring with a wooden spoon, until melted. Add the remaining sugar and cook until it's a lovely caramel color. Pour over the apples.

3. Cover the dish with foil and bake for about 1 hour, until the apples are soft. Stir well and transfer to a colander to drain.

Flambéed Apples

4. Reduce the oven temperature to 350°F (180°C) convection. Melt the butter. Peel, core, and cut each apple into 8 pieces. In a medium bowl, combine the apple pieces with the hot butter.

5. Spread the apples on a rimmed baking sheet and sprinkle with the brown sugar. Bake for about 1 hour, until soft, stirring occasionally. Meanwhile, in a small saucepan, warm the Calvados over low heat. Remove the baking sheet from the oven, pour the Calvados over the apples, and, using a long match or lighter, carefully ignite them. Let the flames subside.

Caramel Powder

6. Line a rimmed baking sheet with parchment paper or a smooth silicone mat. In a small saucepan, cook the sugar with the water over medium-high heat until it's a dark caramel color. Pour on the baking sheet in a thin layer and let cool. Break off 2 to 3 large shards, plus a few smaller pieces, and reserve for decorating. In a food processor, finely grind the remaining caramel until powdery.

Vanilla Chiboust Cream

7. In a medium bowl of very cold water, soften the gelatin. In a separate bowl, whisk the 5 egg yolks with 3½ tablespoons (1½ oz. / 40 g) of the sugar and the cornstarch until combined.

8. In a medium saucepan, heat the milk with the vanilla bean and seeds over medium heat until bubbles appear around the edge; remove from the heat. Remove the bean and whisk the hot milk into the egg yolk-sugar mixture. Return the mixture to the saucepan and cook, whisking constantly, until it returns to a boil. Remove from the heat. Squeeze the gelatin dry and stir into the cream until completely dissolved. Transfer to a large bowl.

9. In a medium bowl, whisk the egg whites, gradually adding the remaining 2½ tablespoons (1 oz. / 30 g) sugar, until they hold a soft peak. Fold half of the whipped egg whites into the creamy mixture, then fold in the second half.

Assembly

10. Line a baking sheet with parchment paper and place the dessert ring in the center. Line the inside rim of the dessert ring with the acetate. Place the almond meringue in the dessert ring.

11. Spread the apple compote in the ring. Arrange the flambéed apples on top. Cover with the Chiboust cream, mounding it slightly. Chill until set, then freeze for 30 minutes.

12. Carefully remove the dessert ring. Using a fine sieve, sift the caramel powder over the cake. Drizzle with half of the Fruity Glaze. Scatter a few small pieces of the reserved caramel over the top and drizzle with the remaining Fruity Glaze. Remove the acetate. Transfer the cake to a platter and chill until needed. Just before serving, decorate with the large caramel shards.

Notes: Instead of preparing this tiny amount of caramel, you can use the same weight of caramel syrup.

Please note that this recipe contains raw egg whites. If you prefer, you can substitute ½ cup (4½ oz. / 135 g) pasteurized egg whites.

Prep:
1 hour

Cook:
25 to 30 minute

Chill:
30 minutes

HAZELNUT TART WITH RHUBARB, PEACHES, AND GRAPEFRUIT

Serves 8

Breton hazelnut pastry

7 tablespoons (3½ oz. / 100 g)
unsalted butter, softened,
plus more for melting

2½ teaspoons (15 g) egg yolk

½ cup (3½ oz. / 100 g)
granulated sugar

Scant ½ teaspoon (2 g) fine salt

¾ cup (2¼ oz. / 65 g) ground
hazelnuts

1 cup plus 1 tablespoon
(4¾ oz. / 135 g)
all-purpose flour

1 scant teaspoon (3.5 g)
baking powder

Assembly

5¼ oz. (150 g)
Pastry Cream (p. 14)

12½ oz. (350 g) Rhubarb
Compote (p. 18)

3 yellow peaches

2 grapefruit

1 orange

2 oz. (50 g) raspberries,
halved lengthwise

Confectioners' sugar
for dusting

Equipment

A 7-inch (18-cm) tart ring or
pan, or eight 2¾-inch (7-cm)
tartlet rings

BRETON HAZELNUT PASTRY

1. In a medium bowl, whisk the butter with the egg yolk, sugar, and salt until smooth.

2. Sift the ground hazelnuts with the flour and baking powder into the butter-egg yolk mixture and fold in using a silicone spatula. Cover with plastic wrap and chill for 30 minutes.

3. Preheat the oven to 340°F (170° C) convection. If using a tart ring, line a baking sheet with parchment paper and place the ring in the center. On a lightly floured work surface, roll out the pastry ⅛ inch (4 mm) thick. Cut out a 7-inch (18-cm) square and place in the tart ring folding it up against the rim if needed. Bake for 25 to 30 minutes. Meanwhile, melt a little butter.

4. As soon the pastry comes out of the oven, brush it with the melted butter. (As it cools and sets, it creates a waterproof layer that prevents the pastry from getting soggy.) Let cool.

ASSEMBLY

5. In a medium bowl, briskly whisk the Pastry Cream until it's as soft as mayonnaise. Spread it in the center of the pastry square, then spread the rhubarb over it. Slice the peaches. Using a small, sharp knife, peel the grapefruit and orange. Cut in between the membranes to release the segments. Arrange the peaches, grapefruit, and orange on the rhubarb. Dot with the raspberry halves. Dust the rim with confectioners' sugar.

Prep:
40 minutes

Chill:
12 hours

Cook:
25 minutes

HAZELNUT BROWNIE CAKE WITH CHOCOLATE CRÉMEUX

Serves 10

Chocolate crémeux

5 oz. (140 g) 64% dark chocolate, chopped

½ cup minus 1 tablespoon (100 ml) whole milk

⅔ cup (150 ml) heavy cream

2 egg yolks

1 tablespoon plus 2 teaspoons (20 g) granulated sugar

Brownie cake

2½ tablespoons (1 oz. / 25 g) all-purpose flour

2½ teaspoons (6 g) unsweetened cocoa powder

2 oz. (60 g) 66% dark chocolate, chopped

1 stick (4 oz. / 115 g) unsalted butter, diced, room temperature

2 eggs, separated

⅓ cup (2½ oz. / 75 g) light brown sugar

⅓ cup (2½ oz. / 75 g) granulated sugar

⅓ cup (1 ½ oz. / 45 g) chopped hazelnuts

Topping

3½ oz. (100 g) blueberry jam, warmed, for spreading

3½ oz. (100 g) blueberries

Equipment

A 3 by 8-inch (8 by 20-cm) oval ovenproof dish or brownie pan

A pastry bag fitted with a Saint-Honoré tip, optional

CHOCOLATE CRÉMEUX

1. Place the chocolate in a medium bowl. In a medium saucepan, heat the milk and cream over medium-high heat until bubbles appear around the edge; remove from the heat. In a medium bowl, whisk the egg yolks with the sugar until pale and thick. Whisk the yolk-sugar mixture into the hot milk mixture. Reduce the heat to low and cook, whisking constantly, until the mixture thickens; do not let boil. Remove from the heat and pour into the chocolate in 3 additions, stirring constantly. Using an immersion blender, process briefly, holding it below the surface to avoid creating bubbles. Let cool, press plastic wrap directly on the surface, and chill for 12 hours.

BROWNIE CAKE

2. Preheat the oven to 340°F (170°C) convection. Line the baking dish with parchment paper. Sift the flour with the cocoa powder.

3. In a medium bowl set over a saucepan of simmering water, melt the chocolate, stirring occasionally, until smooth. Stir in the butter until smooth and lukewarm, then stir in the egg yolks, light brown sugar, and granulated sugar. Fold in the dry ingredients, then the hazelnuts.

4. In a medium bowl, whisk the egg whites until they hold a soft peak. Fold into the chocolate mixture.

5. Spread the batter in the baking dish and bake for 25 minutes, until a tester inserted into the center comes out with moist crumbs. Let cool in the dish.

TOPPING

6. Spread the jam on the cake, then pipe or spread the chocolate crémeux on top. Decorate with the blueberries and chill. This dessert is best served chilled.

Note: A *crémeux* is a relatively recent creation in the French pastry repertoire. With its enriched custard base, it has a silky texture and is firm enough to be piped or used in a layer cake.

ALMOND CASSATA CAKE

Serves 8

Citrus almond paste cake

Ingredients for 1 recipe
Almond Paste Cake (p. 79)

Finely grated zest of ½ orange

Finely grated zest of ½ lemon

¾ cup (3 oz. / 80 g)
sliced almonds

Syrup

⅓ cup plus 2 teaspoons
(90 ml) water

½ cup minus 1 tablespoon
(2¾ oz. / 80 g) granulated sugar

2 tablespoons plus 2 teaspoons
(40 ml) Grand Marnier or
other orange liqueur

Candied fruit

½ oz. (15 g) candied ginger

1½ oz. (40 g) candied
lemon peel

1½ oz. (40 g) candied
orange peel

1½ oz. (40 g) candied cherries

1 tablespoon plus 1 teaspoon
(20 ml) Grand Marnier or
other orange liqueur

Cassata cream

Scant ¼ cup (50 ml) heavy
cream, well chilled

15 oz. (425 g) Pastry Cream
(p. 14)

Finish

Confectioners' sugar
for dusting

Equipment

An 8 by 12-inch (20 by 30-cm)
cake frame or pan, or 10-inch
(25-cm) square pan

CITRUS ALMOND PASTE CAKE

1. Preheat the oven to 350°F (180°C) convection.
If using a cake frame, line a baking sheet with
parchment paper and place the frame in the center.
Brush the frame with butter and dust with flour.
Follow the instructions for the Almond Paste Cake,
stirring in the orange and lemon zest.

2. Spread the batter in the frame and sprinkle with
the sliced almonds. Bake for 20 to 30 minutes, until
a tester inserted into the center comes out clean.
Turn the cake out onto a rack and let cool.

SYRUP

3. In a small saucepan, bring the water to a boil
with the sugar, stirring, until the sugar dissolves.
Remove from the heat and stir in the Grand Marnier.
Let cool.

CANDIED FRUIT

4. Cut the candied fruit into ¼-inch (5-mm) dice
and combine with the Grand Marnier.

CASSATA CREAM

5. In a medium bowl, whip the cream until it holds
a soft peak. In a separate bowl, briskly whisk the
Pastry Cream until it's as soft as mayonnaise. Fold in
the whipped cream.

ASSEMBLY AND FINISH

6. Using a long serrated knife, cut the cake
horizontally in half. Brush both halves generously
with the syrup and let stand until absorbed.

7. Spread the cassata cream evenly on the bottom
cake half and dot with the diced candied fruit
Carefully place the top cake half on the cream.
Dust the rim with confectioners' sugar and chill.

RUM BABA SPONGE CAKE

Serves 10

Sponge cake

Unsalted butter for brushing

1 cup plus scant ½ cup
(4½ oz. / 130 g) cake flour,
plus more for dusting

⅓ cup (1¾ oz. / 50 g)
potato starch

4 eggs, separated

2 whole eggs

¾ cup (5¾ oz. / 170 g)
granulated sugar, divided

⅓ oz. (10 g) trimoline or
1½ teaspoons honey

1 oz. (30 g) 50% almond paste,
well softened

A pinch fine salt

Syrup

1½ cups (350 ml) water

1¼ cups (9 oz. / 250 g)
granulated sugar

2 oranges, juiced and zest
finely grated

1 large lemon, juiced and zest
finely grated

2 tablespoons (30 ml)
aged dark rum

Chantilly Cream

1⅔ cups (400 ml) heavy cream

Scant ⅓ cup (2 oz. / 60 g)
granulated sugar

1 tablespoon pure vanilla
extract or the seeds of
1 vanilla bean

Equipment

A 10-inch (24-cm) cake pan

A pastry bag fitted with a
fluted tip, optional

SPONGE CAKE

1. Preheat the oven to 350°F (180°C) convection.
Brush the cake pan with butter and dust with flour.
Sift the flour with the potato starch.

2. In a stand mixer fitted with the whisk, whip the
4 egg yolks with the 2 whole eggs and scant ⅔ cup (4
oz. / 120 g) of the sugar until pale and thick. Add the
trimoline and almond paste and whip at high speed
for 10 minutes.

3. In a medium bowl, whisk the egg whites with the
salt and remaining ¼ cup (1¾ oz. / 50 g) sugar until
firm and glossy. Carefully fold the egg white mixture
into the egg-almond paste mixture, then fold in the
dry ingredients. Bake for 30 minutes, just until a
tester inserted into the center comes out clean.

SYRUP

4. In a medium saucepan, bring the water to a boil
with the sugar, orange juice and zest, and lemon
juice and zest, stirring, until the sugar dissolves.
Immediately remove from the heat, let cool to barely
lukewarm, and stir in the rum.

CHANTILLY CREAM

5. Ten minutes before making the whipped cream,
place the bowl of a stand mixer, the whisk, and the
cream in the freezer. If you don't have time, place the
bowl in a larger bowl of ice water.

6. Fit the whisk and bowl to the stand mixer and
whip the cream at high speed for 3 to 4 minutes,
gradually adding the sugar and vanilla, until it holds
between the wires of the whisk.

7. Place the cake on a platter. Brush generously
with the syrup. Pipe or spoon dollops or other
patterns of the whipped cream on the sponge cake.

Note: Traditional *baba au rhum* is a yeasted cake, but
this recipe is easier and just as delicious.

Prep:
50 minutes

Chill:
30 minutes

Cook:
20 minutes

RASPBERRY–RICH PASTRY CREAM TART

Serves 8

10½ oz. (300 g) Sweet Almond Pastry (p. 10), room temperature

9 oz. (250 g) Rich Pastry Cream (p. 13)

1 to 2 teaspoons kirsch

7 oz. (200 g) raspberries, halved,
plus a few whole raspberries for decorating

3 sheets (6 g) 200 bloom gelatin

12 oz. (335 g) raspberry purée

3 tablespoons (1¼ oz. / 35 g) granulated sugar

Equipment

A 9-inch (22-cm) tart ring or pan

A pastry bag, optional

1. Preheat the oven to 340°F (170° C) convection. If using a tart ring, line a baking sheet with parchment paper and place the ring in the center. On a lightly floured work surface, roll out the pastry ⅛ inch (3 mm) thick. Line the ring with the pastry. Chill for 30 minutes. Bake for 20 minutes, until golden, and let cool.

2. In a medium bowl, briskly whisk the pastry cream until it's as soft as mayonnaise. Whisk in the kirsch.

3. Pipe or spread the pastry cream in the tart shell. The layer should be ¼ inch (5 mm) deep.

4. If you like, press the raspberry halves into the pastry cream so they don't peek above the surface.

5. In a medium bowl of very cold water, soften the gelatin.

6. In a medium saucepan, bring about one-quarter of the raspberry purée to a boil with the sugar. Remove from the heat. Squeeze the gelatin dry and stir in until dissolved, then stir in the remaining raspberry purée. Let cool to room temperature, but do not let set.

7. Place the tart on a baking sheet, if needed. Spread the raspberry purée over the pastry cream and transfer smoothly to the refrigerator. Chill for 1 hour, until set. Carefully remove the tart ring and decorate with the whole raspberries.

Note: The top of this tart should be as smooth and flat as possible. To avoid jiggling the raspberry mixture as you move it, first make room for the tart in your refrigerator near the door.

Prep:
50 minutes

Chill:
20 minutes
+ 1 hour

Cook:
20 to 25 minutes

RASPBERRY CHEESECAKE

Serves 8

Breton short pastry

2 egg yolks

Scant ½ cup (3 oz. / 85 g) granulated sugar

7 tablespoons (3½ oz. / 100 g) unsalted butter, diced, softened

1 cup plus 1 tablespoon (4¾ oz. / 135 g) all-purpose flour

Scant ½ teaspoon (2 g) fine salt

1 scant tablespoon (11 g) baking powder

Raspberry layer

2½ sheets (5 g) 200 bloom gelatin

9 oz. (250 g) raspberry purée, divided

2½ tablespoons (1 oz. / 30 g) granulated sugar

2 oz. (50 g) assorted raspberries and blueberries

Cream cheese layer

5¼ oz. (150 g) cream cheese

1 cup (250 ml) heavy cream

1 tablespoon plus 2 teaspoons (20 g) light brown sugar

A little finely grated lime zest, optional, plus more for sprinkling

Equipment

An 8-inch (20-cm) tart ring or pan

A 7-inch (18-cm) tart ring

A pastry bag fitted with a Saint-Honoré tip or other tip of your choice, optional

BRETON SHORT PASTRY

1. In a medium bowl, whisk the egg yolks with the sugar until pale and thick. Using a wooden spoon, beat in the butter. Sift in the flour, salt, and baking powder and fold in.

2. Shape the pastry into a disk, cover with plastic wrap, and chill for about 20 minutes.

3. Preheat the oven to 340°F (170° C) convection. On a lightly floured sheet of parchment paper, roll out the pastry ¼ inch (4 to 5 mm) thick.

4. Using the larger tart ring, press out a pastry disk and leave the pastry in the ring. Remove the excess pastry and brush off the flour. Carefully transfer with the paper to the baking sheet. Alternatively, if using a tart pan, transfer the pastry disk to the base of the pan. Bake for 20 to 25 minutes, until golden. Let cool in the ring.

RASPBERRY LAYER

5. Line a separate baking sheet with parchment paper and place the smaller pastry ring in the center. In a medium bowl of very cold water, soften the gelatin.

6. In a medium saucepan, bring about one-quarter of the raspberry purée to a boil with the sugar. Remove from the heat.

7. Squeeze the gelatin dry and stir in until dissolved, then stir in the remaining raspberry purée.

8. Spread the raspberry mixture in the pastry ring, just under ½ inch (1 cm) thick, and dot with raspberries and blueberries. Place in the freezer until set, about 1 hour.

9. Center the raspberry layer in the tart shell.

CREAM CHEESE LAYER

10. In the bowl of a stand mixer fitted with the whisk, whip the cream cheese, gradually adding the cream, then add the light brown sugar and lime zest, if using. Whip until fairly firm, but don't overdo it!

11. Pipe or spread the cream cheese over the raspberry layer and sprinkle with the remaining lime zest.

Note: Instead of using all-purpose flour in the pastry, you can substitute a mix of ¾ cup plus 2 tablespoons (3½ oz. / 100 g) all-purpose flour combined with a generous ⅓ cup (1¼ oz. / 35 g) of almond flour or finely ground hazelnuts.

Prep:

1 hour

Rest:

12 hours

Cook:

25 to 30 minutes

ORANGE–SAFFRON ECLAIR BOATS
Carolines Orange-Safran

Serves 6

Candied oranges

2 oranges

1¼ cups (300 ml) water or
orange juice (see Note)

2 cups (14 oz. / 400 g)
granulated sugar

**Orange-saffron
whipped cream**

1½ cups (350 ml) heavy cream

A few threads saffron

Finely grated zest of 1 orange

2½ tablespoons
(20 g) confectioners' sugar

Assembly

2 oranges

A few saffron threads

Equipment

A pastry bag fitted with a fine
fluted tip, optional

Eclairs

Choux Pastry (p. 12)

CANDIED ORANGES

1. A day ahead, slice the oranges crosswise just
under ½ inch (1 cm) thick. To blanch them, place
in a large saucepan of hot water and bring to a boil.
Drain and repeat 4 times.

2. In a large saucepan, bring the water to a boil
with the sugar, stirring, until the sugar dissolves.
Add the orange slices, reduce the heat, and let
simmer for a few minutes, so the slices absorb the
syrup. Cover and let rest for 12 hours. Reserve 2
teaspoons (10 ml) of the syrup.

ORANGE–SAFFRON WHIPPED CREAM

3. In a large bowl, combine the cream with the
saffron and chill for 3 hours to infuse. Add the zest
and confectioners' sugar and whip until the cream
holds a firm peak. Whip or stir in the reserved syrup.

ECLAIRS

4. Meanwhile, preheat the oven to 340°F (170°C)
conventional. Line a baking sheet with parchment
paper. Pipe or spoon 6-inch (15-cm) logs on the
baking sheet. Bake for 20 to 25 minutes, until golden
and well puffed. Let cool.

ASSEMBLY

5. Dice the candied orange slices. Using a small,
sharp knife, peel the oranges. Cut in between the
membranes to release the segments and drain on
paper towels. Using a serrated knife and working
horizontally, cut off the top third of each eclair.
Divide the candied orange dice among the eclairs
and pipe or spoon in dollops of the whipped cream.
Decorate with the orange segments and a few
saffron threads.

Note: Using orange juice instead of water gives the
candied orange a fruitier taste.

Prep:
1 hour

Rest:
3 to 12 hours

Cook:
25 to 30 minutes

RASPBERRY MADELEINES

Makes 20 madeleines

Madeleines

6 tablespoons (3 oz. / 90 g)
unsalted butter, plus more
for brushing

1 cup (4½ oz. / 125 g)
all-purpose flour, plus more
for dusting

2¾ teaspoons (10 g)
baking powder

3 eggs

⅔ cup (4½ oz. / 125 g)
granulated sugar

½ oz. (15 g) trimoline or
2 teaspoons (15 g) honey

1 teaspoon raspberry eau-
de-vie or orange flower water,
plus more for drizzling

2 oz. (60 g) raspberries,
chopped

Glaze and finish

1⅓ cups (6½ oz. / 180 g)
confectioners' sugar, sifted

¾ oz. (20 g) raspberry purée

1 teaspoon (5 ml)
raspberry liqueur

A little water

A little mauve food coloring

A little Barely Sweet
Raspberry Jam (p. 17)

Edible silver balls, optional

2 oz. (50 g) raspberries, sliced
crosswise

Equipment

20 madeleine pans or mini
muffin cups

A pastry bag, optional

MADELEINES

1. Brush the madeleine pans with butter and dust with flour. In a small saucepan, melt the butter over medium heat and let cool to lukewarm. Sift the flour with the baking powder.

2. In a medium heatproof bowl, using an electric beater, whisk the eggs with the sugar and trimoline. Place over a saucepan of simmering water and whisk constantly until the temperature reaches 104°F (40°C). Remove the bowl from the heat and continue whisking until the mixture cools to room temperature. Beat in the melted butter, eau-de-vie, and chopped raspberries.

3. Let the batter rest at room temperature for at least 3 hours. If you have time, chill it for up to 12 hours.

4. Preheat the oven to 410°F (210°C) convection. Pipe or spoon the batter into the madeleine pans, filling them three-quarters full. Place in the oven and immediately reduce the temperature to 350°F (180°C) convection. Bake for 10 to 12 minutes, until well risen and golden.

GLAZE AND FINISH

5. Meanwhile, in a medium bowl, combine the confectioners' sugar with the raspberry purée, raspberry liqueur, water, and coloring. The texture should be smooth and creamy, but not too runny. Heat the raspberry jam over low heat and keep warm.

6. When the madeleines come out of the oven, switch it off so it begins to cool. Drizzle the madeleines with the eau-de-vie, then brush the tops (the side with the bump) with the jam. Let cool slightly, then carefully turn the madeleines out of the pans onto a rack for a few minutes, until the jam sets.

7. Return the madeleines to the pans, brush the tops with the glaze, and sprinkle with the silver balls, if using. Let dry for a few minutes, then warm in the oven for about 30 seconds to dry the glaze. Decorate with the sliced raspberries.

Note: Instead of the glaze, you can use Fondant Icing (p. 17) and color it pink.

PISTACHIO CAKE WITH PISTACHIO WHIPPED CREAM AND RASPBERRIES

Serves 8

Cake

7 tablespoons (4 oz. / 110 g) unsalted butter, softened, plus more for brushing

½ cup minus 1 tablespoon (1¾ oz. / 50 g) all-purpose flour, plus more for dusting

1 cup minus 3 tablespoons (3 oz. / 80 g) almond flour

1½ tablespoons (15 g) cornstarch

½ teaspoon (2 g) baking powder

1 cup (4½ oz. / 130 g) confectioners' sugar

1 tablespoon plus 1 teaspoon (20 ml) neutral oil

1½ oz. (40 g) pistachio paste, well softened

2 extra-large eggs, separated

2 tablespoons (1 oz. / 30 g) lightly beaten egg

1 tablespoon plus 1 teaspoon (20 ml) whole milk

2½ tablespoons (1 oz. / 30 g) granulated sugar

Pistachio whipped cream

1¾ cups (400 ml) heavy cream

2¾ oz. (80 g) pistachio paste, well softened

Assembly

Barely Sweet Raspberry Jam (p. 17)

8 oz. (180 g) raspberries

¼ cup (1 oz. / 30 g) peeled pistachios, very coarsely chopped

Equipment

A 6- to 7-inch (15- to 16-cm) brioche mold

A pastry bag, optional

CAKE

1. Preheat the oven to 350°F (180°C) convection. Brush the brioche mold with butter and dust with flour. In a medium bowl, whisk the all-purpose flour with the almond flour, cornstarch, and baking powder.

2. In a large bowl, beat the butter with the confectioners' sugar, oil, pistachio paste, egg yolks, beaten egg, and milk. In a medium bowl, whisk the egg whites with the granulated sugar until they hold a soft peak and carefully fold into the butter mixture. Fold in the dry ingredients.

3. Spread the batter in the brioche mold and bake for about 15 minutes, until golden and well risen.

PISTACHIO WHIPPED CREAM

4. In a medium bowl, whip the cream until it holds a firm peak, then carefully fold in the pistachio paste.

ASSEMBLY

5. Scoop out a hollow in the cake and fill with the jam and raspberries, reserving a few for decorating. Cut the reserved raspberries lengthwise in half. Pipe or spoon the pistachio whipped cream on top and decorate with the raspberry halves and pistachios.

Sunday

A day to roll up your sleeves and bake something special for family and friends—a decadent charlotte (p. 277) is a French classic that never fails to impress.

STRAWBERRY CHARLOTTE

Serves 12

1 lb. 8 oz. (700 g) strawberries (see Note)

5 sheets (10 g) 200 bloom gelatin

2 cups (500 ml) heavy cream, well chilled

⅓ cup (2½ oz. / 70 g) granulated sugar

3 tablespoons plus 1 teaspoon water

2 teaspoons (10 ml) kirsch

1 recipe Pink Ladyfinger Sponge Cake (p. 11), biscuits plus two 9-inch (20-cm) disks

A few almonds, preferably green almonds, shelled

Confectioners' sugar for dusting

Equipment
A 10-inch (24-cm) dessert ring, soufflé dish, or other deep bowl

(Recipe continues on the following page)

STRAWBERRY CHARLOTTE

1.   An hour ahead, place a large bowl, preferably metal, in the freezer. You'll need it to whip the cream.

2.   In a food processor or blender, purée 14 oz. (400 g) of the strawberries until smooth and strain through a fine sieve.

3.   In a medium bowl of very cold water, soften the gelatin.

4.   Pour the cream into the chilled bowl and whip, gradually adding ¼ cup (1¾ oz. / 50 g) of the granulated sugar, until it holds a soft peak; chill.

5.   Squeeze the gelatin dry and place in a large metal bowl. Set over a saucepan of simmering water to melt. Remove the bowl from the heat, add 2¾ oz. (80 g) of the strawberry purée, and whisk until smooth. Whisk in 6 oz. (175 g) of the purée. Using a silicone spatula, carefully fold in the whipped cream.

6.   In a small saucepan, combine the remaining 1 tablespoon plus 2 teaspoons (20 g) granulated sugar with the water and bring to a boil. Remove the syrup from the heat and stir in the remaining strawberry purée and the kirsch.

7.   If using a dessert ring, line a baking sheet with parchment paper and place the ring in the center. Stand the biscuits around the rim, smooth side out. Set a disk in the base and brush lightly with the syrup.

8.   Spread a layer of mousse just under ½ inch (1 cm) deep in the ring. Slice the remaining strawberries and arrange some of them on the mousse. Using an offset spatula, smooth the mousse. Set the second disk on top and brush lightly with syrup. Cover with the remaining mousse and chill for 15 minutes.

9.   Mound the remaining strawberries on top, pressing lightly, and decorate with the almonds. Carefully remove the cake ring. Dust with confectioners' sugar. Chill for at least 2 hours, until set.

Note: You'll need 9 oz. (250 g) strained strawberry purée for the mousse in Step 5 and 1¾ oz. (50 g) for the syrup in Step 6.

Prep:
10 minutes

Chill:
1 hour

Cook:
12 minutes

RAISIN SCONES

Makes 10 to 15 scones, depending on size

⅔ cup (3½ oz. / 100 g) raisins

4½ cups (14 oz. / 400 g) cake flour, plus more for dusting

2 tablespoons plus ½ teaspoon (1 oz. / 25 g) baking powder

Scant ½ cup (3 oz. / 90 g) granulated sugar

3 tablespoons plus 1 teaspoon (1¾ oz. / 50 g) unsalted butter, diced, room temperature

1 whole egg

⅔ cup (150 ml) milk

1 egg yolk, lightly beaten

1. A day ahead, soak the raisins in a bowl of hot water (unless you're in a hurry!).

2. In a large bowl, whisk the flour with the baking powder and sugar. Add the butter and rub into the flour mixture until grainy. Switch to a wooden spoon and stir in the whole egg and milk.

3. Drain the raisins and stir them into the dough, then knead lightly. Transfer the dough to a sheet of parchment paper and cover with another sheet. Roll out the dough 1¼ inches (3 cm) thick. Transfer the dough between the parchment to a baking sheet and chill for 1 hour.

4. Preheat the oven to 465°F (240°C) convection.

5. Carefully peel off the top parchment. Cut the dough into triangles. Brush the tops with the beaten egg yolk.

6. Bake the scones for 6 minutes, then reduce the oven temperature to 410°F (210°C) convection and cook for 6 to 7 minutes. To test for doneness, break a scone in half; the inside should be barely done. Let cool on a rack.

Prep:
50 minutes

Chill:
1 hour

Cook:
20 minutes

VANILLA COOKIE TOWER

Makes about 20 cookies

2¾ cups (9 oz. / 250 g)
cake flour

Scant ⅓ cup (1 oz. / 30 g)
almond flour

¾ cup (3⅓ oz. / 95 g)
confectioners' sugar

½ teaspoon fleur de sel

1 teaspoon vanilla bean powder

1 egg

1 stick plus 2 tablespoons
(5¼ oz. / 150 g) unsalted butter,
diced, room temperature

Equipment

Assorted cookie cutters

A pastry tip or skewer

A 12-inch (30-cm) polystyrene
cone with a 5-inch
(12-cm) base

A sheet of white parchment
paper or decorative food-safe
paper to cover the cone

Wooden skewers

1. In the bowl of a stand mixer fitted with the paddle, combine the cake flour with the almond flour, confectioners' sugar, fleur de sel, and vanilla bean powder at low speed.

2. Increase the speed to medium and beat in the egg and butter until the dough forms a ball. Shape into a disk, cover with plastic wrap, and chill for 1 hour.

3. Preheat the oven to 350°F (180C°). Transfer the dough to a sheet of parchment paper and cover with another sheet. Roll out the dough ⅛ inch (4 mm) thick. Transfer the dough between the parchment to another baking sheet and chill for a few minutes, until firm.

4. Carefully peel off the top parchment. Using the cutters, press out cookies. Using the small end of a pastry tip, pierce a hole in each one. Bake for 20 minutes, until light golden.

5. Cover the cone with white parchment paper. Using the wooden skewers, affix the cookies to the cone.

Note: This original, festive recipe was created by Françoise Vauzeilles.

Prep:
20 minutes

Cook (original version):
25 minutes

Chill (new version):
2 to 12 hours

SONIA RYKIEL'S CHOCOLATE POTS

Serves 8

Original version
2 cups (500 ml) whole milk
3½ oz. (100 g) 70% dark chocolate
¾ oz. (20 g) 100% dark chocolate
4 egg yolks
½ cup (3 ½ oz. / 100 g) granulated sugar

Equipment
8 ramekins

New version
6 oz. (175 g) 72% dark chocolate, preferably Valrhona® Guanaja
1 cup (250 ml) whole milk
1 cup (250 ml) heavy cream
4 egg yolks
½ cup minus 1 tablespoon (2¾ oz. / 80 g) granulated sugar

Equipment
8 heatproof cups

ORIGINAL VERSION

1. Preheat the oven to 400°F (200°C) convection. In a medium saucepan, heat the milk with the two chocolates over medium-high heat, whisking constantly, until smooth. Remove from the heat.

2. In a medium bowl, whisk the egg yolks with the sugar until dissolved. Whisk the yolk-sugar mixture into the hot milk mixture. Strain into a medium glass measuring cup. Divide among the ramekins.

3. Place the ramekins on a baking sheet, cover with foil, and bake for 25 minutes.

NEW VERSION

4. Finely chop the chocolate and place in a medium bowl.

5. In a medium saucepan, heat the milk and cream over medium-high heat until bubbles appear around the edge; remove from the heat. In a

medium bowl, whisk the egg yolks with the sugar until pale and thick.

6. Whisk the yolk-sugar mixture into the hot milk mixture. Reduce the heat to low and cook, whisking constantly, until the mixture thickens; do not let boil. Remove from the heat.

7. Gradually pour over the chocolate, stirring constantly with a wooden spoon, until smooth. If necessary, process briefly using an immersion blender. Keep the blender well immersed to avoid creating bubbles.

8. Strain into a medium glass measuring cup. Divide among the cups and chill for 2 to 12 hours.

Note: The late fashion designer Sonia Rykiel kindly shared this recipe with me.

Prep:
30 minutes

Chill:
about 1 hour

Cook:
12 to 20 minutes

RUM–GLAZED ALMOND COOKIES

Makes about 30 cookies

Almond cream

4 tablespoons (2 oz. / 60 g)
unsalted butter, softened

⅓ cup (2 oz. / 60 g)
granulated sugar

¾ cup (2 oz. / 60 g)
almond flour

1½ teaspoons (5 g) cornstarch

1 egg, lightly beaten

½ teaspoon (2 ml) dark rum

Cookie batter

1 cup (3½ oz. / 100 g)
almond flour

1 scant cup (6 oz. / 180 g)
granulated sugar, divided

1 tablespoon plus 1 teaspoon
(10 g) all-purpose flour

7 egg whites

Chopped almonds for
sprinkling

Confectioners' sugar for
dusting

Rum glaze

2 tablespoons plus 1 teaspoon
(35 ml) water

2 tablespoons (30 ml)
dark rum

1¼ cups (6 oz. / 160 g)
confectioners' sugar

Equipment

A pastry bag fitted with a plain
½-inch (10-mm) tip, optional

ALMOND CREAM

1. In the bowl of a stand mixer fitted with the whisk, whip the butter with the sugar, almond flour, and cornstarch until smooth. Gradually whisk in the egg and rum. Cover and chill for 1 hour.

COOKIE BATTER

2. Preheat the oven to 350°F (180°C) convection. Line a baking sheet with parchment paper. Whisk the almond flour with ½ cup minus 1 tablespoon (2¾ oz. / 80 g) of the sugar, and the all-purpose flour.

3. In the bowl of a stand mixer fitted with the whisk, whip the egg whites, gradually adding the remaining ½ cup (3½ oz. / 100 g) sugar, until they hold a soft peak. Fold in the dry ingredients.

4. Pipe or spoon the batter into 1¼-inch (3-cm) rings onto the baking sheet. Sprinkle with the chopped almonds.

5. Pipe or spoon a thin layer of almond cream into the center of the rings. Dust the cookies with confectioners' sugar. Bake for 15 to 20 minutes, until lightly colored and beginning to firm up. Let cool slightly on the baking sheet, then transfer the cookies to a rack to cool completely. Leave the oven on.

RUM GLAZE

6. In a small bowl, stir the water with the rum and confectioners' sugar until smooth. Spoon a little into the center of each cookie. Return the cookies to the baking sheet and bake in the oven for a few minutes, until the glaze forms a crust.

CARROT CAKE
WITH ORANGE MERINGUE FROSTING

Serves 8

Carrot cake

Unsalted butter for brushing

4 eggs, separated

1 cup minus 2 tablespoons
(6 oz. / 175 g) light brown sugar

Finely grated zest and juice
of 1 lemon

1 cup minus 2½ tablespoons
(2½ oz. / 75 g) cake flour

½ teaspoon fine salt

2 cups minus 3 tablespoons
(6 oz. / 175 g) almond flour

Scant ½ cup (1¾ oz. / 50 g)
chopped pecans

1 teaspoon cinnamon

½ teaspoon grated fresh or
ground ginger

1 pinch gingerbread spice mix

10½ oz. (300 g) peeled, finely
grated carrots

2½ tablespoons (1 oz. / 25 g)
raisins

1 tablespoon plus 1 teaspoon
(20 ml) orange juice

Orange meringue

3 egg whites

1 cup minus 1½ tablespoons
(6¼ oz. / 180 g) granulated
sugar, divided

Finely grated zest of ½ orange

Pecan halves for garnishing

Confectioners' sugar for
dusting

Equipment

A springform pan or loaf pan

A pastry bag fitted with a
Saint-Honoré tip, optional

CARROT CAKE

1. Preheat the oven to 350°F (180°C) convection.
Generously brush the springform pan with butter.

2. In a food processor, blend the egg yolks with the
brown sugar until light and thick. Pulse in the lemon
zest, then the cake flour, salt, almond flour, pecans,
cinnamon, ginger, and spice mix.

3. Pulse in the grated carrots and lemon juice.
Pulse in the raisins and orange juice. Transfer to a
medium bowl.

4. In a separate bowl, whisk the egg whites until they
hold a soft peak. Carefully fold into the carrot batter.

5. Spread the batter in the pan and bake for 40 to 50
minutes, until a tester inserted into the center comes
out clean. Transfer to a rack and let cool completely.

ORANGE MERINGUE

6. Increase the oven temperature to 400°F (200°C)
convection. Using an electric beater, whisk the egg
whites until frothy. Gradually whisk in a scant ½ cup
(3 oz. / 90 g) of the granulated sugar until the mixture
holds a firm peak, then whisk in the remaining scant
½ cup (3 oz. / 90 g) granulated sugar and the orange
zest, reserving a little zest for sprinkling. Whisk for
10 seconds.

7. Pipe or spoon the meringue around the rim of
the cake. Garnish the top with the pecans. Dust with
confectioners' sugar and bake for 6 to 7 minutes,
until lightly browned. Sprinkle with the remaining
orange zest.

Note: The cake mixture can also be baked in a muffin
pan to make mini carrot cakes.

Prep:
50 minutes

Chill:
1 hour

Cook:
1 hour 20 minutes

STACKED MATCHA AND PISTACHIO COOKIE CAKE
Mandelbari

∞∞∞∞∞∞∞∞∞∞∞∞∞∞∞∞∞∞∞∞∞∞

Serves 6

Pistachio cookies

⅓ cup (1½ oz. / 40 g) peeled pistachios

1⅔ cups (5¼ oz. / 150 g) cake flour

½ teaspoon (2 g) baking powder

1 teaspoon Pure Pistachio Paste (p. 19),
well softened

1 stick plus 2 teaspoons (4½ oz. / 125 g)
unsalted butter, softened

Scant ⅓ cup (2 oz. / 60 g) granulated sugar

1 egg yolk

Meringue

4 egg whites

1¼ cups (8½ oz. / 240 g) granulated sugar

1 teaspoon (4 g) matcha tea

Assembly

Chopped pistachios

Pumpkin seeds

Confectioners' sugar

Equipment

A set of graduated round cookie cutters

A pastry bag fitted with a fluted
¾-inch (18-mm) tip, optional

STACKED MATCHA AND
PISTACHIO COOKIE CAKE

PISTACHIO COOKIES

1. In a food processor, grind the pistachios into a fine powder. In the bowl of a stand mixer, whisk the cake flour with the baking powder and ground pistachios. Add the pistachio paste, butter, granulated sugar, and egg yolk.

2. Fit the dough hook to the stand mixer and beat the ingredients until smooth. Alternatively, knead with your hands. Shape the dough into a disk, cover with plastic wrap, and chill for at least 1 hour.

3. Preheat the oven to 320°F (160°C) convection. Line 2 baking sheets with parchment paper. On a lightly floured work surface, roll out the dough about ⅛ inch (4 mm) thick. Beginning with the largest cookie cutter plus a size that enables you to cut out a disk to form a ring, cut out two cookie rings.

4. Using the next size down, cut out two cookie rings. Continue to cut out increasingly smaller pairs of rings. Arranging the cookies by size, place on the baking sheets.

5. Bake for about 20 minutes, rotating the pans halfway through, until nicely golden. Let cool slightly on the baking sheet. They should still be warm when you pipe the meringue over them.

MERINGUE

6. Reduce the oven temperature to 195°F (90°C) convection.

7. In the bowl of a stand mixer fitted with the whisk, whip the egg whites until frothy, then add a little of the sugar. Whip until they hold a soft peak. Gradually add the remaining sugar, whisking for 10 minutes, until the egg whites hold a firm glossy peak. Add the matcha and whisk for 1 minute.

ASSEMBLY

8. Pipe or spoon dollops of the meringue onto the cookie rings. Decorate each ring with a few pistachios and pumpkin seeds.

9. Bake for 1 hour, then let cool completely.

10. Just before serving, dust each meringue-topped cookie with confectioners' sugar. Starting with the largest cookies, stack them to make the mandelbari tower.

Original recipe by Christelle Aron.

We have revisited the mandelbari recipe,
adding two of today's subtle flavors,
matcha and pistachio. The meringue here is baked
slowly to give it a crisp crust and a melting texture.
This recipe is dedicated to lovers of new,
sophisticated tastes.

Prep:
1 hour 30 minutes

Chill:
1 to 2 hours

Cook:
25 to 30 minutes

BRETON CAKE
WITH ALMOND BLANCMANGE AND APRICOTS

Serves 8

Breton cake

1 stick plus 2 teaspoons (4½ oz. / 125 g) unsalted butter, softened, plus more for brushing and sautéing

3 tablespoons (1¼ oz. / 35 g) light brown sugar, plus more for sprinkling

1 cup (4½ oz. / 125 g) all-purpose flour

¼ teaspoon (1 g) baking powder

Scant ½ cup (3 oz. / 95 g) granulated sugar, divided, plus more for sautéing

1 pinch fine salt

¼ teaspoon vanilla bean powder

2½ egg yolks

3 egg whites

12 oz. (350 g) ripe apricots

1 tablespoon plus 1 teaspoon (20 ml) apricot eau-de-vie

½ teaspoon lemon juice

Generous ¼ cup (1¾ oz. / 50 g) natural almonds

Almond blancmange

3 sheets (6 g) 200 bloom gelatin

¾ cup (200 ml) whole milk

½ cup minus 1½ tablespoons (100 ml) orgeat syrup

1½ cups (350 ml) heavy cream

Assembly

Apricot jam, warmed, for brushing

Thinly sliced apricots and a few whole or chopped natural almonds for decorating

Equipment

A pastry bag fitted with a ⅓-inch (8 mm) plain tip, optional

A 10-inch (24-cm) cake ring, 1¼ cm (3 cm) deep, or springform pan

BRETON CAKE

1. Preheat the oven to 320°F (160°C) convection. If using a cake ring, line a baking sheet with parchment paper and place the ring in the center. Brush the ring with butter and sprinkle with brown sugar. Sift the flour with the baking powder.

2. In a large bowl, whisk the butter with ⅓ cup (2½ oz. / 75 g) of the granulated sugar until light and fluffy. Whisk in the salt and vanilla bean powder.

3. In medium bowl, whisk the egg yolks with the light brown sugar until thick and creamy, then whisk into the butter mixture.

4. In a separate medium bowl, whisk the egg whites with the remaining 1 tablespoon plus 2 teaspoons (20 g) granulated sugar until they hold a soft peak. Carefully fold into the butter-egg yolk mixture. Fold in the dry ingredients.

5. Pipe or spoon the batter into the ring. Cut about 5 oz. (150 g) of the apricots in half and press into the batter. Bake for 25 to 30 minutes. Drizzle with eau-de-vie.

6. Quarter the remaining apricots and sauté in butter and sugar. Drizzle with the lemon juice.

ALMOND BLANCMANGE

7. In a medium bowl of very cold water, soften the gelatin.

8. In a small saucepan, heat the milk over medium-high heat until bubbles appear around the edge; remove from the heat. Squeeze the gelatin dry and stir into the hot milk with the orgeat syrup; let cool. In a medium bowl, whisk the cream until it holds a soft peak. Fold the whipped cream into the milk mixture. Chill for 1 to 2 hours, until set.

ASSEMBLY

9. Brush a little apricot jam on the Breton cake. Arrange the sautéed apricots on top, leaving a 1-inch (3-cm) border. Pipe or spoon the almond blancmange around the border. Freeze the cake for a few minutes, until the blancmange sets, then pipe or spread the rest over the top.

10. Chill until set. Top with the sliced apricots and almonds.

Prep:
45 minutes

Chill:
12 hours

Cook:
15 minutes

VANILLA–STRAWBERRY CAKES

Makes 8 small cakes

Strawberry jam

1¼ cups (9 oz. / 250 g) granulated sugar, divided

9 oz. (250 g) strawberries

½ teaspoon (2 g) pectin, optional

1 teaspoon (5 ml) lemon juice

Praline cakes

7 tablespoons (4 oz. / 110 g) unsalted butter, softened, plus more for brushing

½ cup minus 1 tablespoon (1¾ oz. / 50 g) all-purpose flour, plus more for dusting

1 cup (4½ oz. / 130 g) confectioners' sugar

1 tablespoon plus 1 teaspoon (20 ml) neutral oil

Pure Hazelnut Praline Paste

1½ oz. (40 g) Hazelnut Praline (p. 16), well softened

2 extra-large eggs, separated, plus 2 tablespoons (1 oz. / 30 g) lightly beaten egg

1 tablespoon plus 1 teaspoon (20 ml) whole milk

2½ tablespoons (1 oz. / 30 g) granulated sugar

Scant ½ cup (1½ oz. / 40 g) almond flour

Scant ½ cup (1 ½ oz. / 40 g) ground hazelnuts, toasted

1½ tablespoons (15 g) cornstarch

½ teaspoon (2 g) baking powder

Assembly

2 vanilla beans

1¾ cups (400 ml) heavy cream, divided

3½ tablespoons (1½ oz. / 40 g) granulated sugar

8 oz. (250 g) strawberries

8 small mint leaves

Equipment

8 individual brioche molds or muffin cups

A pastry bag fitted with a fluted tip, optional

STRAWBERRY JAM

1. Twelve hours ahead, start the jam: Reserve 2½ teaspoons (10 g) of the sugar. In a medium bowl, toss the strawberries with the remaining sugar and chill for 12 hours. In a medium saucepan, cook the strawberries over low heat, stirring constantly, until softened. Combine the pectin NH with the reserved sugar and stir into the strawberries. Let simmer for a few minutes, or longer if not using the pectin, then stir in the lemon juice and remove from the heat.

PRALINE CAKES

2. Preheat the oven to 350°F (180°C) convection. Brush the molds with butter and dust with flour. In a large bowl, beat the butter with the confectioners' sugar, oil, praline, egg yolks, beaten egg, and milk.

3. In a medium bowl, whisk the egg whites with the granulated sugar until they hold a soft peak, then fold into the praline mixture. Whisk the all-purpose flour with the almond flour, ground hazelnuts, cornstarch, and baking powder and fold into the batter.

4. Spread the batter in the molds, set on a baking sheet, and bake for about 15 minutes, until a tester inserted into the center comes out clean.

ASSEMBLY

5. Split the vanilla beans lengthwise and scrape out the seeds. In a medium saucepan, heat ⅔ cup (150 ml) of the cream with the vanilla beans and seeds over medium-high heat until bubbles appear around the edge. Let cool completely. Remove the vanilla beans and whisk in the remaining cream and the sugar. In a medium bowl, whisk the cream until it holds a medium-firm peak.

6. Reserve 8 small strawberries. Scoop out a hollow in the center of each cake and fill with the jam and remaining strawberries. Pipe or spoon the whipped cream on top and decorate with a reserved strawberry and a mint leaf.

ALMOND–CHERRY TARTLETS
Les Amandines aux cerises

Makes 10 tartlets

9 oz. (250 g) Sweet
Almond Pastry (p. 10)

1 stick plus 2 teaspoons
(4½ oz. / 125 g) unsalted butter,
softened, plus more
for brushing

⅔ cup (4½ oz. / 125 g)
granulated sugar

1½ cups (4½ oz. / 125 g)
ground almonds

2 eggs

1 drop kirsch

5 oz. (150 g) sweet cherries
or sour cherries

1½ cups (5 oz. / 150 g)
sliced almonds

1¾ oz. (50 g) candied
cherries, halved

Confectioners' sugar
for dusting

Equipment
10 individual brioche molds or
muffin cups

1. On a lightly floured work surface, roll out the pastry ⅛ inch (3 mm) thick. Line the brioche molds with the pastry, prick with a fork, and chill until needed.

2. Preheat the oven to 340°F (170°C) convection. In a medium bowl, whisk the butter with half of the granulated sugar, half of the ground almonds, and 1 egg until smooth. Whisk in the remaining granulated sugar, ground almonds, and egg, then whisk in the kirsch until very smooth.

3. Remove the cherry stems. Cut the cherries in half and remove the pits. Pipe or spread some of the almond cream in the tart shells.

4. Arrange the cherry halves, packing them tightly, over the almond cream, then fill the tart shells with the remaining almond cream. Decorate with the almond slices, arranging them evenly over the top.

5. Set the tartlets on a baking sheet and bake for about 30 minutes, until the almond cream is set. Let cool slightly in the molds, then carefully remove from the molds and let cool completely on a rack. Dust very lightly with confectioners' sugar and decorate with a candied cherry.

Note: Children enjoy arranging the sliced almonds on top of the almond cream in Step 4.

PÂTISSERIE BOURGUIGNON'S
APRICOT TART

Serves 8

Light brown sugar for sprinkling
9 oz. (250 g) Quick Puff Pastry (p. 12), chilled
1½ 15-oz. (425 g) cans apricot halves, drained(1 lb. 8 oz. / 700 g) net weight
½ cup minus 1 tablespoon (2¾ oz. / 80 g) granulated sugar
4 tablespoons (2 oz. / 60 g) unsalted butter, melted

Equipment
A 10-inch (24-cm) tart ring or pan

1. Sprinkle a work surface with the light brown sugar and roll out the pastry to make an 11-inch (28-cm) disk.

2. Prick the pastry with a fork. If using a tart ring, line a baking sheet with parchment paper and place the ring in the center. Line the tart ring with the pastry and chill for at least 10 minutes.

3. Drain the apricots.

4. Preheat the oven to 400°F (200°C) convection. Cut the apricot halves into two and pack them tightly in the pastry shell.

5. Bake the tart for about 1 hour, sprinkling the apricots occasionally with the granulated sugar and brushing with the butter. Let cool.

Note: This recipe comes from the Pâtisserie Bourguignon in Metz, a store that's been in the same family for generations.

HAZELNUT MERINGUE CAKE
Dacquoise Paris-Brest

Serves 8

Hazelnut meringue

1⅓ cups (6 oz. / 170 g)
confectioners' sugar,
plus more for dusting

1¾ cup (5¼ oz. / 150 g)
ground hazelnuts

6 egg whites

¼ cup plus 1 tablespoon
(2 oz. / 55 g) granulated sugar

3 tablespoons (1 oz. / 30 g)
hazelnuts, chopped

Hazelnut cream

7 oz. (200 g) Pastry Cream
(p. 14), chilled

4 tablespoons plus 1 teaspoon
(2¼ oz. / 65 g) unsalted butter,
room temperature

4 oz. (115 g) Pure Hazelnut
Praline Paste

1¼ oz. (35 g) hazelnut paste,
well softened

Scant ⅓ cup (70 ml)
heavy cream

Equipment

A pastry bag fitted with a plain
⅓-inch (10-mm) tip, optional

HAZELNUT MERINGUE

1. Preheat the oven to 350°F (180°C) convection.
Line a baking sheet with parchment paper. Draw two
9-inch (22-cm) circles on the paper and turn it over.
Sift the confectioners' sugar into a medium bowl and
stir in the ground hazelnuts.

2. In a large bowl, whisk the egg whites, gradually
adding the granulated sugar, until they hold a soft
peak. Fold in the ground hazelnut mixture. Using the
circles as a guide, pipe or spread meringue disks on
the baking sheet.

3. Sprinkle the meringue disks with the chopped
hazelnuts and dust with the confectioners' sugar.
Bake for 20 to 25 minutes, until a thin crust forms
and the disks are springy to the touch.

4. Carefully transfer to a rack and let cool.

HAZELNUT CREAM

5. In a medium bowl, briskly whisk the Pastry
Cream until it's as soft as mayonnaise.

6. Using an electric beater, whisk the butter with
the praline and hazelnut paste until very light and
creamy. Whisk in the Pastry Cream until firm but
pliable. In a medium bowl, whisk the cream until it
holds a soft peak. Using a silicone spatula, carefully
fold the whipped cream into the praline mixture. Let
stand at room temperature until needed.

7. Place a meringue disk on a serving plate. Pipe or
spread the hazelnut cream evenly over the disk.

8. Place the second disk on top and dust with
confectioners' sugar.

Prep:
1 hour

Chill:
1 to 2 hours

Cook:
25 minutes

GLUTEN–FREE VANILLA–MANGO CAKE

∞∞∞∞∞∞∞∞∞∞∞∞∞∞∞∞∞∞∞∞∞∞∞∞∞∞∞∞∞∞∞∞

Serves 8

Pecan sponge cake

1 egg yolk

1 medium egg

1 cup minus 3 tablespoons
(5½ oz. / 160 g) granulated
sugar, divided

Generous ¼ cup (1½ oz. / 45 g)
potato starch (see Note)

3 egg whites

Generous ½ cup (2½ oz. / 70 g)
pecans, chopped

Mango-passion fruit cream

1 sheet (2g) 200 gold
bloom gelatin

3 oz. (90 g) mango purée

1 oz. (30 g) passion fruit purée

2 egg yolks

1 medium egg,
lightly beaten

3 tablespoons (1¼ oz. / 35 g)
granulated sugar

3 tablespoons (45 g) unsalted
butter, softened

Assembly

10½ oz. (300 g) Set Vanilla
Cream (p. 16)

Equipment

A 9- to 10-inch (22- to 24-cm)
cake ring or springform pan, at
least 2 inches (5 cm) deep

A pastry bag fitted with a fluted
tip, optional

PECAN SPONGE CAKE

1. Preheat the oven to 350°F (180°C) convection. If
using a cake ring, line a baking sheet with parchment
paper and place the ring in the center. To encourage
the cake layer to stick to the side, do not brush with
butter. In a medium bowl, whisk the egg yolk with
the whole egg and ½ cup minus 1 tablespoon
(2¾ oz. / 80 g) of the sugar until pale and thick.
Whisk in the potato starch.

2. In a medium bowl, whisk the egg whites with the
remaining ½ cup minus 1 tablespoon (2¾ oz. / 80 g)
sugar until they hold a soft peak. Carefully fold into
the egg-potato starch mixture, then stir in the pecans.

3. Spread the cake batter in the cake ring. Bake for
25 minutes, until lightly golden.

MANGO–PASSION FRUIT CREAM

4. In a medium bowl of very cold water, soften
the gelatin.

5. In a medium saucepan, whisk the mango and
passion fruit purées with the egg yolks and whole
egg and then the sugar. Heat to 162°F (72°C), stirring
constantly. Remove from the heat. Squeeze the
gelatin dry and stir in until dissolved. Let cool to
140°F (60°C).

6. Stir in the butter. Chill until set.

7. Run a small knife around the inside of the ring
and carefully remove. Using a long serrated knife,
slice the cake horizontally in half. Mound half of the
fruit cream in the center of each cake half and pipe
or spoon the Vanilla Cream around it. Carefully stack
the two cake halves.

Note: Don't substitute cornstarch for the potato
starch here!

Prep:
40 minutes

Chill:
30 minutes

Cook:
15 to 20 minutes

SIMPLE VANILLA MILLEFEUILLE

Serves 8

No-turn puff pastry

2¼ cups (7 oz. / 200 g)
cake flour

4 teaspoons granulated sugar

2 teaspoons fine salt

2 sticks (8½ oz./ 240 g)
unsalted butter, diced, room
temperature

Caramel glaze

½ cup plus 1½ tablespoons
(140 ml) heavy cream

1 cup minus 1½ tablespoons
(6¼ oz. / 180 g) granulated
sugar, divided

¼ cup (3¼ oz. / 90 g)
glucose or honey

Assembly

1 lb. 7 oz. (650 g) Pastry Cream
(p. 14), chilled

Equipment

A pastry bag fitted with a plain
⅓-inch (10-mm) tip, optional

NO-TURN PUFF PASTRY

1. In a large bowl, whisk the flour with the sugar and salt. Using your palms, rub in the butter until grainy, like couscous. Work in the water until smooth. Shape the dough into a disk, cover with plastic wrap, and chill for 30 minutes.

2. Preheat the oven to 350°F (180°C) convection. On a lightly floured work surface, roll out the pastry into a rectangle the size of your baking sheet, about ⅛ inch (3 to 4 mm) thick. Line the baking sheet with parchment paper, transfer the pastry to the sheet, and prick with a fork. Cover with a second sheet of parchment and place an oven rack directly on top to keep the puff pastry from rising as it bakes.

3. Bake for 15 to 20 minutes, until golden, then let cool to room temperature.

CARAMEL GLAZE

4. In a medium saucepan, heat the cream with a scant ½ cup (3 oz. / 90 g) of the sugar over medium-high heat, whisking constantly until bubbles appear around the edge and the sugar dissolves; remove from the heat. In a small saucepan, cook the remaining scant ½ cup (3 oz. / 90 g) of the sugar with the glucose over medium-high heat, stirring constantly with a wooden spoon, until it's a light caramel color; remove from the heat. Carefully pour in the warm cream and return to the heat, stirring constantly, until the temperature reaches 230°F (110°C). Remove from the heat, cover the pan with plastic wrap, and let cool to between 130°F (55°C) and 115°F (45°C).

ASSEMBLY AND FINISH

5. In a medium bowl, briskly whisk the Pastry Cream until it's as soft as mayonnaise.

6. Cut the pastry into three equal rectangles. Pipe or spread half of the Pastry Cream over two rectangles. Carefully stack them, then top with the remaining rectangle. Using a thin metal spatula, spread the top with the caramel glaze.

Notes: Remarkably, this no-turn puff pastry's texture is very similar to the traditional variety with much less effort!

Please note that the pastry is a little soft because of the water.

PISTACHIO–RASPBERRY LAYER CAKE

Serves 10

Pistachio cake

1 egg

2 egg yolks

½ oz. (15 g) Pure Pistachio Paste
(p. 19), well softened

Generous ½ cup (2¾ oz. / 75 g)
confectioners' sugar

Scant ½ cup (1½ oz. / 40 g)
almond flour

Generous ⅓ cup (1 oz. / 30 g)
ground pistachios

½ cup minus 1 tablespoon
(1¾ oz. / 50 g) all-purpose flour

3½ egg whites

3 tablespoons (1¼ oz. / 35 g)
granulated sugar

⅓ cup (1¾ oz. / 50 g) peeled
pistachios, chopped

Pistachio cream

2 sheets (4 g) 200
bloom gelatin

2 egg yolks

1½ tablespoons (15 g)
cornstarch

2½ tablespoons (1 oz. / 30 g)
granulated sugar

¾ cup (200 ml) whole milk

3½ oz. (100 g) white
chocolate, chopped

1 oz. (25 g) Pure Pistachio Paste
(p. 19), well softened

1 cup (250 ml) heavy cream

Raspberry syrup

¼ cup (60 ml) water

3 tablespoons (1¼ oz. / 35 g)
granulated sugar

¾ oz. (20 g) raspberry purée

2 teaspoons (10 ml) kirsch

Assembly

7 oz. (200 g) raspberries

Barely Sweet Raspberry Jam
(p. 17), lightly warmed,
for dipping

PISTACHIO CAKE

1. Preheat the oven to 350°F (180°C) convection. Line a 12 by 16-inch (30 by 40-cm) rimmed baking sheet with parchment paper. In a medium bowl, whisk the whole egg with the egg yolks and pistachio paste. Whisk in the confectioners' sugar, then the almond flour and ground pistachios. Sift in the all-purpose flour and fold in.

2. In a medium bowl, whisk the egg whites with the granulated sugar until they hold a soft peak. Carefully fold into the pistachio paste mixture. Spread the batter evenly over the baking sheet and sprinkle with some of the chopped pistachios. Bake for 15 minutes, until a thin crust forms and the pistachio cake is springy to the touch. Let cool.

PISTACHIO CREAM

3. In a medium bowl of very cold water, soften the gelatin. In a separate medium bowl, whisk the egg yolks with the cornstarch. In a medium saucepan, heat the milk over medium-high heat until bubbles appear around the edge. Gradually whisk half into the egg yolk mixture.

4. Return the mixture to the saucepan, stirring constantly, until thickened. Stir in the white chocolate and Pistachio Paste until smooth. Squeeze the gelatin dry and stir in until dissolved. Remove from the heat and let cool to 85°F (30°C). Meanwhile, in a medium bowl, whisk the heavy cream until it holds a soft peak. Fold the whipped cream into the cooled pistachio cream.

RASPBERRY SYRUP

5. In a small saucepan, simmer the water with the granulated sugar and raspberry purée, stirring until the sugar dissolves. Add the kirsch and let cool.

ASSEMBLY

6. Invert the pistachio cake on a clean sheet of parchment paper and peel off the top parchment. Cut the cake in half crosswise. Brush one half with some of the syrup and spread with the pistachio cream. Brush the smooth side of the other half with the syrup and invert on the pistachio cream. Dip the raspberries in the jam and decorate the top of the cake. Sprinkle with the remaining pistachios.

HAZELNUT TART
WITH CITRUS FRUIT

∞∞∞∞∞∞∞∞∞∞∞∞∞∞∞∞∞∞∞∞∞

Serves 8

Breton hazelnut pastry

7 tablespoons (3½ oz. / 100 g) unsalted butter,
softened, plus more for brushing

1 medium egg yolk

½ cup (3½ oz. / 100 g) granulated sugar

Scant ½ teaspoon (2 g) fine salt

¾ cup (2¼ oz. / 65 g) ground hazelnuts

1 cup plus 1 tablespoon (4¾ oz. / 135 g) all-purpose flour

1 scant teaspoon (3.5 g) baking powder

Topping

3 oranges

3 limes

10½ oz. (300 g) Light Citrus Pastry Cream (p. 15)

2 oz. (50 g) redcurrants or raspberries

Confectioners' sugar for dusting

Mint leaves for decorating

Equipment

A 9-inch (22-cm) tart ring or pan

BRETON HAZELNUT PASTRY

1. In a medium bowl, whisk the butter with the egg yolk, sugar, and salt until smooth.

2. Sift the ground hazelnuts with the flour and baking powder into the butter-egg yolk mixture and fold in. Cover with plastic wrap and chill for 30 minutes.

3. Preheat the oven to 340°F (170°C) convection. If using a tart ring, line a baking sheet with parchment paper and place the ring in the center. On a lightly floured work surface, roll out the pastry ⅛ inch (3 mm) thick. Cut out a 9-inch (22-cm) disk and place in the tart ring. Bake for 25 to 30 minutes. Meanwhile, melt a little butter.

4. As soon as the pastry comes out of the oven, brush it with the melted butter. (As it cools and sets, it creates a waterproof layer that prevents the pastry from getting soggy.)

TOPPING

5. Using a small, sharp knife, peel the oranges and limes. Cut in between the membranes to release the segments and drain on paper towels. Spread the pastry cream over the pastry disk and arrange the orange and lime segments and the redcurrants on top.

6. Dust the rim with confectioners' sugar and decorate with mint leaves.

Note: Do try to weigh out the ingredients for the Breton hazelnut pastry. Weight measures are more accurate than volume, so you'll get a better result.

Prep:
20 minutes

Chill:
30 minutes

Cook:
40 to 45 minutes

PISTACHIO–ALMOND CUSTARD TART
Mirliton à la Pistache

Serves 8

10½ oz. (300 g) Sweet
Almond Pastry (p. 10), room
temperature

2 tablespoons plus 1 teaspoon
(1¼ oz. / 35 g) unsalted butter,
melted and cooled

4 eggs

3 tablespoons (15 g)
almond flour

¼ cup (20 g) ground pistachios

1 tablespoon all-purpose flour

¾ cup minus 1 tablespoon
(180 ml) heavy cream

2¼ oz. (65 g) Pistachio Paste
(p. 19), or store-bought,
well softened

1 tablespoon kirsch

10 oz. (300 g) assorted
red berries

Equipment

A 10-inch (24-cm) cake ring
or pan, 1½ inches
(3 to 4 cm) deep

A paper decorating
cone (p. 157)

1. If using a cake ring, line a baking sheet with parchment paper and place the ring in the center. On a lightly floured work surface, roll out the pastry ⅛ inch (3 mm) thick. Line the ring with the pastry. Chill for 30 minutes. If you like, prebake the tart shell; if not, make sure the baking sheet is perforated or very thin aluminum so the pastry bakes all the way through.

2. Preheat the oven to 350°F (180°C) convection. Melt the butter in the microwave or in a small saucepan and let cool.

3. In a medium bowl, whisk the eggs with the almond flour, ground pistachios, all-purpose flour, melted butter, sugar, cream, 1¼ oz. (35 g) of the pistachio paste, and the kirsch.

4. Spread the berries in the tart shell and pour in the custard, filling to the rim.

5. Bake for 40 to 45 minutes, until set and golden. Let the tart cool completely. Using the paper cone, drizzle lines with the remaining 1 oz. (30 g) pistachio paste over the tart.

Note: If you prebaked the pastry and see there are small holes, fill them in with a little custard (⅛ inch / 2 to 3 mm deep) and bake for a few minutes, until set. Then proceed as above.

ALMOND–CHOCOLATE CHIP CAKE
WITH BLACK CURRANT WHIPPED CREAM

⋯⋯⋯⋯⋯⋯⋯⋯⋯⋯⋯⋯⋯⋯⋯⋯⋯

Serves 8

Cake

1 stick plus 2 tablespoons
(5¼ oz. / 150 g) unsalted butter,
softened, plus more
for brushing

½ cup minus 1 tablespoon
(1¾ oz. / 50 g) all-purpose
flour, plus more for dusting

1 cup minus 3 tablespoons
(3 oz. / 80 g) almond flour

1½ tablespoons (15 g)
cornstarch

½ teaspoon (2 g) baking
powder

1 cup (4½ oz. / 130 g)
confectioners' sugar

1 tablespoon plus 1 teaspoon
(20 ml) neutral oil

2 extra-large eggs, separated

2 tablespoons (1 oz. / 30 g)
lightly beaten egg

1 tablespoon plus 1 teaspoon
(20 ml) whole milk

2½ tablespoons (1 oz. / 30 g)
granulated sugar

Generous ½ cup
(3½ oz. / 100 g) chocolate
chips or chopped chocolate

Cherry jam

1 cup (7 oz. / 200 g) granulated
sugar, divided

8 oz. (250 g) sweet cherries

½ teaspoon (2 g) pectin NH,
optional

1 teaspoon (5 ml) kirsch

Topping

1¾ cups (400 ml) heavy cream

10½ oz. (300 g)
black currant purée

2 oz. (50 g) black currants

3½ oz. (100 g) cherries, halved
and pitted

Equipment

A 6- to 8-inch (15- to 20-cm)
brioche mold

A pastry bag fitted with a
fluted tip, optional

CAKE

1. Preheat the oven to 350°F (180°C). Brush the brioche mold with butter and dust with flour. In a medium bowl, whisk the all-purpose flour with the almond flour, cornstarch, and baking powder.

2. In large bowl, beat the butter with the confectioners' sugar, oil, egg yolks, beaten egg, and milk. In a medium bowl, whisk the egg whites with the granulated sugar until they hold a soft peak and carefully fold into the butter mixture. Fold in the dry ingredients.

3. Spread the batter in the brioche mold and add the chocolate chips. Bake for about 15 minutes, until golden and well risen.

CHERRY JAM

4. Reserve 2½ teaspoons (10 g) of the sugar. Halve and pit the cherries. In a medium bowl, combine them with the remaining sugar.

5. In a medium saucepan, cook the cherries over low heat, stirring frequently, until well softened. In a small bowl, combine the pectin NH with the reserved 2½ teaspoons (10 g) sugar and stir into the cherries. Let simmer for a few minutes, or longer if not using pectin, then remove from the heat and stir in the kirsch. Let cool.

TOPPING

6. In a medium bowl, whip the cream until it holds a firm peak, then carefully fold in the black currant purée.

7. Scoop out a hollow in the cake and fill with the cherry jam, black currants, and cherry halves, reserving a few for decorating. Pipe or spoon the black currant whipped cream on top and decorate with the remaining cherry halves.

HAZELNUT–CHOCOLATE BARS
Fondant Pralin Feuilleté

Serves 15

Feuillantine base
A little neutral oil for brushing
13¼ oz. (375 g) Pure Hazelnut Praline Paste (p. 16), well softened
4½ oz. (125 g) 35% white chocolate, melted
8 oz. (225 g) feuillantine flakes or wafer cookies, finely crushed

Ganache
4½ oz. (125 g) 70% dark chocolate,
preferably Valrhona® Guanaja, chopped
3¼ oz. (95 g) 100% dark chocolate, chopped
⅓ cup plus 1 tablespoon (90 ml) heavy cream
4 egg yolks
Scant ⅓ cup (2 oz. / 60 g) sugar
6 tablespoons plus 1 teaspoon (3¼ oz. / 95 g)
unsalted butter, diced, softened
¾ cup (180 ml) lukewarm water

Equipment
A 6 by 8-inch (15 by 20-cm) confectionery frame
or brownie pan

FEUILLANTINE BASE

1. If using a confectionery frame, line a baking sheet with parchment paper and set the frame in the center. Brush with oil. In a large bowl, stir the praline paste with the white chocolate. Stir in the crushed feuillantines. Spread the feuillantine mixture evenly in the frame just under ½ inch (1 cm) thick.

GANACHE

2. In a medium bowl, combine the two chocolates. In a medium saucepan, heat the cream over medium-high heat until bubbles appear around the edge. Pour over the chocolate and stir until smooth. Using an electric beater, whisk the egg yolks with the sugar for 5 minutes, until pale and thick. Stir into the ganache, then stir in the butter. Carefully whisk in the water in several additions.

3. Spread a ¾-inch (1.5-cm) layer of ganache over the feuillantine. Chill for 2 hours, until set. Cut into bars just under ½ inch (1 cm) wide—you can decide on the length.

Note: These melt-in-your-mouth chocolate treats can be stored in the refrigerator or freezer. Just wrap them well.

Prep:
20 minutes

Chill:
2 hours

Cook:
1 hour 10 minutes

STREUSEL–APPLE TART

Serves 8 to 10

Streusel topping

¾ cup plus 2 tablespoons (3½ oz. / 100 g) all-purpose flour

½ cup (3½ oz. / 100 g) granulated sugar

1 cup plus 3 tablespoons (3½ oz. / 100 g) ground almonds

½ teaspoon (2 g) fleur de sel

¾ teaspoon (2 g) cinnamon

7 tablespoons (3½ oz. / 100 g) unsalted butter, diced

Apple tart

2 tablespoons plus 2 teaspoons (1½ oz. / 40 g)
unsalted butter, plus more for brushing

3 lb. (1.5 kg) Belle de Boskoop or other baking apples

3 tablespoons granulated sugar

12 oz. (350 g) Crisp Plain Pastry (p. 9), room temperature

Equipment

A 10-inch (24-cm) tart pan

STREUSEL TOPPING

1. In a medium bowl, whisk the flour with the sugar, ground almonds, fleur de sel, and cinnamon. Squeeze in the butter until the dough forms large crumbs. Chill until needed.

APPLE TART

2. Preheat the oven to 350°F (180°C) convection. Brush the tart pan with butter. Peel and core the apples and cut into large cubes. In a large skillet, melt the butter and cook the apples with the sugar over medium-low heat, stirring often, for about 20 minutes. Remove from the heat.

3. On a lightly floured work surface, roll out the pastry ⅛ inch (3 mm) thick. Line the pan with the pastry and prick with a fork. Shape any remaining pastry into a disk, cover in plastic wrap, and chill to use in another recipe.

4. Cover the pastry with parchment paper and fill with baking beans. Prebake for 30 minutes. Carefully remove the paper with the beans. Spread the apple filling in the shell and sprinkle the streusel over the top.

5. Bake for 40 to 45 minutes. Let cool completely.

RHUBARB–MERINGUE CAKE

Serves 8 to 10

Rhubarb cake

1 lb. (450 g) rhubarb

1 cup minus 2 tablespoons
(6 oz. / 175 g) granulated sugar,
divided

1 stick plus 2 tablespoons
(5¼ oz. / 150 g) unsalted butter,
softened, plus more
for brushing

1⅔ cups (5¼ oz. / 150 g)
cake flour

½ cup (2½ oz. / 75 g) cornstarch

1½ teaspoons (6 g)
baking powder

2 egg yolks

1 whole egg

Vanilla meringue

4 egg whites

1 cup minus 3 tablespoons
(5½ oz. / 160 g)
granulated sugar

1 teaspoon pure vanilla extract

1 teaspoon cornstarch

1 teaspoon white vinegar

Decoration

Sliced rhubarb sprinkled with
vanilla sugar

Confectioners' sugar for
dusting

Equipment

A 10-inch (24-cm) cake pan,
preferably springform

A pastry bag with a decorative
tip of your choice, optional

RHUBARB CAKE

1. Peel the rhubarb and thinly slice. In a medium bowl, toss with 2 tablespoons (1 oz. / 25 g) of the sugar and place in a colander to drain for 2 to 3 hours.

2. Preheat the oven to 350°F (180°C) convection. Brush the cake pan with butter and line with parchment paper. Sift the flour with the cornstarch and baking powder.

3. In a medium bowl, whisk the butter with the remaining ¾ cup (5 ¼ oz. / 150 g) sugar. Whisk in the egg yolks and whole egg. Gradually fold in the dry ingredients.

4. Spread the batter in the cake pan. Smooth the top and spread the rhubarb on top. Bake for 40 minutes. Let cool. Reduce the oven temperature to 320°F (160°C) convection.

VANILLA MERINGUE

5. Meanwhile, in a medium bowl, whisk the egg whites until they hold a firm peak. Gradually whisk in the sugar until smooth and glossy. Whisk in the vanilla, cornstarch, and vinegar.

6. Pipe or spoon the meringue over the cake and bake for 30 minutes. Let the cake cool slightly in the pan, then carefully remove from the pan and let cool completely. Leave the oven on.

DECORATION

7. Spread the rhubarb on a baking sheet and bake for 10 minutes, until tender. Let cool. Arrange on the meringue and dust the rim with confectioners' sugar.

LEMON–POPPY SEED MADELEINES

Makes 12 madeleines

3 tablespoons plus 1 teaspoon (1½ oz. / 45 g) unsalted butter,
plus more for brushing

1 cup (4½ oz. / 125 g) all-purpose flour

1 teaspoon (4 g) baking powder

2 eggs

Scant ⅔ cup (4 oz. / 120 g) granulated sugar

Finely grated zest of 1 lemon

1 tablespoon plus 2 teaspoons (25 ml) whole milk

1 teaspoon (5 ml) lemon juice

⅓ cup (75 ml) extra virgin olive oil

Poppy seeds for sprinkling

Equipment

12 madeleine molds or mini muffin cups

A pastry bag, optional

1. Preheat the oven to 350°F (180°C) convection. Brush the pans with butter. In a small saucepan, melt the butter over medium heat and let cool to lukewarm. Sift the flour with the baking powder.

2. In a medium bowl, briskly whisk the eggs with the sugar for 1 minute, then whisk in the lemon zest.

3. Briskly whisk in the melted butter, then whisk in the milk, lemon juice, and olive oil.

4. Carefully fold in the dry ingredients. If the batter's lumpy, using an immersion blender, mix for a few seconds.

5. Sprinkle the pans with the poppy seeds, then turn upside down and rap gently to remove any excess. Pipe or spoon the batter into the pans, filling three-quarters full.

6. Bake the madeleines for 15 to 20 minutes, until well-risen and golden. Let cool to room temperature in the pans, then carefully turn out onto a rack.

Funday

Any occasion is a good excuse for baking
at home. For special events and celebrations,
why not add a bit of humor with these funny
treats that are sure to make guests smile?

Prep:
1 hour

Chill:
12 hours

Cook:
1 hour

BASIC ROUND CAKE

Serves 6

Vanilla cream

3½ sheets (7 g) 200 bloom gelatin

¾ cup plus 1 tablespoon (190 ml) whole milk

2 vanilla beans, split lengthwise and seeds scraped

8 oz. (225 g) white chocolate, preferably Valrhona® Ivoire, chopped

1⅔ cups (385 ml) heavy cream

Vanilla sponge cake

Neutral oil for brushing

1¼ cups (5½ oz. / 160 g) all-purpose flour

2 tablespoons (20 g) cornstarch

Seeds of ½ vanilla bean

6 eggs

1 cup minus 2½ tablespoons (6 oz. / 170 g) granulated sugar

1 tablespoon plus 1 teaspoon (20 g) unsalted butter

Caramel syrup

1 cup (7 oz./ 200 g) granulated sugar

Seeds of 1 vanilla bean

1¼ cups (300 ml) mineral water

Caramelized apples

2 Golden Delicious or other baking apples

¼ cup (1¾ oz. / 50 g) granulated sugar

Seeds of 1 vanilla bean

2 tablespoons (1 oz. / 30 g) unsalted butter

Assembly

1 lb. 2 oz. (500 g) about 35% almond paste, white or colored, well kneaded

Equipment

A 7-inch (18-cm) domed silicone mold

A fondant smoother

Vanilla cream

1. A day ahead, make the vanilla cream: In a medium bowl of very cold water, soften the gelatin. In a medium saucepan, heat the milk with the vanilla beans and seeds over medium-high heat until bubbles appear around the edge, then remove from the heat. Remove the vanilla beans. Squeeze the gelatin dry and stir in until dissolved. Place the white chocolate in a medium bowl. Stir in the hot milk until smooth. Let cool to about 85°F (30°C), then stir in the heavy cream. Press plastic wrap directly on the surface of the vanilla cream. Let cool and chill, preferably for 12 hours, until needed.

Vanilla sponge cake

2. Preheat the oven to 350°F (180°C) convection. Brush the mold with the oil and place in the center of a baking sheet. Sift the flour with the cornstarch and vanilla seeds.

3. In the bowl of a stand mixer fitted with the whisk, whip the eggs at low speed, gradually adding the sugar. Increase the speed to maximum and whisk for 15 minutes. Meanwhile, melt the butter in a saucepan. Detach the bowl from the mixer and carefully fold in the dry ingredients with a silicone spatula, then the melted butter.

4. Spread the batter in the mold and smooth the top. Cover with foil and bake for 15 minutes. Let the cake cool in the mold, then turn out carefully onto a rack.

Caramel syrup

5. In a medium saucepan, cook a little of the sugar over medium heat until lightly colored. Gradually add the remaining sugar, cooking until it's a lovely caramel color. Stir in the vanilla seeds and cook until it darkens to a deep caramel. Remove from the heat. In a small saucepan, gently heat the mineral water and carefully stir into the caramel. Return the pan to low heat and cook, stirring constantly, until syrupy.

Caramelized apples

6. Peel, core, and cut the apples into small dice. In a medium skillet, cook a little of the sugar over medium heat until lightly colored. Gradually add the remaining sugar, cooking until it's a lovely caramel color. Stir in the vanilla seeds and butter and cook until the butter melts. Stir in the diced apples. Reduce the heat to low and cook for 10 minutes, stirring often. If the caramel thickens too much, stir in a few drops of water. Remove from the heat and let cool.

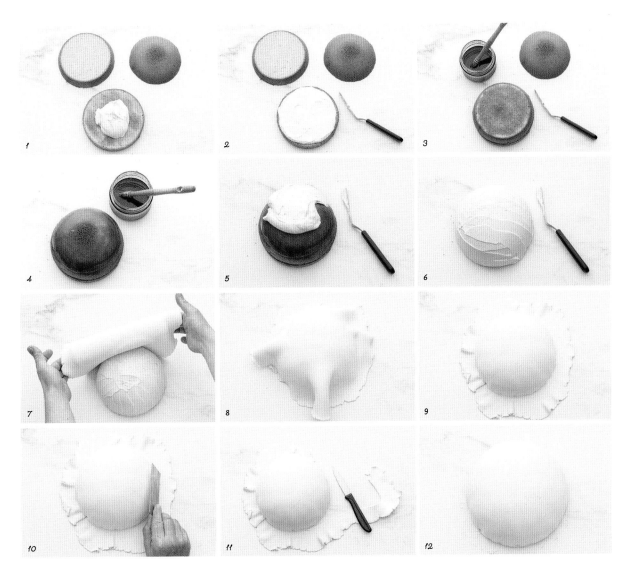

Assembly

1. Using a long serrated knife, cut the cake horizontally into 3 equal layers. Brush the cut side of the bottom layer with the caramel syrup. Whisk the vanilla cream lightly. Spread a thin layer of the cream on top.

2. Dot a few pieces of caramelized apple on the cream and spread with a little more cream.

3. Brush both sides of the middle layer with the caramel syrup. Place on the bottom layer.

4. Repeat with the middle layer, alternating vanilla cream, diced apple, and vanilla cream on top. Lightly brush the cut side of the top layer with caramel syrup and invert it onto the middle layer. Press gently so the cake holds together.

5. Spread the remaining vanilla cream all over the cake.

6. On a lightly floured work surface, roll out the almond paste 1/16 inch (2 mm) thick. Make sure it will cover the cake, allowing some overhang.

7. Carefully wrap the almond paste around a rolling pin and position it to cover the cake evenly.

8. Unroll it to cover the cake entirely. (You can use any excess to make decorations).

9. Gently press the almond paste to remove any air bubbles.

10. Using a fondant smoother, flatten out the paste; the covering should be as even as possible, including around the sides.

11. Using a sharp knife, neatly trim the excess.

12. And voilà, your cake is ready to decorate!

MADAME CHICKEN LICKEN CAKE

Serves 6

About 35% red, orange, white, and black almond paste,
well kneaded

Confectioners' sugar for dusting

Edible glue or water

1 recipe Basic Round Cake (p. 326)

Equipment
Round ⅓-inch (8-mm), 1¼-inch (4-cm), and 2-inch (5-cm) cookie cutters

A fine paintbrush

1. Begin with the red crest. On a work surface dusted with confectioners' sugar, roll out the red almond paste about ⅓ inch (6 to 7 mm) thick. Use a small, sharp knife to cut out the waves and base.

2. To make the orange feet, roll out the orange almond paste just under ¼ inch (4 mm) thick. Using the 2-inch (5-cm) cutter, cut out 2 disks. Press lightly on the sides and use the knife to make 2 incisions to shape the 3 claws. For the beak, cut a diamond that you can pinch a little on the upper half so that it protrudes when you affix it.

3. To make the wings, roll out the white almond paste 1/16 inch (2 mm) thick and cut them out as shown in photo 3.

4. To make the tail, roll 5 balls of white almond paste, each one slightly smaller than the previous one. Pinch one end and lengthen each ball to make 5 cones, each one slightly shorter than the previous one.

5. To make the eyes, roll out a little white almond paste 1/16 inch (2 mm) thick. Repeat with a little black almond paste. Cut out two 1½-inch (4-cm) white

disks and two ⅓-inch (8-mm) black disks. Using a little edible glue, stick a black disk on each of the white disks.

6. Your decorations are now ready to be attached to the cake. Using the paintbrush and a little edible glue, stick the crest, eyes, wings, feet, tail, and beak on the cake. Your cute little chicken is now ready to be presented and eaten.

CLOWNING AROUND CAKE

Serves 6

About 35% red, plain, brown, black, green,
and yellow almond paste, well kneaded

Confectioners' sugar for dusting

Edible glue or water

1 recipe Basic Round Cake (p. 326)

Equipment

A fine paintbrush

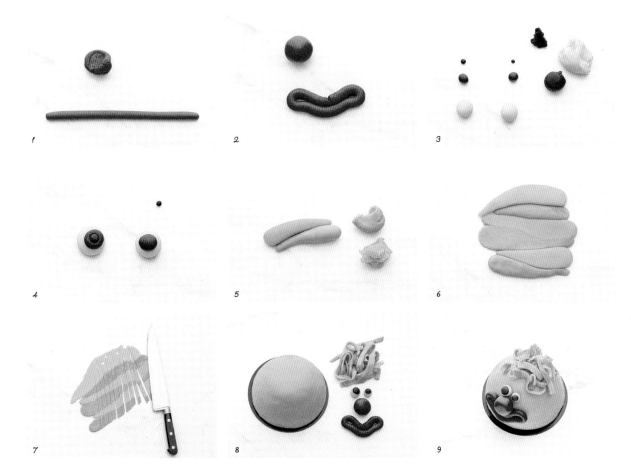

1. You'll need 2 pieces of red almond paste, a small piece for the nose and a long strip for the mouth.

2. Roll the small piece into a ball. Roll the long strip into a thin noodle and join the ends to form the mouth.

3. For the eyes, you'll need plain, brown, and black almond paste. Make 2 balls with the plain paste, 2 smaller balls with the brown paste, and 2 very small balls with the black paste. The balls don't need to be exactly the same size for each color—odd shapes will give your clown an even funnier expression!

4. Make a small indentation in each brown ball. Insert a smaller black ball into each one. Repeat with the plain colored balls, inserting the brown balls. This will result in 2 bulging eyes—even more amusing if differently sized.

5. To make the hair, shape 1 long cone of the same size from a little of both the green and yellow almond paste. Stick one against the other.

6. Repeat to make a slab of cones with alternating colors.

7. On a work surface dusted with confectioners' sugar, roll out the green-and-yellow slab 1/16 inch (2 mm) thick. Using a sharp knife, cut thin strips of striped paste to make yellow and green hair for the clown.

8. And here you have the elements to decorate the cake.

9. Using the paintbrush and a little edible glue, stick the hair, eyes, nose, and mouth on the cake.

Note: For a variation, instead of the vanilla cream, caramel syrup, and caramelized apples called for in the Basic Round Cake (p. 326), swap in fresh raspberries and Raspberry Mousseline Cream (p. 14) with no added sugar, and moisten the sponge layers with raspberry syrup.

FUNNY BUNNY CAKE

About 35% deep pink, white, pale pink, purple,
and green almond paste

Confectioners' sugar for dusting

Edible glue or water

1 recipe Basic Round Cake (p. 326)

Equipment

A fine paintbrush

1. To make the cheeks, shape 2 large deep pink almond paste balls and flatten them slightly to make 2 thick disks. Using the tip of a ballpoint pen cap, make round indentations in the rounded part of each cheek.

2. For the eyes, shape 2 white balls, 2 smaller dark pink balls, and 2 even smaller white balls. Using the paintbrush and a little edible glue, stack them from large to small. Using a little more of the dark pink almond, shape a nose.

3. If necessary, dust the work surface with confectioners' sugar. For the teeth, roll out a piece of white almond paste $\frac{1}{16}$-inch (2 mm) thick. Using a small knife, cut out a V shape.

4. For the hair, roll out a piece of pale pink almond paste $\frac{1}{16}$-inch (2 mm) thick. Cut into thin strips.

5. For the ears, roll 2 pieces of dark pink almond paste to make 2 large cones. Shape the tip of each into a point. Roll very lightly on the work surface. Using the tip of a small knife, make an incision in each cone. Curve them slightly so they look floppy.

6. For the carrot, shape the purple almond paste into a ball, then roll it into a cone. Using the small knife, make horizontal incisions along the length.

7. The green almond paste must be particularly well kneaded. Place a piece in a small sieve.

8. Push the paste through the mesh to make fine threads.

9. There you have it! All the elements to decorate the bunny are ready: the ears, hair, eyes, nose, cheeks, teeth, and even the carrot. All you need to do now is stick them on the cake using the paintbrush and a little edible glue.

TEDDY BEAR CAKE

Serves 8

Chocolate-hazelnut cake

2 sticks plus 1½ tablespoons
(9 oz. / 250 g) unsalted butter,
room temperature,
plus more for brushing

1⅔ cups (7¼ oz. / 210 g)
all-purpose flour,
plus more for dusting

1 generous cup (7 oz. / 200 g)
hazelnuts

1½ teaspoons (6 g) baking powder

⅓ cup (1½ oz. / 40 g) unsweetened
cocoa powder

1 cup (7 oz. / 200 g)
granulated sugar

1 tablespoon vanilla sugar

4 eggs

A pinch fine salt

½ cup (120 ml) whole milk

Glaze

7 oz. (200 g) chocolate-hazelnut
spread

⅔ cup (160 ml) heavy cream

Decoration

10 oz. (300 g) chocolate curls

About 35% black, white,
and brown almond paste,
well kneaded

Confectioners' sugar for dusting

Edible glue or water

Equipment

A 9-inch (22-cm) springform pan

Round ⅓-inch (8-mm), ¾-inch
(2-cm), and 4-inch (9.5-cm)
cookie cutters

A fine paintbrush

Chocolate-hazelnut cake

1. Preheat the oven to 345°F (175°C) convection. Brush the springform pan with butter and dust with flour. Spread the hazelnuts on a baking sheet and toast for about 10 minutes, then let cool. Wrap the hazelnuts in a kitchen towel and rub off the skin. In a food processor, finely grind the hazelnuts until powdery. Sift the flour with the baking powder and cocoa powder.

2. Increase the oven temperature to 350°C (180°C) convection.

3. Combine the granulated sugar with the vanilla sugar. In the bowl of a stand mixer fitted with the whisk, whip the butter, gradually adding the sugar mixture. Beat in the eggs, one by one, then whip for 5 minutes.

4. Stir in the ground hazelnuts and salt.

5. Carefully fold in the dry ingredients, then gradually stir in the milk until smooth, but do not overmix.

6. Spread the batter in the springform pan and bake for 10 minutes. Reduce the oven temperature to 340°F (170°C) convection and bake for 40 to 50 minutes, until a tester inserted into the cake comes out clean. Carefully remove the pan side and let the cake cool on a rack.

Glaze

7. Meanwhile, in a medium saucepan, heat the chocolate-hazelnut spread with the cream over low heat, stirring frequently, until smooth. Let cool completely.

Decoration

8. Place the cake on a rack set over a rimmed baking sheet. Using a long serrated knife, trim the top of the cake so it's flat.

9. Heat the glaze to 85°F (30°C). Using a flat metal spatula, spread the glaze over the entire cake. Pat the top and sides with the chocolate curls, pressing them in gently so they stick.

Note: Every kid loves a teddy bear. This one, with its cute round face, is sure to win hearts. And the cake is so simple you can easily prepare it with your little ones for a fun, delicious activity.

1. For the teddy bear features, dust a work surface with confectioners' sugar. Roll out the black almond paste ¹⁄₁₆-inch (2 mm) thick. Roll out the white almond paste to the same thickness. Shape 2 balls of brown almond paste.

2. Using the ¾-inch (2-cm) cutter, cut out 3 black disks, 2 for the eyes and 1 for the nose. Using a small, sharp knife, cut 2 thin black strips for the mouth.

3. Roll out the white almond paste ¹⁄₁₆-inch (2 mm) thick. Using the ⅓-inch (8-mm) cutter, cut out 2 disks. Using the paintbrush and a little edible glue, stick them on the larger black disks to finish the eyes.

4. Using the largest cutter, make a white disk for the snout.

5. Center the black disk for the nose on the white snout to help position the 2 lines for the mouth. Using the paintbrush and a little edible glue, stick the black strips on the white disk to make the teddy's mouth.

6. For the nose, stick the ¾-inch (2-cm) black disk on the center of the white disk where the ends of the mouth meet.

7. To make the ears, shape two balls of the brown almond paste. Using your thumb, press firmly into each to make an indentation.

8. Stick the ears above and to the side of each eye.

9. And there you have your teddy bear: as delicious, chocolaty, and endearing as you could wish for.

TEDDY BEAR CAKE

FRIENDLY LION CAKE

Prep:
2 hours

Cook:
45 minutes

Chill:
2 to 12 hours

FRIENDLY LION CAKE

Serves 12

Lemon cream

1 egg

2 tablespoons (1 oz. / 30 g)
unsalted butter

¼ cup (1 ¾ oz. / 50 g)
granulated sugar

Finely grated zest and
juice of 1 lemon

Vanilla cake

2 sticks plus 1½ tablespoons
(9 oz. / 250 g) unsalted butter,
room temperature, plus more
for brushing

3⅔ cups (16 oz. / 450 g)
all-purpose flour

2 tablespoons (22 g)
baking powder

1¾ cups (11½ oz. / 330 g)
granulated sugar

1 teaspoon pure vanilla extract

4 eggs

1 cup (250 ml) reduced-fat milk

1 pinch fine salt

Buttercream frosting

5 egg whites

1¼ cups (9 oz. / 250 g)
granulated sugar

3¾ sticks (15 oz. / 430 g)
unsalted butter, diced, room
temperature

2 teaspoons pure vanilla extract

Orange food coloring

Decoration

White, brown, pink, and yellow
sugar paste

Confectioners' sugar
for dusting

Equipment

Three 8-inch (20-cm) cake pans

Round ⅓-inch (8-mm),
¾-inch (2-cm), and
4-inch (9.5-cm) cookie cutters

A fine paintbrush

A pastry bag fitted with
a fluted tip

Lemon cream

1. In a medium bowl, lightly beat the egg with a fork. In a medium saucepan, melt the butter over low heat. Stir in the sugar and egg, then the lemon zest and juice. Whisk continuously for 5 minutes, until thickened. Transfer the lemon cream to a bowl and press plastic wrap directly on surface. Chill for at least 2 hours or, preferably, 12 hours.

Vanilla cake

2. Preheat the oven to 340°F (170°C). Brush the 3 cake pans with butter and line the base of each with a parchment paper disk. Sift the flour with the baking powder. In the bowl of a stand mixer fitted with the whisk, whip the butter and sugar until light and fluffy. Beat in the vanilla, then the eggs, one by one, until smooth. Incorporate the dry ingredients, then beat in the milk

and salt. Divide the batter between the 3 pans and bake for 45 minutes, until a tester inserted into the center comes out clean. Let cool for 10 minutes in the pans, then transfer to a rack to cool.

Buttercream frosting

3. Bring a medium saucepan of water to a simmer. In the bowl of a stand mixer, combine the egg whites with the sugar. Set the bowl over the hot water and whisk for 5 to 10 minutes, until the sugar dissolves. Fit the whisk to mixer, attach the bowl, and whip until the mixture is firm and glossy.

4. Replace the whisk with the paddle. Gradually add the butter and beat until smooth. Beat in the vanilla and enough orange food coloring to make a light orange buttercream.

Decoration

5. Follow steps 1 to 7.

Assembly

6. Using a long serrated knife, trim the top of each cake so it's flat. Place the first cake on a plate. Spread the side and top with the lemon cream. Set the second cake on top and repeat with the lemon cream. Place the third cake on top. Follow steps 8 to 14.

1. Roll out the white and brown sugar paste ¹⁄₁₆-inch (2 mm) thick.

2. Using the largest cutter, make a white disk for the snout. Using the medium cutter, cut out a brown disk. Using a knife, cut 2 narrow brown strips.

3. Using the paintbrush and a drop of water, attach the brown disk to the white disk. Add the brown strips to make the lion's mouth.

4-5. To make the eyes, use the smallest cutter to cut out 2 white disks. Roll 2 small brown balls and attach them to the white disks. Cut out 2 yellow disks and 2 very small pink disks to form the ears.

6-7. Roll a log of yellow sugar paste to shape the tail. Roll a ball of brown fondant into a small ball, flatten slightly, and cut strips into it. Press into the end of the tail. To make the whiskers, shape 6 very small brown balls.

8-10. Spread the buttercream all over the cake, reserving enough to make the lion's mane, and smooth all over.

11-12 Add more orange coloring to the remaining buttercream. Pipe out small dollops of buttercream to make the lion's mane.

13-14. Place the sugar paste decorations on the top of the cake, pressing very lightly. Attach the tail to the base.

Indexes

Recipes by Category

*Page numbers in italics indicate photographs.

Index of Recipes

Editor's Notes on Precision & Preparation

PRECISION IN PASTRY-MAKING

An accurate scale is indispensable to a pastry chef, and professionals use scientific precision when they prepare their ingredients. All the metric measurements in this book have been converted to the imperial system and to cups and spoons, as well as sticks for butter. Conversions inevitably require a little rounding up or down, and so we recommend you use a digital scale. Choose either metric or imperial and use the same system for any given recipe.

PREPARING PANS

Don't skimp on the few minutes it takes to prepare a pan. Melt some butter and brush the pan all over, including corners and angles. When the butter's set, dust the pan very lightly with flour, tilting it so the flour is evenly distributed. Turn the pan upside down and rap it lightly to eliminate any excess flour. Some recipes may give other instructions for pan prep, like brushing the pan with butter before lining it with parchment paper.

Notes on Temperature & Folding In

TEMPERATURE OF INGREDIENTS

Ingredients usually combine best when they're at room temperature. Take your eggs and butter out of the refrigerator about 30 minutes before you start baking. For some recipes, butter may need softening before it's incorporated—in this case, whisk it a little. If you're in a hurry and want to take the chill off your butter, soften it using very brief pulses in the microwave oven, taking care it doesn't melt.

Whipping cream and egg whites

The exception to recommendation to use room temperature ingredients is cream for whipping: it must be well chilled. For some of our recipes (mousses, for example, where a stable mixture is particularly important), you'll see that we recommend chilling the equipment beforehand to help the cream stay cold while you whip it. It's best to use a metal bowl. Be careful not to overwhip!

When whipping egg whites, the golden rule is to use a bowl that's not only spick and span but completely dry. Separate your eggs one by one using different bowls from the one you'll be whipping in to make sure that not a drop of yolk slips in.

FOLDING IN

Two kinds of ingredients require the technique known as 'folding in': whipped cream and egg whites, and dry ingredients, such as flour or ground nuts. For both, it's best to use a flexible spatula, preferably silicone, as you incorporate them into a preparation of a different texture or density.

Many French pastry recipes use the air bubbles in whipped eggs, often the whites, as a leavening agent, so it's important to preserve them. You may also need to fold airy whipped cream into a mousse or other light preparation. To preserve their frothiness, it's key to work gently. Add the whipped egg whites or cream in several additions. Each time, lift your spatula up to bring the batter over the whites or cream to gently mix it in while you rotate the bowl a quarter-turn. You don't want to squash those bubbles against the side of the bowl and deflate them. The moment the mixture is smooth, stop!

To incorporate dry ingredients, either all at once or in several additions, use the same lifting, stirring, and rotating motions, and stop as soon as there are no traces left of the flour, cocoa powder, etc. It's important not to overmix when you add flour as it might alter texture of the baked cake.

Acknowledgments

Christophe would like to thank:

All the members of the team at Éditions de la Martinière, the new Boss included, for their competence.

Laure Aline, special thanks to you for your useful comments, to-the-point opinions, and legendary sense of humor. Working with you is like working with my family.

Agathe Masson, for your fine intelligence, for always going the extra mile, for your availability from early morning to late at night, Sundays included. I'm delighted to have the privilege of working with you.

Laurent Fau, for your incredible talent, your professionalism, and your entertaining stories. And Sarah Vasseghi, who's always available for us, even after we've changed everything.

Benjamin Heuzé, for all the talent we've admired in you for so many years.

Sylvie Kempler, for your close rereading and highlighting!

Françoise Vauzeilles, for your cutting-edge creations, your ideas, and your speedy, efficient help; Christelle Aron, the queen of mandelbari and our cakes for kids; Laetitia Troesch, Virginie Breuse, Virginie Masse and Huck! Sandrine Pascolini, Fabienne Clauss, Maggie Galbraith, and especially to the one and only Lily.

Patricia Ropartz and Julia for your fine communications work.

Henri Charpentier's team, dear, talented President Goki Arita, Komai Takahiro, Henri Charpentier's main chef, winner of the second prize at the World Pastry Cup, for his recipe featured here and for his wonderful, forward-looking ideas.

Hatsumi, for all the straightforward advice and experience, and Mirai, a talented pastry chef.

All the pastry chefs in Mutzig, and our sales staff for their attentive service.

My children Louis, Marie, and Lucie.

Camille Lesecq, for all the time spent putting together and making the recipes.

Camille would like to thank:

Christophe Felder, who enabled me to make my dream of this pastry shop come true. Our Petite Pâtisserie wouldn't be what it is without him. His constant striving for perfection and the way he helps all those around him grow mean he's a very special person.

The wonderful team of pastry chefs in Mutzig.

Laetitia, for her generosity, and who has given me the sweetest treat ever: Romane.

Little Camille, who loves coconut cookies.

My dear family in Normandy.

And all the members of the wonderful team who helped bring this fine book to fruition.